HEXCUR

Daytripping in and around Pennsylvania's Dutch Country, the Delaware Valley and Poconos

by Sally M. and David C. Keehn

HASTINGS HOUSE · PUBLISHERS
New York 10016

Library of Congress Cataloging in Publication Data

Keehn, Sally M.
   Hexcursions: daytripping in and around Pennsylvania's Dutch country, the Delaware Valley and Poconos

   Includes index.
   1. Pennsylvania Dutch Country (Pa.)—Description and travel—Guide-books.   I. Keehn, David C.   II. Title.
F157.P44K43   1982   917.48'10443   82-952
ISBN 0-8038-3061-0

Published simultaneously in Canada by
Saunders of Toronto, Ltd., Don Mills, Ontario
Printed in the United States of America

Contents

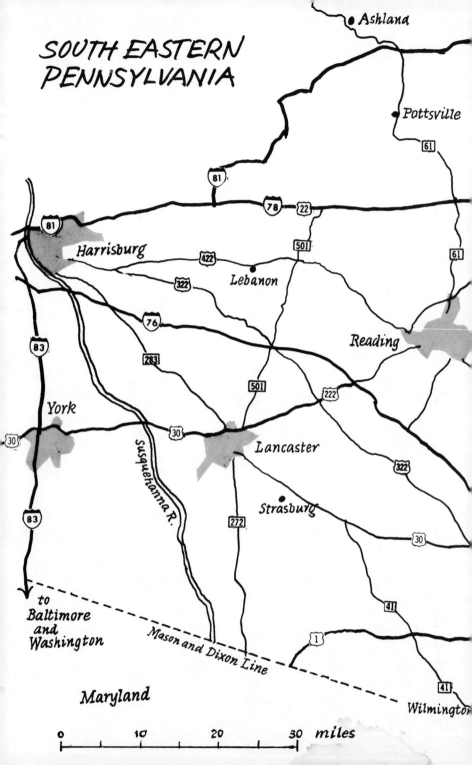

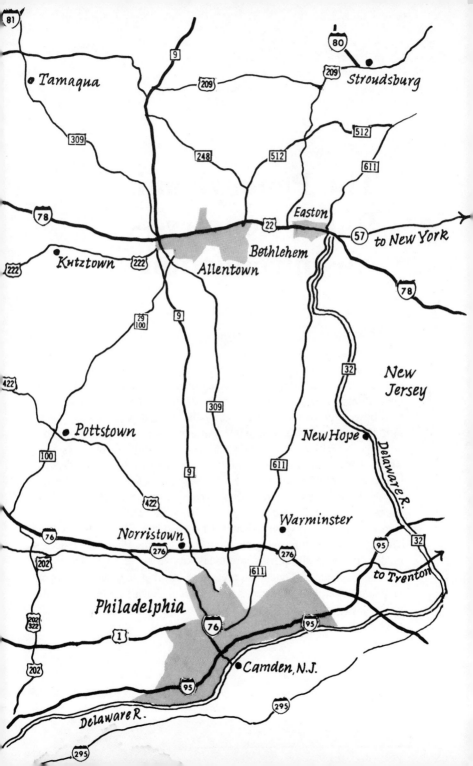

The Pennsylvania Dutch Country— An Introduction

The word "Dutch" in the term "Pennsylvania Dutch" is really an Americanism for the word "Deutsch" meaning German. It refers to the wave of immigrants coming from Germany and the German-speaking part of Switzerland who by 1750 comprised more than half of the population of Pennsylvania. From Switzerland came the Mennonites or followers of Menno Simons who believed and practiced simplicity in their work, dress, and worship. An even more disciplined offshoot were the Amish who completely shunned the frivolities of the outside world. Today, these sects are known collectively as the "Plain Dutch" in recognition of the austere lifestyle they still follow. William Penn's "Holy Experiment" in religious freedom also attracted a flood of Lutheran and Reformed immigrants from the Palatinate region of Germany who brought with them their own customs, food and dialect. These thrifty, yet fun-loving people who unlike the Plain Dutch accept modern life with all its frills, are today known as the "Gay Dutch."

Pennsylvania's Dutchmen are proud of what they are and appreciative of what their forebears have left them. Each year they welcome millions of tourists to their picture-book region to see their many attractions that revolve generally around four basic themes:

1. Pennsylvania Dutch Folkways

The simple and austere life style of Lancaster's "plain people" has become a source of fascination for "outsiders" caught up in the frantic complexities of modern day living. Through a variety of tourist attractions, festivals, and "in spots" to visit, the folkways and religious beliefs of these people can be better understood and appreciated. In a number of re-created Amish houses and farms, the visitor can get a sense of what it is like to live without electricity, telephones, and other modern conveniences. Several folkcraft centers display implements and show pictures of the Amish and Mennonites at work and play. They try to impart an understanding and respect for these close-knit people who live without insurance, relying upon a community of believers who will come to their aid should their barn burn down or tragedy strike. Buggy rides are offered at two locations so that the visitor can experience what it's like to travel in Amish style. In places such as the Green Dragon Farmers Market and the New Holland Sales Stables, the Amish and Mennonites can be seen going about their daily business, and in scenic drives through the Lancaster area, their rural life style may be observed from afar. It is good to remember during any foray to respect the Amish desire to be left alone.

The Gay Dutch primarily reside in Berks, Lebanon and Lehigh Counties, and are well known for their food, handicrafts and festivals. These are the folks who brought us sauerkraut un schpeck (pork), funnel cake, smearcase (cottage cheese), pot pie, schnitz un knepp (dried apples and dumplings), and Lebanon Bologna. Numerous festivals such as those at Kutztown, Kempton, and Schaefferstown, feature these culinary delights along with handicrafts, music, hoedowns, and displays of customs, past and present.

These Gay Dutch are proud of their German heritage and have retained a good portion of it. Many of them speak the Pennsylvania Dutch dialect, a curious mixture of German and English. Their folk art has been preserved, reflected in their painted toleware, pottery, fraktur printing (*see glossary*), and colorful quilts. Once heard, their music is not easily forgotten. It is lively and fun-loving, featuring polkas, brass bands and boom-bas (*see glossary*).

The landscape of this region—which is dotted with bank barns (*see glossary*) sporting gaily painted Hex Signs, rich and fertile farms, covered bridges, one-room school houses and folk-life museums reflects the influence of the Pennsylvania Dutch. They are a thrifty and industrious people who love the earth, and its bountiful harvests. The ethnic traditions of later residents, such as the Poles and Ukrainians, have added to the area's colorful appeal.

Other sects that came to Pennsylvania to avoid the religious persecution suffered in Europe are the Moravians of Bethlehem and Lititz, the Cloister established at Ephrata, and the Quakers who settled in the counties surrounding Philadelphia. Each transplanted its own unique beliefs and culture to the New World. The structures of the early self-sufficient community established at Ephrata by the German Pietists and in Bethlehem by the Moravians remain largely intact. While present-day Moravians still continue with their beautiful musical festivals, Christmas Putzes, and lovely Christmas light displays, the Brotherhood and Sisterhood at Ephrata has long since died out due to, in part, their mystical leader's belief in celibacy.

2. Gateways to History

In addition to religious groups, William Penn's land grant offerings attracted early explorers and settlers. While Penn was building Pennsbury, his country home on the Delaware River, pioneers like Conrad Weiser moved inland to make peace with the Indians and settle the land. The homesteads of these early settlers can still be seen at Conrad Weiser Park, the Brinton 1704 House, the Hans Herr House near Lancaster, and Susanna Wright's mansion in Columbia. The mother of famed explorer Daniel Boone was raised at the Morgan Log House in Montgomery County. She later married and moved inland towards Birdsboro where young Daniel was born and raised.

The constant efforts of the British to entrap the Continental Congress in Philadelphia ensured Pennsylvania's role in the American fight for independence. The first Pennsylvania encampment of Washington's ragtag army took place in the winter of 1776 at Washington Crossing State Park along the Delaware River. It was from here that Washington staged his daring raid back across the Delaware on Christmas Eve to take the Hessians at Trenton by surprise. During the summer of 1777, the British tried to outflank the Americans by sailing from New York City to Head of the Elk, Maryland and approaching Philadelphia from the south. The Continental Army met their advance at the Battle of Brandywine but suffered defeat due to faulty intelligence reports. The British then moved into Philadelphia and drove the Continental Congress to Lancaster and the Liberty Bell to Allentown. Washington moved his battered troops to the high ground near Valley Forge to dig in for the bitter winter of 1777. Here the Prussian Baron von Steuben relentlessly drilled the undisciplined Continental Army and forged them into the integrated fighting machine that finally defeated the British at Yorktown four years later.

The Pennsylvania Dutch region also played a significant role in the development of the fledgling nation. The Pennsylvania Long Rifle and Conestoga wagon that were developed here aided in further western expansion. Houses like that of the Peter Wentz Farmstead, the ironmaster mansions at Hopewell and Pottsgrove, and Donegal Mills Plantation were once inhabited by the rugged individuals who with agricultural and industrial knowhow forged the new nation. Towns like Bethlehem, Allentown, Lititz and Lancaster (which was the home of Pennsylvania's only President, James Buchanan) were centers for a burgeoning culture. Their rich architectural heritage is evident even today as seen on the respective walking tours that are offered.

3. Those Industrious Dutchmen

The remarkable industrial development that has taken place in the Pennsylvania Dutchland over the last 350 years resulted initially from agricultural needs. The bountiful harvests, which are still attractively displayed at farmers' markets throughout the area, created the demand for the earliest industries. Grain had to be ground before it could be used in baking, so grist mills were built of which four are still in operation today. Soon commercial bakeries developed, the best known being that of Julius Sturgis who created a successful pretzel business. Corn and rye were plentiful and whiskey was soon being made at places similar to Michter's Distillery near Schaefferstown. Beer was carefully blended from barley and hops in breweries like A. Bube's in Mount Joy. The meat from the cattle was made into bologna at Lebanon while the hides were prepared in tanneries such as the one in Bethlehem's historic area. Later on, the milk was used to make delicious chocolate candy by Milton Hershey and Candy Americana in Lititz (which is famous for its "Wilbur Buds").

The plentiful iron ore, limestone, and timber for making charcoal led to early iron-making furnaces such as the ones at Cornwell, Lockridge, and the restored village at Hopewell. Due to the efforts of miners like those at Eckley Miner's Village, the charcoal was replaced by coal. An example of the mines they worked can still be visited at Ashland. The black gold caused towns like Mauch Chunk (now Jim Thorpe) to spring up overnight and created a need for a transportation infrastructure that made men like Asa Packer rich. Canal boats, like those still operating at Hugh Moore Park and New Hope, were used initially to take the coal to market. Then came the heyday of the railroad. The Railroad Museum at Strasburg chronicles these early days of railroading, and four steam trains which operate in the Dutch region take visitors for excursions.

The Dutchman's inventiveness and fascination with gadgetry led to further industrialization. Charles Duryea produced and tested his hill-climbing gas-driven autos near Reading, Robert Fulton of Lancaster invented the steamboat, and David Saylor first learned how to produce cement out of limestone. The interest in gadgets lead to the establishment of the National Watch and Clock Museum in Columbia, Koziar's spectacular Christmas light display near Bernville, and the miniature railroads at Strasburg and Roadside America. In a more artistic vein, Henry Mercer crafted intricately designed tiles near Doylestown, Martin hand-produced his superior guitars at Nazareth, and artists' colonies sprang up at Brandywine and New Hope.

The early origins of the region and the fine craftsmanship and frugality of the Pennsylvania Dutch combine to make the area a bargain hunter's paradise. Thousands of dealers show everything from the finest antiques to creatively inspired junk at flea markets such as those located at Adamstown and Kutztown. House and farm auctions are prevalent where the discriminating buyer can pick up beautiful items at cut-rate prices. For avid bargain seekers, there are countless factory outlets in the region. The greatest majority of them are concentrated in the city of Reading.

4. An Outdoor Funfest

Besides supporting the agricultural and industrial base, the land provides its own attractions and recreational opportunities. Interesting geological formations like the Blue Rocks and Delaware Water Gap as well as the region's four limestone caves give physical evidence of changes that took place millions of years ago. The two sets of waterfalls in the area are noted for their rugged beauty. There's an excellent system of State Parks offering lakes, boating, swimming, camping, and picnicking facilities, while the Pocono Mountains are made to order for hiking, skiing, canoeing and whitewater rafting.

Nature lovers will be inspired by the climb to the top of Hawk Mountain or a visit to the Audubon home and wildlife preserve. For those who like to see animals close up, there are zoos and a game preserve. The excellent trout fishing is supported by a number of public nurseries where children can feed the rainbow and brown trout. The area also contains some of the most splendid gardens on the East Coast, including the rose gardens at Hershey, the Oriental Garden at Swiss Pines, and the magnificent 300-acre country estate at Longwood. In terms of man-made recreation, there are five amusement parks and a creative play park for children called Sesame Place. For speedsters, there's horse racing at Penn National, bicycle racing at the Lehigh County Velodrome, and auto racing at the Duryea Hill Climb and Pocono Raceway. The Pennsylvania Dutchland is truly an Outdoor Funfest that will satisfy virtually every type of sportsman's appetite.

Glossary

Bank barn: a barn, usually built into the side of a hill, that is two stories high on the lower side and one story high on the upper. This enables the farmer to drive his truck up the hill to the second floor of the barn to unload and store his feed with relative ease.

Boom-bas: a musical instrument of German origin which resembles a modified pogo stick with a variety of percussion instruments, such as a tambourine, wood block, sleigh bells etc., attached.

Christmas Putz: a manger scene.

Fraktur: illustrated sayings written in a style noted for its dramatic use of scrolled letters.

Funnel cake: a Pennsylvania-Dutch pastry made from dough poured through a funnel into a pan of hot oil, fried until brown, then rolled in powdered sugar.

Hex signs: prevalent throughout the Gay Dutch area, these are the colorful geometric designs most commonly seen painted on barns. They are a form of folk art, and not, as some believe, symbols of charms against the powers of darkness.

Old Order Amish: one of many divisions within the Amish religion, this sect is considered to be the most strict in shunning modern conveniences and adhering to the old ways.

Sgraffito: a method of decoration in which a design is scratched through layers of paint, clay, plaster etc.

Slipware pottery: earthenware which is covered by a thin layer of diluted clay and often decorated with superimposed designs.

Team Mennonites: "plain people" who dress in a fashion peculiar to their sect and primarily use the horse and buggy for transportation (although one division within this sect permits the use of cars with painted black bumpers). Unlike the Amish, Team Mennonites hold services in meetinghouses rather than in their homes.

Toleware: a type of painted tinware often elaborately decorated in gay colors.

Tulip ware: slipware pottery decorated with the tulip motif.

Lancaster, Land of the Amish and Mennonites

KEY TO MAP—AREA I (*overleaf*)

A – A. Bube's Brewery and Catacombs

B – Anderson Pretzel Bakeries

C – Amish Farm and House

D – Amish Homestead

E – Amish Village

F – Lancaster Carriage Tours

G – Abe's Buggy Rides, Bird-In-Hand Farmer's Market

H – Donegal Mills Plantation

I – Dutch Wonderland and National Wax Museum

J – Eagle Americana Museum

K – Ephrata Cloister, Ephrata Farmer's Market

L – Folkcraft Museum at Witmer

M – Green Dragon Farmer's Market

N – Hans Herr House

O – Heritage Center Museum of Lancaster County

P – Intercourse: The People's Place, Kitchen Kettle, and Noah Martin Emporium

Q – Nissley Vineyards

R – Lancaster County Winery

S – Lancaster Walking Tour, Lancaster's Farmer's Markets

T – Lititz Walking Tour, Sturgis Pretzel House, and Candy Americana Museum

U – Mill Bridge Craft Village

V – National Watch and Clock Museum, Columbia Farmer's Market

W – New Holland Sales Stables

X – Phillip's Lancaster County Swiss Cheese Shop

Y – Plain 'n Fancy Farm and Dining Room

Z – Pork Chop Farm

a – Railroad Museum of Pennsylvania, Strasburg Steam R.R., Strasburg's Railroads in Miniature

b – Rock Ford

d – Rome Mill

e – Rough 'n Tumble Engineer's Museum

f – Weaver Poultry Tours

g – Weavertown One Room Schoolhouse

h – Wheatland

i – Wright's Ferry Mansion

j – Meadowbrook Farmer's Market

k – Roots Country Market

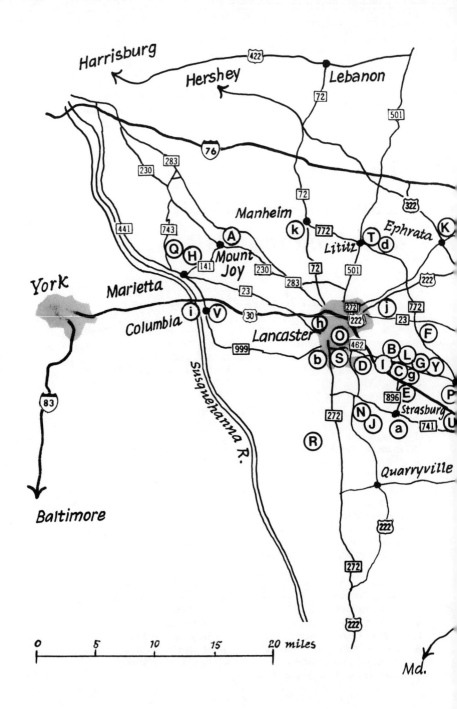

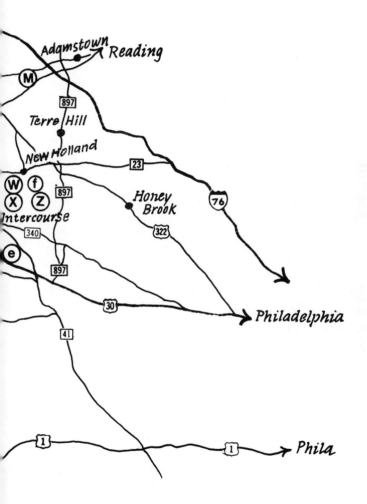

Lancaster, Land of the Amish and Mennonites

When the Amish and Mennonites left their native Europe to seek religious freedom and workable farm land in the New World, they found the answer to their prayers in Lancaster County. Its fertile and gently rolling land was perfect for farming, and William Penn's invitation to the religiously persecuted was a Godsend. There would be freedom for all to worship here. That they found this area conducive to their needs is evident, for everywhere you look there are visible signs of their ongoing culture.

As you drive down scenic roads past neat farms with windmills and freshly painted white houses, you'll see farmers using horse- and mule-drawn plows to work the fields; buggies taking families on outings; and young boys dressed in overalls fishing in a local stream. When you come to the numerous small towns that dot the countryside, stop and look around. Many small shops have quilts and handmade items for sale. Maybe you'll spy a white-capped Mennonite making a purchase, or a bonneted youngster loading the family wagon. Keep your eyes open, for there's always something to be seen and learned.

The attractions listed in the Lancaster area are all relatively close together except for those in the western portion of the county. It is feasible then to consider including attractions other than those listed as "nearby" in planning a day's excursion.

A. BUBE'S BREWERY AND CATACOMBS

Open daily May–Oct. 15th, 10–5 p.m. After mid-Oct. by appointment only. Fees: Adults, $2.50; children 6-12, $1.50. Group rates for ten or more. Bar. Gourmet meals by reservation, June—August. Gift shop. A. Bube's Brewery, 102 N. Market St., Mount Joy, Pa. 17552. (717) 653-2160.

Lancaster County was once known as the "Munich of the New World," and for no small reason. During the 19th century, over twenty breweries operated throughout the area and supplied beer locally as well as to such "far away" places as Boston and Baltimore. Sadly, none of these breweries is in operation today. All have been destroyed or converted into another type of operation save one, the A. Bube Brewery.

Built prior to the Civil War, this old-time brewery was in continual use until Prohibition forced its closing. In 1968 it was reopened, but this time as a museum. It is a unique attraction, for it has retained its historicity with much of the actual equipment used in the age-old brewing process still intact.

Guided tours commence on the upper floor of the brewery where the entire brewing process as practiced in the old days is described. You'll see collections of antique beer bottles, large wooden barrels, and samples of beer-making equipment all carefully displayed in the wood-floored 54-inch-thick stone walled rooms.

As you descend the steep wooden steps which lead to the underground catacombs, your interest will quicken. These subterranean rooms (some 43 feet below the ground) were honed from natural underground caverns and lined with cut stone to form the walls and ceilings. Their rough surfaces have a certain beauty and mystery about them reminiscent of those underground catacombs used as burial sites in ancient Rome. You won't see any bodies here, though. What you will see are the well-preserved remains of what was once a flourishing business. Ten-foot-high barrels that once held 1,900 gallons of fermenting brew fill an entire vault. Another area, known as the Lagering Cellar, houses massive vats built in place in 1810 to hold the ageing beer. You'll walk through underground passages that lead beneath the adjacent Central Hotel (erected by Bube in 1880–1884 to complement his Brewery) to an upper brick-floored vault. In this cool but attractive area decorated with old brick floors and small stalactites, you can enjoy a gourmet meal (prepared in the adjacent Central Hotel) during June, July and August.

Directions: From Lancaster, follow Rt. 30 West to Rt. 283 West. From 283, take the Mount Joy-Manheim Exit. In Mount Joy, take Main St. to N. Market and turn right. The Brewery will appear on your left directly behind the Central Hotel (N. Market St. is directly after you see the U.S. Post Office on Main St.).

Nearby Attractions: See Donegal Mills Plantation, and Lancaster Wineries-Nissley Vineyards. A fifteen-minute drive away is Columbia, which features the National Watch and Clock Museum and Wright's Ferry Mansion.

AMISH HOUSE TOURS

THE AMISH FARM AND HOUSE

Open daily year round: Summer, 8:30 a.m. to 8:00 p.m.; Spring and Fall, 8:30 a.m. to 5:00 p.m.; mid-Nov.—Feb., 8:30 a.m. to 4:00 p.m., weather permitting. Fees: Adults, $3.00. children 6-11, $1.00 Rest rooms. Gift shop. Picnics. Amish Farm and House, 2395 Lincoln Hwy. East, Lancaster, Pa. 17602. (717) 394-6185.

The customs and life style of the Amish have fascinated "outsiders" for years. Their emphasis on independence (carried to such a degree they refuse to use electricity because the power lines link them up to the rest of the world), their reverence for the simple plain life, and their neat farms with horse-drawn plows and buggies, pique the tourist's curiosity. In 1955, the doors of the Amish Farm and House, a replica of an Old Order Amish farmstead, were opened in response to this interest, and since then thousands have come away with a greater appreciation of these plain folk who shun the modern-day world and its conveniences.

A lecture and tour of this ten-room stone farm house, built in 1805, lasts a good 45 minutes. Amish customs are described in detail, from marriage and funeral rites, to Sunday services and courting practices. The setting for the lecture and subsequent tour is an austere one. There are rooms lit only by kerosene lamps and heated by coal stoves. Unadorned windows (curtains are considered too frilly) break the monotony of bare walls, and all is painted in the earth colors of brown, green, blue or white. Plain clothes (none having buttons or decorative trim) hang from pegs lining the walls. Everything in the house exists for a nondecorative utilitarian purpose.

An added highlight is the self-guided tour of the farmyard itself (maps are available). There are the authentic outbuildings and equipment associated with an Amish farm. These include a springhouse, barn, bake oven, smoke house, cucumber pump with water wheel, chicken house and buggies. In addition, there are exhibits featuring a furniture making shop, Christmas Putz, lime kiln, and antique doll and Indian museum. Throughout the farm tour, animals may be seen frolicking in the fields or busily eating in the barn and sheds. The last Thursday and Friday of April feature the annual sheep shearing which the public may view, and through the warmer months Conestoga and buggy rides are available.

Directions: Take Route 30 (Lincoln Highway) six miles east of Lancaster. The Amish Farm and House is directly on this route, adjacent to the red covered bridge.

Nearby Attractions: See Dutch Wonderland, National Wax Museum, and Amish Homestead.

THE AMISH HOMESTEAD

Open daily year round: Summers, 9–7 p.m.; After Labor Day, 9–4 p.m. weather permitting. Tours leave every 10 minutes. Last tour leaves one hour before closing. Fees: Adults, $2.00; children 6-12, 50¢. Rest rooms. Gift shop. Picnics. The Amish Homestead, 2034 Lincoln Highway East, Lancaster, Pa. 17602. (717) 392-0832.

Authenticity is the key word used to describe this tourist attraction in the Amish countryside. The scenic 73-acre farm is actually used by an Amish family who inhabit two sections of the 200-year-old farmhouse. Their Amish buggies and sleighs occupy the sheds, their crops are growing in the fields, and their animals live in the outbuildings. This is about as close as you'll get to these Amish, however, except perhaps for a fleeting glimpse of a bonneted youngster harvesting the vegetables. The Amish are by tradition shy of outsiders, and these are no exception. You will, however, get a good second-hand look into their lives and traditions through the excellent tours provided at this site.

Knowledgeable guides lead you through the five unoccupied rooms of the "three generation" farm house. These are authentically furnished in the Old Order Amish style and include a large kitchen, living room, two bedrooms, and a summer or kettle kitchen. In each room the customs and life styles of the ''plain people'' are described and illustrated through the objects displayed. After the house tour, you are taken on a walk through the working farm. There is a Swiss Bank Barn (banked on three sides) which is used as a stable for the horses and as storage for hay and straw. A tobacco barn stands nearby with curing stalks of tobacco hanging from the rafters. New-born piglets squeal and grunt in the pig shed, and lazy cattle chew their cud in the field. The setting is a bucolic one conducive to a relaxing picnic at the end of the tour.

Directions: The Homestead is located three miles east of Lancaster on Lincoln Highway East (Rt. 462), 1,000 feet beyond the junction of Rts. 30 and 462. The farm will be on your left.

Nearby Attractions: See Anderson Pretzel Factory, Dutch Wonderland, and The National Wax Museum.

THE AMISH VILLAGE

Open daily 9–5 p.m. in spring and fall; 9–8 p.m. during the summer months. Fees: Adults, $2.50; children 6–12, 75¢. Rest rooms. Gift shop. Snacks. The Amish Village, Route 896, P.O. Box 105, Strasburg, Pa. 17579. (717) 687-8511.

Unlike the other house tours, the Amish Village emphasizes local institutions that figure in the Amish life as well as the house and farm. Tours commence in the 1840 farm house which is authentically furnished in the tradition of the Old Order Amish. The guided tour underlines the history and customs of these people and furnishes fascinating details of their strictly-ordered existence. Outside the house can be seen the spring house, which serves as a refrigerator; the Smoke House where meats are preserved; an ingenious windmill and water wheel that pump water to the livestock in the barnyard; and a bevy of animals including pigs, goats, and horses.

The ''village'' section of this attraction features an Amish Store that sells souvenirs along with such Pennsylvania Dutch goodies as apple schnitz (dried apples), freshly baked bread, shoo-fly pie, dried beef and pepper cabbage; a Blacksmith Shop (considered an integral part of the Amish life) furnished with the tools of the trade; a one-room school house which was built by Amish craftsmen and authentically furnished as an example of how Amish children are educated today; and a field which provides the setting for short buggy rides costing 50¢ a person.

Directions: The village is located on Pa. Route 896, two miles north of Strasburg, and one mile south of the juncture of Routes 30 and 896.

Nearby Attractions: See Strasburg Steam Railroad, Strasburg's Railroads in Miniature, The Railroad Museum of Pennsylvania and Mill Bridge Craft Village.

THE ANDERSON PRETZEL BAKERIES, INC.

Open for tours Mon.-Fri., 9 a.m. to 3:30 p.m. No admission fee. Rest rooms. Retail store. Anderson Pretzel Bakeries, Inc. 2060 Old Philadelphia Pike, P.O. Box 779, Lancaster, Pa. 17604. (717) 299-2321.

Children are mesmerized, adults fascinated by the wheels, belts, and intricate equipment all working in unison to produce the world-renowned pretzel at the Anderson Pretzel Bakeries. Through glass partitions, the entire art of pretzel manufacturing can be observed in air-conditioned comfort. Sixty-eight mechanical fingers twist 1,700 Bavarian Pretzels in a minute. A 160-foot conveyor belt carries the dough to the baking area, where it is put through a hot soda solution and baked in one of the five ovens for 3½ to 6½ minutes (depending on the size of the pretzel). Then, carried by cooling conveyors, the pretzels are taken to the packaging area, a room filled with the action of vibrating machine hoppers, conveyor belts, and bags and boxes being filled with pretzels of different shapes and sizes.

The entire pretzel manufacturing process, from the loading of the mixer to the packing of bags in cartons, takes one hour and forty minutes. At the commencement of your tour, you are given a sheet which explains the process step by step, so you are free to linger at each stop for as long as you wish. When you have finished your tour, there is a tourist lounge where hot soft pretzels and cold drinks are offered for sale. Directly below the lounge is a display room and retail shop where the Anderson products may be purchased and mail orders arranged.

Directions: The bakery is located at 2060 Old Philadelphia Pike (Route 340) one block east of the Route 30 Bypass.

Nearby Attractions: See Folkcraft Museum at Witmer, Dutch Wonderland, National Wax Museum, and Amish House Tours—The Amish Farm and House, Amish Homestead.

BUGGY RIDES THROUGH THE AMISH COUNTRYSIDE

The chief mode of transportation for the Old Order Amish and certain Mennonite Sects is the horse and buggy. Throughout the Lancaster area, these carriages may be seen being pulled by high-stepping spirited horses. The buggies come in varying colors and shapes, from the common black closed carriage to an open buckboard, to a small cart being pulled by a pony.

An entertaining way to gain an Amish perspective of travel on today's roads is to take a buggy ride of your own through this scenic countryside. For an hour or a day, you can travel at a slower pace and get a glimmer of what life is like for these "plain people."

LANCASTER CARRIAGE TOURS

Tours available year round, weather permitting. Fees: One hour's ride, adults, $5.25; children, half price. Half day tour with picnic lunch, adults, $15.00; children, half price. In winter, sleigh rides offered. Reservations recommended. Group rates for ten or more persons. Robert or Sandra Herman, Lancaster Carriage Shop, Main Street, Leola, Pa. (717) 656-9448.

Commencing at the shop of Lancaster Carriage, which specializes in designing horse-drawn vehicles and in restoring antique ones, Lancaster Carriage Tours offers the visitor a choice of five different tours through the countryside. These range in length from three to twelve miles, and bypass the commercial tourist spots to view the resplendent farms of the Amish and Team Mennonites, as well as a number of small businesses owned by these people (such enterprises as broommaker, book binder, horse dealer and farrier). The guides are well-informed about the lives and beliefs of these people, and your leisurely ride is peppered with an entertaining and educational commentary. The longer tours include a picnic lunch and provide an excellent opportunity to view this pastoral life close at hand. There are both open and closed buggies that may be taken, and the larger open vehicle can accommodate up to six people (including the driver).

Directions: The shop is located on Main Street (Rt. 23) in Leola, Pa., near the junction of Rts. 772 and 23.

Nearby Attractions: See Folkcraft Museum at Witmer, Farmers' Markets–Bird-in-Hand, and Plain & Fancy Farm and Dining Room.

ABE'S BUGGY RIDES

Rides available year round. Closed Sundays. No reservations needed. Fees: Adults, $6.00; children, $3.00. Abe's Buggy Rides, 2596 Philadelphia Pike, Lancaster, Pa. 17505. (717) 392-1794.

This concession operates along Route 340 and has a number of manned buggies operating continuously throughout the day. These rides in Amish carriages go for a two-mile tour through the farm country and provide a twenty-minute educational look into the life and travel styles of the "plain people."

Directions: Abe's is located along Rt. 340 (you can't miss the buggies on the side of the road) about ⅓ of a mile west of Bird-in-Hand.

Nearby Attractions: See Farmers' Markets—Bird-in-Hand, Weavertown One-Room School, Folk Craft Museum at Witmer, and Plain & Fancy Farm and Dining Room.

DONEGAL MILLS PLANTATION

Guided tours daily Tues.–Sat., 10–4:30 p.m.; Sun. 1–5 p.m. from Easter Weekend to Columbus Day. Closed Mondays. Open weekends in Oct. through third weekend in Nov. Other times by appointment. Fees: Adults, $2.75; children 6–12, $1.00. Rest rooms. Overnight accommodations. Gift shop. Donegal Mills Plantation, P.O. Box 204, Mount Joy, Pa. 17552. (717) 653-2168.

A 19th century Georgian mansion in the heart of Pennsylvania Dutch country? No, you haven't strayed too far south, you're at Donegal Mills Plantation. This is a unique ongoing restoration of an 18th and 19th century community originally settled in the early 1700's by a Scotch-Irish adventurer, Mr. David Byars, who found the valley with its meadows, streams and woods an ideal spot for a settlement.

In 1779 the land was sold to a group of Pennsylvania Germans who set up a thriving community composed of two grist mills, a blacksmith shop, cider press, creamery and ice pond. Through the years some of these buildings were destroyed, some added onto, which explains the columned facing of classic Greek revival architecture built over the original 18th century farm house.

Guided tours of the existing buildings are conducted by gracious hostesses in colonial garb. Lasting over an hour, the tour includes the lovely mansion with its authentic antiques dating from the Empire and Victorian periods; the 1760 Colonial Miller's House with its furnishings typical of the era and class of people; the three-story Brick Grist Mill which replaced the original one-story stone mill in 1830; and the bake kitchen with squirrel tail oven (another original building on the grounds). There is also a charming German Kitchen Garden laid out in the shape of a cross, and a trout hatchery. Peacocks, deer and barnyard animals can be seen in adjoining fields.

During certain times of the year festivities are held at Donegal Mills which bring the colonial past to life. There is an Apple Festival in the fall with homemade bread and apple butter, and a Christmas candlelight tour in late November. Often lunches are served in the old mill during these occasions, but reservations must be made in advance. Each season of the year has its festivities, so write for times and details. Overnight lodging in the authentically furnished Miller's House is also available.

Directions: From Lancaster take Route 283 West. Exit onto 230 West (Mt. Joy Exit). ½ block past the first traffic light in Mount Joy turn left onto 141 South. Go approximately three miles to Musser Road, turn right, go ¼ mile, turn left onto Trout Run Road which leads to the plantation.

Nearby Attractions: See A. Bube's Brewery & Catacombs and Lancaster's Wineries—Nissley Vineyards. A short distance away is Groff's Farm which serves excellent Penn.-Dutch food in a farm house setting. Reservations must be made well in advance. Groff's Farm Dining Room, Pinkerton Road, Mt. Joy, Pa. 17562. (717) 653-1520.

DUTCH WONDERLAND

Open Easter Weekend to Memorial Day Weekend, Sat. 10–6 p.m., Sun. 12–6 p.m.; Memorial Day through Labor Day, Mon.–Sat. 10–8 p.m., Sun. 11–6 p.m., Day after Labor Day through October, Sat. 10–6 p.m., Sun., 12–6 p.m. weather permitting. Fees: Admission Plan A, including 5 designated rides and all park entertainment, $3.95; Plan B, including 18 designated rides and all park entertainment, $6.75. Additional ride tickets may be purchased in park. Rest rooms. Concessions. Restaurant. Gift shops. Dutch Wonderland, 2249 Lincoln Highway East, Lancaster, Pa. 17602. (717) 291-1888.

When visitors come to the Lancaster area, they frequently ask, "What do you have that would be fun for the children?" The answer is, "Dutch Wonderland," an amusement park built with the specific needs of children in mind. Situated on forty-four tastefully landscaped acres (the colorful tulips, flower gardens and fountains are a treat to behold), the park offers a multitude of rides, most of which even a toddler can enjoy. A ride on the monorail provides a good overview of the park. You can see the old-fashioned river boat putt-putting down the stream, dolpins performing in the marina, miniature trains chugging through covered bridges, and the graceful gondolas making their way through the lovely Botanical Gardens.

Children of all ages will delight in the fantasy prevalent throughout this wonderland. The entrance to the park is a white medieval castle seemingly straight out of Cinderella. Numerous storybook characters are situated throughout the park. These include the "Old Woman in the Shoe" slide and Hansel and Gretel's famous gingerbread house with an animated candy factory inside. During the day, marionette shows are held which will tickle any child's funnybone.

This clean, attractive amusement park is geared to the whole family and has none of the frenetic glitter of the fast-paced carnival midway, although there are a few "spine chilling" rides such as the giant slide and double splash flume. It is a unique attraction, combining amusement rides with a Pennsylvania Dutch theme as evidenced by the covered bridges, miniature Amish farmhouse, animated scenes from an Amish quilting bee, and aerial views of the surrounding "Dutch" farm land.

Directions: The park is located on Route 30, four miles east of Lancaster.

Nearby Attractions: See The National Wax Museum, Amish House Tours–The Amish Farm and House and Amish Homestead, and The Anderson Pretzel Factory Tour.

EAGLE AMERICANA MUSEUM

Open daily from 10:00–5:00 from April through October (longer hours on weekends and during July and August). Weekends only during March and November. Fees: $1.75 for adults—50¢ for children 6 through 11 (five and under free). The Eagle Museum, Strasburg, PA. 17579. (717) 687-7931.

Weapon collectors and admirers will get a charge out of the Eagle Museum at Strasburg. Established in 1965 by nationally recognized firearms authority Vincent Nolt, the museum is best known for its fine collection of Pennsylvania (AKA Kentucky) flintlock rifles. The superior accuracy, range, and firepower of these rifles played a key part in winning the American Revolution and more than 300 Lancaster County gunsmiths crafted these rifles during the flintlock and percussion period (1725–1875). Today, it's the sheer beauty of their curly maple stocks and intricately designed brass ornamentation which is most revered.

Special firings are sometimes arranged on summer holidays where visitors can try their own hand at measuring powder from a horn and stuffing it, together with a ball and patchcloth, down the barrel with a ramrod. They say there's quite a kick when the flint strikes the frizzen and ignites the powder. The museum also contains an assortment of more bizarre weapons such as an ancient French crossbow, "harakiri" swords, a tripwire anti-poaching gun, and a World War II anti-aircraft gun. There's also a display of the type of Derringer used to assassinate Lincoln and rifle used in President Kennedy's slaying.

Wives may be more interested in the collection of antique toys, clocks, housewares, and glassware of the type originally manufactured by Baron Von Steuben in nearby Manheim. The Eagle Museum is also well-known for its large collection of Indian artifacts, which include an original Cree birchbark canoe. For history buffs there's an assortment of Lancaster County memorabilia but none as impressive as the 1740 stone mill itself which houses the Museum's collection. Scenically located, the mill was built by the brother of Lancaster's first settler and had been used for grinding flour, sawing lumber, distilling whisky, and producing electricity before serving its present function.

Directions: The Eagle Museum is located one mile west of Strasburg, PA. on Route 741.

Nearby Attractions: See Hans Herr House, Strasburg Steam Railroad, Strasburg's Railroads in Miniature and Railroad Museum of Pennsylvania.

EPHRATA CLOISTER

Open year-round, daily except Mondays, 10 a.m.–4:30 p.m., Sun. 12–4:30 p.m. Slightly longer hours during summer. Fees: Adults, $1.50; children under 12 free. Rest rooms. Gift shop. Ephrata Cloister, 632 W. Main St., Ephrata, PA. 17522. (717) 733-6600.

Vorspiel Performance: Sat. evenings late June to Sept. Fees: Adults, $3.50; children, $1.25. Includes Candlelight Tour of Cloister. Reservations Recommended.

Men wearing the long gown and cowl of the Capuchin order and women in white wool dresses stand in the doorways of medieval-looking buildings surrounded by neat wooden fences. There is a certain quiet atmosphere here, reminiscent of a monastery during the Middle Ages. This is the Ephrata Cloister—a unique restoration of a colonial religious commune brought to us in the twentieth century by Pennsylvania's Historical and Museum Commission.

The Cloister at Ephrata was founded in 1732 by Conrad Beissel, a German Pietist seeking spiritual and physical regeneration through practice of the ascetic lifestyle, esoteric teachings, and mystical rites of the ancient religious philosophers. He came to America with his followers and organized a communal society dedicated to self-denial and simplicity. The community was divided into three orders—the celibate Brotherhood, chaste Sisterhood, and the married order of householders for whom sex was discouraged but not forbidden. All followed Beissel's strict precepts and practiced such rigorous disciplines as sleeping on board benches with wooden blocks for pillows and eating one meal a day.

Despite this austere lifestyle, the group was extremely productive. They farmed, grew fruit, made baskets, did carpentry and milled. The Cloister became renowned throughout the colonies for the excellence of its book production, and its original printing press is still in operation at Ephrata today. Equal fame emanated from the sophisticated quality of its music. Beissel wrote numerous hymns exalting his mystical beliefs and claimed his followers could only achieve the purity of voice required for their a cappella performance by maintaining strict dietary controls. At its height in 1750, the society numbered about 300 souls. Nevertheless, its unity and strength began to decline when Beissel died, and by 1800, the celibate orders were virtually extinct. The remaining householders formed the Seventh Day German

Baptist Church in 1814 and continued worshipping in the remaining Cloister buildings until 1934.

A tour of the Cloister begins with a slide show contrasting life at the commune with that of the surrounding colonial settlers. A guide, dressed in the white habit of the Brothers or Sisters, then takes you through the Saron (Sisters' house) and Saal (chapel). From there on you're free to explore the other surviving buildings which include Beissel's log house, the Almonry (alms and bake house), the Print and Weavers Shops, a householder's cabin, and the graveyard where many of the original believers are buried. If you can arrange to be in Ephrata on a Saturday (or selected Sunday) evening from late June to September, don't miss the Vorspiel at dusk. This one-hour musical drama depicts life at the Cloister after the death of Beissel when the commune's charitable care for wounded soldiers from the Battle of Brandywine leads to yearning for the outside world. The production is highlighted with many original Cloister hymns performed by talented local professionals.

Directions: The Cloister is located off Rt. 322 in Ephrata shortly before it intersects Rt. 272 (the Oregon Pike).

Nearby Attractions: See Green Dragon Farmers Market.

THE FOLKCRAFT MUSEUM AT WITMER

Open April 1 to Dec. 1: Mon.–Sat., 10–5 p.m.; Sun., 11–5 p.m. Fees: Adults, $3.00; children 6–14, $1.50; families, $7.00. Rest rooms. Gift shop. Folkcraft Museum, Mt. Sidney Rd., Witmer, Pa. 17585. (717) 397–3609.

It's an intriguing building made of timber and old bricks. It looks straight out of the 1700's, yet has existed for only a few years. The secret? It was built of old materials salvaged from throughout Lancaster County and features the half-timbered and brick construction which was a popular style of architecture in Berks County during the early 1700's. Inside, old beams support the ceilings, bricks line the floors, and a massive stone fireplace graces one wall. Adjacent to this unusual structure is a small log cabin. It is an original one, built in 1762 near the Ephrata Cloister and hauled to the small town of Witmer to be used as the "Loom Haus" in this interesting complex known as the Folkcraft Museum.

Visits commence here in the small auditorium which is designed as an Old Order Mennonite meeting house. Wooden benches provide the seats for a twelve minute slide-tape presentation which depicts through beautiful slides (taken by Mel Horst, the owner of the Folkcraft Museum and a professional photographer) the lifestyles and crafts of the Amish, Mennonites, and other Pennsylvania Dutch peoples. Hanging on the wall in this meeting room is the only known copy of the Declaration of Independence printed in German on linen-backed parchment by C. A. Elliot of Philadelphia for the German speaking Pennsylvanians.

In the upstairs balconies of the gallery and museum is a collection of tools and household objects that were integral to life in the early days. Each set of items is accompanied by a written text and blown-up black-and-white photographs which illustrate how these tools were utilized. There are photographs of logging operations, butchering, iron working, broommaking, farming and old time printing techniques among others. There are some fascinating examples of old ballads and broadsides including "The Ballad of Susanna Cox," who was accused of infanticide.

The downstairs hall features a rotating collection of "folk art." On display here have been such well-known local artists as Abner Zook, an Amish artist who specializes in three-dimensional dioramas, and James T. Rexrode, "The Grandpa Moses of the Mountains." Along the walls of this room (which was made from an old garage) are a wagon, sleigh, a collection of Stiegal Apothecary glass, old photography equipment and other antiques.

Periodically during the season, craft demonstrations are conducted. In the "Loom Haus" a weaver operates the 100-year-old loom. Nearby is a woodworking shop where a craftsman fashions items like bells, rattles, and jewelry boxes using a lathe. There is also a print shop which operates out of these buildings.

Directions: The museum is located on Mount Sidney Road in the village of Witmer. Mount Sidney Road starts at Route 340 just west of Smoketown and east of Route 30. Follow Mount Sidney until you see the museum on your right.

Nearby Attractions: See Anderson Pretzel Factory, Amish House Tours—The Amish Farm and House and Amish Homestead, Dutch Wonderland, The National Wax Museum, and Lancaster Carriage Tours.

THE GREEN DRAGON FARMERS MARKET & AUCTION

Held every Friday from 10 a.m. to 10 p.m. No admission fee. Rest rooms. Food concessions. Green Dragon Farmers Market, R.D. 4, Ephrata, Pa. 17522. (717) 733-2334.

Need an odd-size bolt to repair your ailing lawn mower? Want a butter churn to decorate your kitchen? How about some fresh fruit or vegetables for your larder, a ton of hay for your horses, or a bull for your herd of cows? You can purchase all these things and much more at the Green Dragon Farmers Market where the in people say, "If you can't buy it at the Green Dragon, it chust ain't for sale."

The Green Dragon is one of the best and largest farmers' markets in the Pennsylvania Dutch area. Farmers may come from fifty miles away to attend this melange of flea markets, livestock auctions, fresh fruit, vegetable, cheese and meat stands. It is a fun place to visit, and not only for the bargains you might find. The atmosphere is a colorful one, with farmers in denim overalls checking over the cattle for sale, Amish girls selling homemade ice cream, and children in sun bonnets and straw hats helping their father load the family buggy. The market is an interesting meeting ground for the diverse cultures within the Pennsylvania Dutch region. Plain Dutch, such as the Amish and Mennonites, shop alongside the Gay Dutch, the Germans of Lutheran persuasion.

Shopping at the Green Dragon is a unique experience, untainted by the commercialism of a tourist attraction. You could spend an hour or a day here. There are livestock, hay and straw, and dry goods auctions to attend, food concessions to serve you lunch, and over 250 local growers, merchants and craftsmen to tempt you with their wares. There are twenty acres of free parking, with a separate area designated for Amish buggies.

Directions: The market is located on Garden Spot Road off Rt. 272 (look for the Green Dragon directional sign) north of Ephrata in Lancaster County.

Nearby Attractions: See the Ephrata Cloisters.

THE HANS HERR HOUSE

Open daily except Sunday 9–4 April through October, 10–3 Nov. through March. Fees: Adults, $2.00; children 7–12, $1.00. Rest rooms. Gift shop. Special Heritage Days held here during the year. Hans Herr House, 1849 Hans Herr Drive, Willow Street, Pa. 17584. (717) 464-4438.

On a windy hill overlooking the fertile valley below stands a small medieval stone house. Its rugged but lovely brown, gold and tan exterior, so beautifully portrayed in a 1970 painting by Andrew Wyeth, reflects the simple austere tastes of its builders, Swiss Mennonites who came to William Penn's promised land seeking religious freedom. A steeply pitched roof, covered in wood shingles, is cunningly laid so as to provide protection from the prevailing north-west winds. The windows are small and utilitarian, and a sturdy stone chimney rises from the center of the roof providing a unique central heating system. It is remarkable that this fine example of medieval German architecture still exists, for it is the oldest house in Lancaster County, dating from 1719.

A one-hour guided tour of the Hans Herr House not only provides an edifying look at techniques of Early European design and construction, but it reveals interesting details in the lives of religious pioneers in early America. Primitive implements and furnishings reflect a life of religious simplicity. A large central fireplace, which provides heat for at least two floors of this surprisingly spacious house, reveals an energy consciousness only recently being felt today. Hand-hewn stairs, each step hand-carved from individual logs and pegged into place with wooden wedges display the ingenuity of a people who came here with only the clothes on their backs. The large German Bible, hymn book and Martyr's Mirror, which lay on the wooden table in the "family room" converted to a place of worship each Sunday, attest to the religious consciousness of these devout people.

On the grounds of the Hans Herr House are located other buildings which house information and artifacts of early settlers in the Lancaster area. In the Visitor's Center there is a pictorial display with commentary depicting the history of the early Mennonites and the persecution they suffered. In a nearby bank barn are housed implements used by early farmers. Ask to see the restored Conestoga Wagon housed in the chicken coop. It is a beauty! Also, lining the walkway leading to the Hans Herr House is a unique collection of stone millstones, some made in the European fashion, others, the American counterpart.

Directions: Take U.S. Rt. 222 south from Lancaster for about 4.5 miles. Bear left onto Pa. 741, then turn right at the directional sign for the house.

Nearby Attractions: See Eagle Museum, Strasburg Steam Railroad, Railroad Museum of Pennsylvania, and Strasburg's Railroads in Miniature.

THE HERITAGE CENTER MUSEUM OF LANCASTER COUNTY

Open May–Nov., Tues.–Sat. 10–4. Sun. 1–4. Closed Mon. Fees: Adults, $1.00; students 12–18, 75¢; Senior Citizens, 75¢; under 12, free. Group rates. Rest rooms. The Heritage Center Museum of Lancaster County, Center Square and Queen Sts., Lancaster, Pa. 17604. (717) 299-6440.

Housed in Lancaster's Old City Hall and adjoining Masonic Lodge (both buildings dating to the mid-1790's), the Heritage Center Museum features arts and crafts made locally by generations of Lancaster County artisans widely noted for their skill and ingenuity. In well-organized exhibits, you will see 18th century tall clocks, Lancaster Chippendale furnishings, large clothes presses which can be taken apart, corner cupboards, and an assortment of furniture often elaborately decorated. This "high style" of furniture is complemented by the cases of folk art also displayed. Wood carvings, Chalk figures, "Tramp Art" elaborately carved from cigar boxes, and gaily painted tinware accent the warm tones of the wood furnishings.

In the upstairs Masonic Meeting Hall of Lodge 43 (built in 1798), items that were locally produced are arranged in a series of "rooms" by similarity of style rather than by time period. These rooms include parlor settings, living areas, kitchens and the like. In the other upstairs exhibition areas rotating exhibits relating to Lancaster County arts and crafts are displayed.

Directions: The museum is in the center of Lancaster on the corner of Center Square and King and Queen Sts.

Nearby Attractions: See Lancaster's Walking Tour, Wheatland and Rock Ford.

INTERCOURSE:
THE PEOPLE'S PLACE, KITCHEN KETTLE AND NOAH MARTIN EMPORIUM

In the very center of the Amish countryside stands the interesting small town called Intercourse. The origin of the town's curious name is hazy, although two theories have been offered to explain it. One theory proposes that it was named after the "entercourse" or entrance stretch of an old race track nearby; the other, that two famous roads, the old Kings Highway (the east-west road from Philadelphia to Pittsburgh), and the north-south road from Wilmington to Erie, intersected here, forming a joining or "intercourse" of roads. Whatever the reason, this area is a delightful place to visit. Quaint shops such as the Old Curiosity Shop, Nancy's Corner (with lovely quilts for sale) and the Country Store line the main street, and throughout the day the black and gray buggies of the local Amish can be seen traversing the roads.

Listed below are the town's major attractions which are all within walking distance of each other.

THE PEOPLE'S PLACE

Open daily except Sunday, 9:30 a.m.–9:30 p.m. Nov.–March, 9:30–4:30. Fees: Amish Story Museum: Adults, $1.75; children 6–12, $.90. "Who are the Amish?": Adults, $1.75; children, $.90. Combination tickets: Adults, $3.25; children, $1.50. Full-length movie, "Hazel's People": Adults, $3.00; children, $1.50. Rest rooms. Gift shop. Snacks and meals at nearby Kitchen Kettle. The People's Place, Rt. 340, Intercourse, Pa. 17534. (717) 768-7171.

During the 16th century in Zurich, Switzerland, a group of radical Christians, calling themselves the Anabaptists, started a religious movement that declared infant baptism invalid, and stressed the rebaptizing of believing members. Generally a simple and pious people, they emphasized a life that shunned the state and worldly things. They were bitterly persecuted in both Protestant and Roman Catholic countries for these beliefs. In 1536, a Dutch Catholic priest, Menno Simmons, joined this movement, but his teachings were more moderate and a splinter group, which became known as the Mennonites, was formed. Still later in 1693, Jacob Amman, a young Swiss Mennonite Bishop, broke away from the Mennonites to form another sect called the Amish. These Amish were more strict than their parent Mennonite Church, and practiced "shunning" (staying away from) their excommunicated members.

Today, the Mennonites and Amish live in 43 different countries, and have communities in 23 of the fifty states in America. The world's largest Mennonite community and the second largest Amish community are found in Lancaster County, Pennsylvania. At the People's Place, the history, customs and quaint lifestyles of these people are explained through an Amish Story Museum, a series of films, and a craft and book shop. The owners, Merle and Phyllis Good, are both Mennonites who have a sincere desire to share the hows and whys of their faith with those who visit.

A nice way to commence a visit is to watch the 25-minute documentary entitled "Who are the Amish?" Shown continuously throughout the day, this slide show, which uses three screens and nine projectors, is a beautiful commentary on the "plain people." The film deals with such topics as their history, customs, education, death and burial rites, farming and religion. It dispels many of the misconceptions about them, and brings to "outsiders" a greater understanding of the Amish way of life.

In the upper story of the People's Place is housed the studio and display area of Aaron Zook, a self-taught Amish craftsman. His creation, The Amish Story Museum, depicts through large three-dimensional wood-carved paintings events in the life and history of the "plain people." Through this unusual medium, you'll see a barn raising, spring plowing, corn husking, a wedding ceremony, the early years in Europe and other significant occurrences. This permanent collection of paintings presents a unique opportunity to see an "insider's" view of what it is like to be Amish.

In all but the winter season, the dramatic color motion picture called "Hazel's People" is shown here at 6 and 8 p.m. Based on Good's novel, the movie reveals what happens in a quiet Mennonite community when a stranger comes to visit and falls in love with a strong-willed Mennonite girl named Hazel. The confrontation that results from their respective cultures is used as an effective tool to demonstrate the rich spiritual life of these people.

THE KITCHEN KETTLE

Open every day but Sunday, year round, from 9:30 a.m.–5 p.m. Rest rooms. Snacks. Restaurant. Shops. The Kitchen Kettle, Intercourse, Pa. 17534. (717) 768-8261.

Surrounding a flower-bordered courtyard is a quaint village of 15 small shops, featuring crafts, baked goods, flowers, jams and jellies, leather goods and fudge. Here you can sample and buy homemade goodies, and discover unusual gifts for friends and family. Often local craftsmen can be observed demonstrating their skills, and in the kitchen you can see the delicious jams, jellies and fudge being made.

The Kitchen Kettle is located directly behind the People's Place and is a convenient place to grab a quick lunch or snack.

NOAH MARTIN EMPORIUM

Open Mon.–Sat., 8 a.m. to 5 p.m. Closed Sunday. Noah Martin Emporium, Rt. 340, Intercourse, Pa. 17534. (717) 768-3531.

An emporium is defined as a center of trade, a marketplace, a large store selling many different things. Noah Martin's certainly fits this description. Outside the entrance can be seen old buggies, sleighs, plows, desks and harness, while inside anything and everything can be purchased from a player piano to old baby bottles to meat grinders, sausage stuffers and butchering kettles.

Eighty percent of Noah Martin's business is conducted with the local Amish. Often they will bring items here for sale and in return buy needed fixtures such as parts for their windmill pumps or tin cupolas for their barn roofs. Martin's houses a plumbing section and tin shop to fulfill the needs of these local residents.

Farmers from as far away as Idaho and Connecticut also trade with this emporium. Often they can obtain parts for old farm equipment and other unusual items by sending requests to the store. One man from the Midwest phoned Martin's and asked them to build him a buggy and ship it to him. A few months later he called again and asked them to buy him a horse to pull it. They did this without even flinching, which attests to the ingenuity of this unusual and interesting store.

Noah Martin's Emporium is located on the same side of Rt. 340 as the People's Place and is only a few blocks away. You can't miss it!

Directions: Intercourse is located along Rt. 340 about nine miles east of Lancaster.

Nearby Attractions: See Plain & Fancy Farm and Dining room, the Weavertown One-Room School, Farmer's Markets—Bird-in-Hand, and Peterson's Lancaster County Swiss Cheese Shop. You may also want to visit J. Ebersole's Chair Shop, which is a short distance away at the juncture of Rt. 772 and Centerville Rd. Here you can observe local craftsmen making primarily children's furniture such as rocking chairs and tables. These are all for sale.

LANCASTER COUNTY WINERY TOURS

NISSLEY VINEYARDS

Open year round Mon.–Sat. 12–6 (last tour starts at 5:00). Closed Sundays, Election Day, July 4, Thanksgiving, Christmas and Jan. 1. No admission fees. Under 21 must be accompanied by adult. Groups of 15 or more need reservations. Wine shop. Picnics (limited table space). J. Richard Nissley Family, R.D. 1, Bainbridge, Pa. 17502. (717) 426-3514.

A family-owned and -operated winery, Nissley Vineyards has been in existence for ten years. Situated in the scenic rolling farmland near the Susquehanna River, the winery and its grounds provide a lovely setting for picnics and tours. Guides (often family members) will show you the vineyards where the grapes are grown and explain the techniques of wine production. You'll visit the modern wine-making facilities (housed in a massive barn-like structure recently constructed using old materials salvaged from throughout the area), and afterwards enjoy a tasting of red, white and rosé wines in the wine cellar.

Over 30,000 gallons of wine are produced here annually with one of the white wines, Aurora, being a medal winner. Depending on the time of year you visit, you'll be able to watch different phases of the production. In the spring, the wine is bottled and corked. During the late summer months, the grapes are picked, crushed and pressed—an interesting process to observe. Throughout the year, festivities are held at the winery including a Great Wine Race and Barrel Roll Competition and a harvest festival.

Directions: From Rt. 30 west of Lancaster, take Route 441 northwest towards Marietta. Follow Rt. 441 north 8 miles to Wickersham Road. Turn right on Wickersham and follow the signs to the Winery.

Nearby Attractions: See Donegal Mills Plantation, A. Bube's Brewery and Catacombs, and, a fifteen minute drive—The National Watch & Clock Museum and Wright's Ferry Mansion in Columbia.

LANCASTER COUNTY WINERY, LTD.

Tours available Mon.–Sat., April–Nov., 10–4. Store open for sales and sampling year round, Mon.–Sat. 10–4. No admission fee. Under 21 must be accompanied by adult. Large tours by reservation only. Wine and Gift Shop. Lancaster Co. Winery, Ltd., Rawlingsville Rd., Willow St., Pa. 17584. (717) 464-3555.

Situated only a few miles south of the city of Lancaster, this winery is surrounded by fields of vineyards and produces much of its wine from locally-harvested grapes. Tours take you through these fields, where, in the autumn, you can watch the grapes being harvested, and into the winery itself. In the wine-processing rooms and cool cellars you will see how the fresh grapes are slowly processed and converted into the refreshing red, white and rosé wines. This winery still utilizes the massive oaken casks to age its "sleeping" wines. After a leisurely and educational tour of the facility, you are treated to a tasting of a number of the wines bottled here.

An assortment of festivals are held at this winery throughout the year. These may include May vineyard tours (complete with hayrides, country music and wine tastings), an Octoberfest, and Holiday Candlelight Wine and Cheese Parties.

Directions: From Lancaster, take Route 272 South to Baumgardner Road. Turn right (west) onto Baumgardner and follow the signs to the winery.

Nearby Attractions: See Hans Herr House.

LANCASTER, PENNSYLVANIA

Lancaster, the oldest inland city in the United States, is steeped in historical tradition. It twice served as the Capitol of Pennsylvania and was even the Capitol of the United States for one day (September

27, 1777) when the Continental Congress was driven out of Philadelphia. Originally named Hickorytown, the expanding settlement was subsequently named after the Red Rose City of Lancaster, England. It was laid out in 1730 to extend one mile in all directions from Penn Square in the center of town. The downtown streets were named King, Queen, and Duke in deference to the royal family but from thereon the fruits (*e.g.* Lime St.) and nuts (*e.g.* Chestnut) took over.

It was in Lancaster that many of the most eminent personalities from the Republic's first century lived or visited. One can almost reach back into the pages of history and sense what it was like to be among notables like Thomas Paine; George Washington and his Adjutant General Edward Hand; Peggy Shippen, the future wife of Benedict Arnold; abolitionist Thaddeus Stevens; and former President James Buchanan. Lancaster was also the site for many of America's early technological achievements ranging from the Pennsylvania (AKA Kentucky) long rifle, to the steamboat invented by Lancaster local Robert Fulton. The Conestoga Wagon was also developed in Lancaster, which served as a gateway for westward expansion throughout the 1800's. Last but not least, Lancaster continues as the focal point where the Amish and Mennonite farmers in the surrounding countryside bring their produce to market and buy their staples and other necessities. While Lancaster's role in national affairs may no longer be what it once was, the city still preserves its charm and ambiance and remains justifiably proud of its heritage.

LANCASTER WALKING TOUR

Guided tours daily April through October, Mon.–Sat. 10 a.m. and 1:30 p.m., Sundays 1:30 only, twilight tours available Mondays at 6:30 p.m. during July and Aug. Fees: Adults–$2.50, seniors–$2.25, children (6–18) $1.25, under 6 free, group rates also available. Maps and brochure for self-guided tours can be purchased for $2.50 with markers posted at most significant points. Gallery and gift shop at tour headquarters: Historic Lancaster Walking Tour, 15 West King Street, Lancaster, Pa. 17603. (717) 392-1776. A free guided tour of Historic Trinity Lutheran Church at 13 S. Duke St. is provided on Sundays at 10:00 a.m. and 12:15 p.m. and special group tours can be arranged by calling (717) 397-2734.

More than 50 points of historic, architectural, and cultural interest are included on the walking tour of Lancaster City. The guided tours provided by Historic Lancaster Walking Tour Corporation begin with an introductory slide-tape at the Information Center. Then the visitors are broken into smaller groups and led by one of several guides dressed in traditional 19th century Germanic costumes on a fascinating 1¾ mile stroll along the streets and alleyways of historic Lancaster.

One notable feature of the tour is the variety and splendor of architectural styles in evidence. The Georgian style is reflected in the buildings of early Lancaster such as the old City Hall; the Neff-Passmore House, home of Lancaster's first mayor; and Trinity Lutheran Church with its magnificent tower and steeple. The Oppenheimer Townhouse with its metallic ceilings and spiral staircases is a good example of the Federal period, while the ornate decor of the Fulton Opera House reflects the Victorian era. The Romanesque and Queen Anne Revivals are respectively illustrated by the Central Farmers Market and Steinman Mansion, and for more modern tastes Lancaster even has its own skyscraper—the Griest Building.

The homes of the average citizenry are interesting in themselves. For example, there are the L-shaped houses where the householder first built the back half to provide essential living space such as the kitchen and bedrooms. Then as he accumulated more wealth, the front half was added to provide less utilitarian rooms like the dining room and parlor. The quaint story-and-a-half houses were specifically designed to escape the higher property taxes then imposed on two-story dwellings. Especially curious are various embellishments such as the elf-like "eavesdroppers" perched upside-down on the cornices of the Bausman House or the "Busy Lizzies" hanging from top story windows for the purpose of inspecting visitors calling at the front door.

As one might expect, given Lancaster's early beginnings, many of the structures are the earliest or longest operating of their kind. This is true of the Demuth Tobacco Shop where the weekday visitor can still browse amid the type of merchandise offered to the original clientele, the Steinman Hardware Store, and the Royal House Tavern billed as America's first motel. You'll see the site of houses of such notables as Timothy Matlock, the scribe who wrote the Declaration of Independence from Jefferson's dictation, and Thaddeus Stevens, the famous emancipationist and statesman. The guides add a great deal of spice to the tour with stories such as the liaison originally established in Lancaster between Major John Andre who was then held as a British prisoner and Peggy Shippen, the future wife of Benedict Arnold. Andre later used Shippen to convince Benedict Arnold to attempt his treasonous betrayal of the American cause. There's also the tragic story of Anne Coleman whose father forced her to break off her engagement with future President James Buchanan only to see her contract hysteria and die a few days later probably from the laudanum used in treatment. Finally, there's the shameful 1763 massacre by the Paxton Boys of the last remaining Conestoga Indians while they were held in the Old County Jail. All in all, the walking tour of Historic Lancaster is an invigorating and fascinating experience.

Directions: Tour Headquarters are at 15 West King Street, just west of the intersection of King with Penn Square, in the southern portion of the center city area. Center city is accessible via Rts. 222 & 272, Rt. 462, Rt. 23 and Rt. 501. King Street runs parallel to, and is south of Orange, Chestnut and Walnut Streets, and perpendicular to Prince, Queen, Duke and Lime Streets.

Nearby Attractions: See Heritage Center Museum, Wheatland, and Rock Ford.

LITITZ, PENNSYLVANIA— WALKING TOUR, STURGIS PRETZEL HOUSE AND CANDY AMERICANA MUSEUM

WALKING TOUR

Maps available at General Sutter Inn or Johannes Mueller House on East Main Street.

Lititz is a quaint little town founded by Moravians in 1756. Its charm lies in the old 18th century buildings that still line the streets and Church Square, the lovely trees that shade the roadways, and the peaceful atmosphere that permeates the area. For an hour or more you can leisurely stroll down its historic byways and inspect the many old homes, boutiques, and craft shops. The Historical Foundation of Lititz has maps available which describe what you will be seeing. This tour will take you past the famous Linden Hall School for girls (founded in 1767 and one of the two oldest girls' schools in the country); the Johannes Mueller House with its four authentically-furnished rooms and three museum displays (open Mon.–Sat., 10–4); the stately Moravian Church Square which includes the 1759 Brethren's House, the 1758 Sisters' House, the 1787 Moravian Church (rebuilt several times), and the Corpse House, a small colonial structure in which the dead were laid out for viewing; the old Moravian graveyard with headstones dating as early as the 1770's; and thirteen other buildings of interest. While taking your tour, notice that every other house along the street looks old. It is said that an early local ordinance mandated that a vacant lot be left between every two houses built.

Across town lies the scenic Lititz Springs Park which contains picnic pavilions, a playground, rest rooms and food concessions. What is unusual about the park is the Fourth of July festival held here annually. Lititz is known as the City of Lights, and on this special day presents a lovely display of a thousand lit candles. These are placed along the stream running through the park, and their flickering lights are reflected in the flowing water, lighting up the entire area.

Directions: Lititz is located seven miles north of Lancaster at the junction of Routes 501 and 772.

Nearby Attractions: See Rome Grist Mill.

THE JULIUS STURGIS PRETZEL HOUSE

Open all year: Mon.–Sat., 9–5. Fees: Adults, 50¢; children, 35¢; groups, 35¢ per person. Gift shop. Julius Sturgis Pretzel House, 219 East Main St., Lititz, Pa. 17543.

A pretzel ticket is your admission to this popular museum which depicts the early equipment and methods of pretzel making. It is in this house (dating back to 1784) that the first commercial pretzel bakery in the United States was started. Legend has it that in the late 1850's, a tramp stopped at this bakery, and in exchange for some food, gave the baker the recipe for the German hard pretzel. The baker ignored the recipe, but his far-sighted apprentice, Julius Sturgis, used this formula to bake his own pretzels. They were a great success and became the basis upon which Sturgis built his thriving bakery business.

On your tour of this old-time factory, you really do step into the past and see how Sturgis made those first pretzels. With the help of your baker-tour guide, you get the chance to roll and twist your own pretzel dough. After this technique is mastered, you walk over to the massive 200-year-old brick ovens in which the handmade pretzels are still baked. It is here that the difference between soft and hard pretzels is explained as you watch the bakers load the baking pans and place them in the ovens where the pretzels are then cooked for seven to ten minutes. After your twenty-minute tour, you are free to buy your own pretzels and browse through the large gift shop.

Directions: The Pretzel House is located on Main Street (Rt. 772) in Lititz directly across the street from the Linden Hall School for girls.

THE CANDY AMERICANA MUSEUM

Open Mon.–Sat. 10–5. Closed Sundays. No admission fee. Wilbur Chocolate's Factory Candy Outlet here. Rest rooms. Candy Americana Museum, 46 N. Broad St., Lititz, Pa. 17543. (717) 626-1131.

Begun as the brainchild of the owner's wife, this museum features all phases of the candy industry from manufacturing to advertising. It represents a unique opportunity to see how candy was made and packaged in the old days. You'll see displays of equipment used by the country's first candy makers, an early 1900 candy kitchen, shelves filled with unusual candy containers, antique and modern molds, and a collection of over 150 chocolate pots. In the rear of the museum, you can watch workers hand dipping and decorating candies through a glass partition. When you're finished browsing, you may purchase the Wilbur candies at economical prices in the adjacent candy outlet.

Directions: From the Julius Sturgis House on East Main Street, go west on Main St. to the fountain in the square and turn right onto Broad St. The museum will be a couple of blocks away on your left.

MILL BRIDGE CRAFT VILLAGE

Open April–Dec. 1, 9:30–5:30 daily except Sunday. Fees: Adults, $2.50; children, $1.50. Rest rooms. Public cafeteria. Picnics. Campsites. Mill Bridge Craft Village, Box 73, Soudersburg, Pa. 17577. (717) 687-8181.

This small village of craft shops and campsites is located in a scenic area adjacent to a stream which is spanned by one of the longest covered bridges in the area—The Soudersburg Covered Bridge. In the village itself is a lovely old stone mill built in 1738 for Ben S. Herr, the nephew of Hans Herr, one of the earliest and most prominent settlers in Lancaster County. The mill is still working, and the large water wheel provides the power for the millstones to grind the corn into meal. You can see the mill in operation as well as buy the stone ground corn. Also in the mill are housed a variety of craft shops and craftsmen. You can watch the broom maker or candlemaker handcraft their products. There are women spinning wool and hooking rugs, and artists at work painting Lancaster landscapes. Near the mill there is an animal petting area filled with rabbits, chickens, goats, ponies, and other farm animals to keep the children entertained, as well as a number of other craft shops, one of which features a large assortment of colorful quilts handmade by local Amish. A number of country festivals are held at this location throughout the season.

Directions: The village is on Ronks Rd. between Rt. 30 and Rt. 741 east of Strasburg.

Nearby Attractions: See Strasburg Railroad, Strasburg's Railroads in Miniature, Railroad Museum of Pennsylvania, and The Amish Village.

THE NATIONAL WATCH AND CLOCK MUSEUM

Open year round Mon.–Fri. 9–4, Sat. 9–5. Closed Sundays and holidays. Fees: Adults, $1.50; children 8–17 and Senior Citizens, 75¢. Group rates. Rest rooms. Library. Handicapped: Museum is barrier free. National Association of Watch and Clock Collectors, Inc., Box 33, 514 Poplar St., Columbia, Pa. 17512. (717) 684-8261.

The White Rabbit with his blinking eyes gazes at you from his glassed-in shelf. Nearby, a mouse slowly makes his way up to one o'clock only to be sent running down again when he reaches it. A turtle floats in a mineral oil bath, pointing out the hours with his snout, while the splish-splash of water trickling down chutes to mark off seconds is heard in the background. Suddenly, at the hour on the hour, the room comes acoustically alive, not only with tick tocks, but with ping pings, musical tunes, chimes, the clacking of falling marbles, resonant bongs and cuckoos, leaving no doubt that despite your suspicions of being in Wonderland, you have really made it to the National Watch and Clock Museum.

Boasting over 34,000 members from all over the world, the National Association of Watch and Clock Collectors chose Columbia, Pa. as its headquarters and center for their fascinating museum of time pieces. Guided tours lead through numerous clock exhibits ranging from the traditional American tall clocks to novelty items such as the wandering eye clocks, to ornate European time pieces, and to the highly sophisticated atomic time clock. The inner mechanism of many of these clocks is displayed so that you can see the intricate movements of the wheels and gears, a number of them made from wood.

From the moment you punch in your time card at the old Postal Clock until the time you punch out, you will be submerged in an imaginative and precise world that man has created to mark his time. Children as well as adults will enjoy this sojourn from 17th century watches to 20th century water clocks, for there is continual motion; and professional and amateur watch and clock collectors will not be disappointed with the immense variety and sophistication of time pieces on display.

Directions: Take Route 30 west of Lancaster to Rt. 441 Columbia. Take Route 441 towards Columbia, and follow it into town where it becomes N. Third Street. Take N. Third to Poplar Street and turn left (Poplar Street is about three blocks into town). Go two blocks, and the museum will be on the right at the corner of Poplar and N. Fifth Streets.

Nearby Attractions: See Wright's Ferry Mansion. A fifteen-minute drive away is Nissley Vineyards (see Lancaster Co. Winery Tours).

THE NATIONAL WAX MUSEUM OF LANCASTER COUNTY HERITAGE

Open daily all year: Jan. & Feb., 9–6; Memorial Day to Labor Day, 9–9; and remainder of year, 9–8. Fees: Adults, $2.25; children 5–11, $1.25. Rest rooms. Gift shop. Handicapped: Exhibits are all on one level and aisles can accommodate wheelchairs. National Wax Museum, Rt. 30 East, Lancaster, Pa. 17602. (717) 393-3679.

George Washington sits regally at a table listening to his trusted aide General Edward Hand. Martha Washington, in a lovely pale blue dress, holds her cup while Mrs. Hand is serving the tea—a moment in history preserved indefinitely through the technological and artistic efforts of the National Wax Museum of Lancaster County Heritage. Important events, both national and local from the 1600's to the present, figure in this museum's lifelike recreations. All are viewed primarily through a Lancaster County perspective. You will see Benjamin Franklin purchasing the famous Conestoga Wagon; President James Buchanan greeting people at his Pennsylvania home, Wheatland; William Penn receiving his grant to Pennsylvania from King Charles II; and many more. One of the most impressive scenes is a huge diorama depicting a typical Lancaster County Amish farm scene on the day of a "barn raising." The wax figures seem to come alive through the clever use of sound, lighting, image projecting techniques, and animation.

The authentically detailed scenes and lifelike wax figures are so realistic you can easily become a part of the illusion and for an hour or more relive these moments in history. The special effects, such as figures that actually talk, and dramatic lighting techniques, add to the appeal. School-age children and adults will find a tour of this attraction both educational and entertaining.

Directions: The museum is located on Route 30, four miles east of Lancaster and adjacent to Dutch Wonderland.

Nearby Attractions: See Dutch Wonderland, Amish House Tours—The Amish Homestead, and the Anderson Pretzel Bakeries.

NEW HOLLAND SALES STABLES

Horse Auction held Mondays starting at 10 a.m.; Cattle and Pig Auction Weds. at Noon; Sheep and Cattle, Thurs. at 11:00. No fees. Rest rooms. Snacks. (717) 354-4341.

To get a true flavor of Dutch country life, come to the New Holland Sales Stables on Monday mornings beginning at 10:00 a.m. for the horse, mule, and pony auction. But be warned—one can sit mesmerized for hours watching the bustle and color. Farmers and dealers from miles around (including the Amish, for this is where they buy and sell their carriage and work horses) come here to barter. The parking lot is full of cars, horse trailers, and Amish buggies. Blacksmiths are hard at work in nearby sheds rasping hooves and fitting horseshoes. High-stepping ponies pull flashy gigs down the road. There's a flea market where bridles, brushes, old tools and sleigh bells are sold. And grey-bearded Amish men eat hot dogs in the crowded restaurant while children scurry about trying to get a coke.

Up in the beef barn there's an extensive system of plank walkways where visitors can gaze down at the animals below. Sheep, cattle, and pigs with numbers attached to their hindquarters root about while prospective buyers discuss their merits, next year's crops, and the weather.

The atmosphere in the main barn grows heady as the auction begins. Horses of all shapes and sizes—quarter horses, ponies, donkeys, mules, and mixed breeds—are trotted down the center aisle closely watched by the bidders in the surrounding grandstands. A man with a whip stands nearby to keep the horses trotting and to control the unruly ones. A fast-talking auctioneer rattles off the age and credentials for each horse. The crowd gets excited when the bidding ranges into the thousands but a horse can go for as little as $100.00. (Don't wave your hand or you might go home with a workhorse!) Most of the horses are sold. Their destination? Another farm, horse dealer, riding stable, and sometimes even the meat market. The auction lasts as long as there are horses to sell. If you can't make the horse auction on Monday, a cattle and pig auction is conducted on Wednesdays starting at noon while sheep and cattle are also auctioned off on Thursday beginning at 11:00 a.m.

Directions: The sales stables are located in the town of New Holland. If you approach from the east along Route 23, go into town and take a left onto Railroad Avenue (Robinson's Department Store will be on one side, Kauffman's Country Store on the other). Go over the railroad tracks, then take a right at the chain link fence onto Fulton.

Nearby Attractions: See Porkchop Farm, Weaver Poultry Tours, and Peterson's Lancaster Co. Swiss Cheese Shop. While in New Holland, stop at Kauffman's old-time Country Store for a *unique* shopping experience.

PHILLIPS LANCASTER COUNTY SWISS CHEESE COMPANY

Retail store open 8–5 p.m. Mon.–Sat. Best times to see cheese making operation, Mon.–Fri. 9 a.m. to noon. No admission fee. Phillips Lancaster County Swiss Cheese Company, 435 Centerville Rd., Gordonville, Pa. 17529. (717) 354-4424.

"Little Miss Muffet sat on her tuffet, eating her curds and whey . . ." How many times have you heard that nursery rhyme and wondered what it was all about? Well, here is your chance to find out, for the notorious curds and whey are an important part in the making of Swiss cheese.

Mornings are the best time to observe the cheese-making process. Through a glassed-in window, you can see huge copper vats, each filled with 300 gallons of milk to which has been added cheese-making ingredients including a coagulating agent called rennet. When the milk has formed a solid state called junket, it is cut with a cheese harp into small "curds" about the size of a kernel of wheat. Then, when all is mixed and heated, the knowledgeable cheese makers take large sheets of cheese cloth and lift out the solid curds from the liquid whey that is made in the process. The curds, which eventually become the cheese, (200 pounds from the 300 gallons of milk) are then wrapped with cheese cloth and pressed into forms weighing up to 100 pounds. These blocks are soaked in a brine solution for a few days, placed in a cold cellar for a week, then moved to a hot curing center for six weeks (this is the place where the expanded CO_2—carbon dioxide—forms the holes in the cheese). The process is quite similar to that practiced in Switzerland several hundred years ago, and produces 4–7 cheeses a day.

After watching the cheese makers and taking a guided tour of the cooling and ageing rooms, you can purchase a variety of cheeses in the small retail store. These even include a new low fat, low salt and low cholesterol Swiss-type cheese which is quite tasty!

Directions: From the town of New Holland and Rt. 23, go south on Dillar Ave. which turns into Hollander Road. Follow Hollander Rd. to Zeltenreich Road and turn right. Cross Peters Road, then turn left onto the next road you come to, Centerville Rd. The cheese shop will appear on your left.

Nearby Attractions: See New Holland Sales Stables, Weaver Poultry Tours and Intercourse (The People's Place, Noah Martin Emporium, and Kitchen Kettle), and Pork Chop Farm. If you continue down Centerville Road you will come to J. Ebersole's Chair Shop, which specializes in handmade children's furniture. If you come at the right time, you can watch the skilled carpenters at work. (717) 768-8820.

THE PLAIN & FANCY FARM AND DINING ROOM

Restaurant open year-round Mon.–Sat. 11:30–8:00, Closed Sunday and Christmas. Reasonable prices. Large groups need reservations. Shops and museums open Mon.–Sat. 10–6 (some 10–8 in the summer). Fees for museums: moderate. Handicapped: easy access to dining room, some steps leading into shops and museums. Plain & Fancy Farm and Dining Room, Bird-In-Hand, Pa. 17505. (717) 768-8281.

A nice way to top off a day spent in the Amish countryside is to have a home-cooked country meal at the Plain & Fancy Dining Room.

Meals are served family style (children are welcome) at large tables and include a variety of meats and vegetables all cooked by the "plain people." There is no limit to the servings (empty platters are continuously refilled) and even the most hearty of appetites will be satisfied.

In addition to the dining room there is an assortment of shops and museums you may visit. These include an ice cream parlor, Bake Shop, Fudge Shop, toy store, clothing outlet, jewelry store, print shop and flower store. Be sure to visit the Clay Distelfink. Here you can see Pennsylvania Dutch tulip ware bowls and plates slip painted and sgraffitoed by talented artisans. Plates may be custom ordered. The Gay 90's Museum houses an interesting collection of 19th century artifacts including old-style nickelodeons which can still be played, an assortment of buggies and wagons, and America's first coin-operated juke box! Four of the museum's rooms are completely furnished in the Victorian style. If you like dolls, there's an Antique Doll Museum that features over 450 dolls from the early 1800's to the present.

The Plain & Fancy complex could easily be termed a Lancaster County in miniature, for it offers the visitor a variety of opportunities to learn about the Amish and their customs. Attached to one of the gift shops is a re-creation of an Old Order Amish house. Guided tours are conducted through this seven-room home. The customs of the "plain people" are described, and the manner in which the Amish live and worship is explained. In the warmer months, 15-minute buggy rides that start at the Plain & Fancy may be taken. Seated in an Amish courting buggy, you see the roads and automobiles from an Amish perspective. Finally, there is an animal barn and farm to acquaint you with the rural life, and a miniature railroad both children and adults will enjoy.

Directions: The Plain & Fancy Farm is located on Rt. 340, 7½ miles east of Lancaster at Bird-In-Hand.

Nearby Attractions: See Weavertown One Room School, Buggy Rides through the Amish countryside—Abe's Buggy Rides, Farmer's Markets—Bird-In-Hand, Intercourse, and Phillips Lancaster County Swiss Cheese Shop. Another restaurant that serves family style home-cooked meals (but without the added shops and attractions) is the nearby Good 'N Plenty Restaurant, Rt. 896 in Smoketown: (717) 394-7111.

PORK CHOP FARM

Farm open daily from May 15–Sept. 15, 10 a.m. to dusk. Fees: Adults, $1.00; children, 50¢. Pork Chop Farm, R.D. 2, New Holland, Pa. 17557. (717) 354-5054 or 354-9557.

Did you ever see a newborn pig? A boar weighing close to 1,000 pounds? A concrete building filled with nursing sows? You can see all of these and more at Pork Chop Farm, an educational attraction that is also primarily a working farm. Purebred Duroc and Chester White Breeding Stock are raised here for breeding stock and feeder pigs. There can be up to 600 pigs at the farm at any one time with as many as 200 being born each month.

One-half-hour guided tours take you through buildings in which you'll see all phases of pig raising. The Farrowing House will delight the youngsters. Countless newborn piglets, all squealing and wiggling their curly tails, nurse gustily at their mother's sides. In the Gestation House, 130 pregnant pigs lie in their narrow stalls, indolently awaiting the birth of their babies. A sow must average two litters of 8½ piglets each to remain on the farm. In another section of the building are the ones responsible for all the pregnant pigs, the massive boars. These great creatures with mean-looking tusks are said to be quite ill-tempered and dangerous.

Up to 10,000 visitors each summer come to visit this farm and get a taste of the rural life. It provides the ideal educational opportunity to view the modern "production line" method of raising pigs commercially.

Directions: The farm is near New Holland. Take Rt. 23 to New Holland and turn south on Brimmer Rd. Continue for two and one-half miles. Bear left at the "Y" and look for the farm on the right.

Nearby Attractions: See Weaver Poultry Tours, Phillips Lancaster County Swiss Cheese Shop, and New Holland Sales Stables. After your visit ask your guide to point the way to Lapp Valley Farm only 1 mile away. The farm is run by an Amish family and has delicious ice cream cones for sale.

RAILROAD MUSEUM OF PENNSYLVANIA

Open daily 10 a.m. (11 on Sundays) to 5 p.m. Closed most major holidays.
Fees: Adults, $1.50; children under 12 and seniors over 65—free. Rest rooms.
Library. Railroad Museum of Pennsylvania, Box 15, Strasburg, Pa. 17597.
(717) 687-8628.

If, after your ride on the Strasburg Steam Railroad, you've caught
railroad fever and want to get a closer look, walk across the street to
the Railroad Museum of Pennsylvania. Here you can see massive steam
locomotives, coal-carrying tenders, and a large variety of railroad cars
from every conceivable vantage point. There's an overhead balcony
from which you can peer down into the giant smokestacks, a grease
pit where you can gaze up at the pistons and valves that comprise the
engine's inner workings, and of course walk-on opportunities so you
can get the feel of what it's like behind the firebox. The museum,
operated by the Pennsylvania Historical and Museum Commission, is
the only one in the nation specifically designed and constructed to
house a rolling stock collection.

The trains on display were used to perform every imaginable task.
Naturally, there are trains used to move passengers and baggage including the second oldest known piece of passenger equipment in the
United States—an 1885 Cumberland Valley Railroad car. Then there
are trains used in logging, quarrying, and hauling a variety of other
types of freight. Many trains were dedicated to the service of a specific
industry such as the fireless cooker used in Bethlehem Steel's yards.
There's even a post office on wheels and a $1/6$ scale steam engine used
for backyard excursions. In the yard behind the museum are 15 additional pieces of rolling stock being restored for future display in a
proposed second wing of the museum.

In addition to the trains themselves, there's a variety of other
paraphernalia and exhibits on the history and background of railroading. You'll see old-time tickets, lanterns, surveying equipment, conductor's uniforms, dining car china and silver, and numerous pictures
and slides showing the people and equipment which contributed to the
heyday of the iron horse. Graphic displays focus on bridges, trestles,
and viaducts that carried the trains; celebrated railroad catastrophes
such as fires, floods and derailments; and a description of how a steam-
driven locomotive actually works. For the true railroad scholar, there's

even a research library of written railroad memorabilia on the second
floor of the museum.

Directions: Take Rt. 30 East from Lancaster about 7 miles to Rt. 896 South.
Follow 896 S. about 4 miles until it intersects Rt. 741 in Strasburg. Take 741
East about one mile and you'll see the museum on your right.

Nearby Attractions: See Strasburg Steam Railroad (across the street), Strasburg's Railroads in Miniature, Eagle Museum, Hans Herr House, and Mill
Bridge Craft Village.

ROCK FORD PLANTATION

Open weekdays, except Monday, 10–4, Sundays noon–4, April–Nov. Special
evening candlelight tours conducted several times a year, private candlelight
tours for groups also available. Fees: Adults, $2.00; children 6–18, $1.00.
Gift shop. Picnics and snacks at nearby park. Rock Ford, Box 264, 881 Rock
Ford Road, Lancaster, Pa. 17602. (717) 392-7223.

Along the wooded banks of the lovely Conestoga River stands
the stately home of General Edward Hand, an Irish physician who
became George Washington's Adjutant General. Almost two hundred
years old, this brick Georgian mansion was built in a simple style
popular at the time, a center hall with four corner rooms. Scrupulously
preserved, Rock Ford still has most of its original 18th century floors,
shutters, stair rails, doors, panelings and window glass (that includes
1,400 window panes!). Great care has been taken to restore the interior rooms to their original vibrant colors, as seen in the deep gold
walls of the family room and study, and the brillliant blue of the parlor. All furnishings are authentic, although not all are Hand family
pieces.

Guided tours, lasting about 45 minutes, cover three floors of this
house. Costumed hostesses relate the story of General Hand's life and
escort you through the elegantly furnished rooms. There are a variety
of lovely antiques, including a magnificent 1757 clock manufactured
by David Rittenhouse. Scattered throughout the house are memorabilia
of General Hand's. These include his own writing desk which accompanied him throughout the revolution, his set of surgical equipment
which served him after the war when he became a Lancaster physician, and his portrait. In the basement of the mansion is a spacious
brick-floored kitchen with walk-in fireplace. Its large doors provided

easy access for the produce man who was said to drive his horse and wagon directly into the room for easy unloading!

Across the field from the main house is a large restored barn. In it is housed the Rock Ford-Kauffman Museum. On display here is a fine collection of folk artifacts, mostly from Southeastern Pennsylvania, and dating from 1750 to approximately 1900. The museum features an interesting assortment of rifles, pewter, copper, brass, tinware, fraktur, and typical Dutch furniture such as decorated chests and cupboards. Admission to this is included in the Rock Ford fee, and you may browse at will through the many exhibits.

Rock Ford Plantation is surrounded by over 600 acres of the Lancaster County Central Park. There are scenic hiking trails, picnic areas, playgrounds, flower gardens, swimming pool (for a moderate fee), rest room and snack bar, all open and available to the public.

Directions: Rock Ford is within the Lancaster city limits. From Lancaster, take South Duke Street and follow signs to Rock Ford. You will turn right onto Rock Ford Road at the junction of South Duke and the Conestoga River.

Nearby Attractions: See Wheatland, Lancaster Walking Tour, and Heritage Center Museum.

ROME MILL

Open daily with tours conducted from 9 a.m. to 5:30 p.m. Fees: Adults, $1.50; children 6–12, $1.00. Picnics. Rome Mill, Rt. 772, Lititz, Pa. (717) 626-4520.

This old stone mill was in operation for over two centuries. In the 1920's industrialization brought a halt to stone ground milling, and the structure lay neglected. Then, in 1976, it was completely restored as a tourist attraction so that others could see how corn and wheat were ground in "the good ol' days." Today as in those days gone by, the 22-foot water wheel turns inside the building, powering the millstones and several other machines such as the corn roaster, flour sifter, and saw mill apparatus. In our energy conscious days, it is gratifying to watch the power of a natural flowing river performing a feat nowadays accomplished by energy draining machines. What's even nicer is that the nutritious corn and wheat ground here are also for sale.

Adjacent to the mill are several outbuildings also contained in the tour. There is a wheelwright's shop, blacksmith shop, and partially restored up-and-down saw mill which will soon be in operation. Throughout the buildings, old and interesting tools are displayed. There is a fascinating collection of millstones near the picnic grounds, an old log barn that was moved here from New York, and a small petting zoo with donkeys and goats.

Directions: The mill is one half mile east of Lititz on Route 772.

Nearby Attractions: See Lititz, Pa.

THE ROUGH & TUMBLE ENGINEERS MUSEUM

Open daily 10–5 during the summer. Winter hours, Oct.–March, Sat. 10–5. Fees: Adults, $1.00; 10 and under, free. Rest rooms. Gift shop. Picnics. Handicapped: Paved areas lead to most of sheds housing machinery. For schedule of events write: Rough & Tumble Engineers Museum, Box 9, Kinzer, Pa. 17535. (717) 442-4249.

If you like machines and are intrigued by the ingenious way man has harnessed energy throughout the past 100 years, you will certainly enjoy a visit to the Rough & Tumble Museum. Formed after World War II by the Rough and Tumble Engineers Historical Association, Inc., this museum is dedicated to the preservation of steam and gasoline engines as well as other clever labor-saving devices used on the farm and in the home. Here you will see an assortment of machines from massive steam-powered tractors to dog-powered washing machines to a stone crusher, saw mill, miniature steam train and all sorts of gasoline engines. These are housed in buildings throughout the grounds, and although the machinery is not identified, most of its uses are self-evident.

Although it is interesting to browse through the museum on "off days," the most worthwhile time to come is during its annual celebrations: the spring steam-up, the last Saturday in April; the annual four-day Threshers Reunion the third week in August (the main event of the year); and the Enschine-O-Rama in October. At these times, engines are fired up and the grounds are alive with the cacaphony of hundreds of working machines. Massive steam tractors let off hot air, a calliope provides a musical background and over a hundred steam whistles let loose. A miniature train provides rides for the youngsters while all about motors chug, gears go round and round, and old engines perform a variety of feats. There are antique car and fire engine displays, parades featuring Conestoga wagons pulled by work horses, steam threshing exhibits, flea markets, and an abundance of good home-cooked Pennsylvania Dutch food. All ages will enjoy a visit during these celebrations when the engines of the past come to life. Write for exact times and dates.

Directions: The museum is located 18 miles east of Lancaster on Route 30 near the town of Kinzer.

Nearby Attractions: See Strasburg Steam Railroad, Pennsylvania Railroad Museum, and Strasburg's Railroads in Miniature (all about a 10–15 minute drive away).

STRASBURG STEAM RAILROAD

Open daily from May through Oct. with hourly trains beginning at 11:00 (12:00 on Sundays) to 5:00, June–Aug. and at 12:00 to 3:00 during May and Sept.–Oct. Weekends only from 12:00 to 3:00 during April, Nov. and 1st two weeks of Dec. (Santa Claus Days). Fees: Adults, $2.00; children under 12, $1.00. Picnics. Snacks. Gift shop. Rest rooms. Strasburg Railroad, P.O. Box 96, Strasburg, Pa. 17579. (717) 687-7522.

Whether you're a committed railroad buff or just like a good ride through the picturesque Amish countryside, the 4½ mile trip on the Strasburg Railroad to the village of Paradise is truly heavenly. The excitement begins to build as you park your car in the spacious lot and approach the century-old train platform to buy your ticket. Then, suddenly one of the Strasburg line's 100-ton coal-fired iron horses pulls into view with shrieking whistles and a billowing cloud of smoke trailing behind it. And when the conductor finally says all aboard and you climb on one of the celebrated coaches or open observation cars, the excitement is contagious.

The 130-year-old Strasburg is America's oldest short-line railroad, which provided essential short hop transit before the advent of the automobile. Each of its locomotives and coaches has a tale of its own. For example, Engine No. 1223 appeared in the movies "Broadway Limited" and "Hello Dolly" (which also featured Strasburg's elegant observation coach). The closed wooden coaches, such as the Willow Brook that appeared in MGM's "Raintree Country," contain authentic coal oil lamps and pot belly stoves which are still used on colder days.

The train takes you on a 25-minute ride through the rolling Dutch landscape and immaculately-kept Amish farms to the hamlet of Paradise which is the turnaround point. On the way back a stop is also made at Groff's Picnic Grove which can only be reached by train. Here visitors can disembark, enjoy a leisurely lunch, and then return on a later run.

Before leaving, be sure to take time (and 25¢) to stroll through the luxurious President's car. Built in 1916 at a cost of $100,000 (equivalent to about $1 million today), this traveling mansion was used by railroad as well as real Presidents such as Harry S Truman during his famous whistle-stop campaign of 1948. The accommodations are spacious—observation room, master plus two other staterooms, dining room, stainless steel kitchen, and crew and steward areas. And the details are beyond first class—rosewood inlaid woodwork, stained glass windows, air conditioning, and radio and telephone communication links.

Directions: Take Rt. 30 East about 7 miles from Lancaster to Rt. 896 South. Follow 896 about 4 miles until Strasburg where you'll intersect Rt. 741. Take 741 East about a mile beyond Strasburg and the train platform will appear on your left.

Nearby Attractions: See Railroad Museum of Pennsylvania (right across the street), Strasburg's Railroads in Miniature, Eagle Museum, Hans Herr House, and Mill Bridge Craft Village.

STRASBURG'S RAILROADS IN MINIATURE: THE CHOO CHOO BARN AND THE TOY TRAIN MUSEUM

THE CHOO CHOO BARN

Open daily June, July and August, 10–6; May, Sept. and Oct., 10–5; Nov. and April, weekends only, 11–5. Fees: Adults, $1.50; children 7–12, 50¢. Rest rooms. Gift shop. The Choo Choo Barn, Rt. 741, Strasburg, Pa. 17579. (717) 687-7911.

A miniature circus with the "world's smallest sword swallower," a pint-size rifle-toting farmer matching wits with a ground hog ducking in and out of his hole—these are just two of the many delights which await you at the Choo Choo Barn in Strasburg, Pa. Known as America's most unique model railroad, this fully-automated display combines an expert and intricate model train layout with a multitude of scaled-down scenes from Lancaster County. Ten model trains, eight "O" gauge, one "HO" and one "N" are featured here. But most noteworthy is the animation of the hundreds of tiny figures moving in a variety of settings: skiers going downhill, parades, firemen putting out a house fire, children playing baseball, acrobats walking the tightwire, and much more. An added highlight to the display is when the lights dim and a nighttime beauty descends. Glowing house and street lights come on and the glittering moon revolves slowly in the center of this tiny world.

People of all ages will find much to entertain them here (small children love all the movement, although you may have to lift them up to the level of the display at times). The layout covers over 1,700 square feet, and you may spend as much time as you wish gazing at the diminutive scenes.

Directions: The Choo Choo Barn is located on Route 741 about a mile east of the junction of Rts. 741 and 896.

THE TOY TRAIN MUSEUM

Open daily 10–5, May 1–Oct. 31; Weekends in April, Nov. and first two weekends in Dec. plus Good Friday, Easter Monday, Thanksgiving Friday and Christmas Week (weather permitting). Fees: Adults, $1.50; children 7–12, 50¢. Handicapped: Museum is barrier free. Rest rooms. Gift shop. Museum Director, P.O. Box 248, Strasburg, Pa. 17579. (717) 687-8976.

A short distance from the Choo Choo Barn, the Toy Train Museum is the actual headquarters of the Train Collector's Association, an organization dedicated to the preservation and history of toy trains, and, not surprisingly, composed of ardent model railroad fans. The Museum has on display toy trains from before the turn of the century to the present, many of them operating in realistic villages. You will see the prize achievements of many manufacturers dating from the 1800's on. There are the early tin and wood trains, live steam cast–iron engines, early electric engines, and the standard gauge (2 gauge) trains.

This is the spot for all those men, who, when their first-born son takes his first breath, go out and buy him a model train. In fact, the current movie being shown at the museum, entitled "Model Railroading At Its Best" presents a humorous look at a man who goes bananas over model trains, and the trials and tribulations of his wife who has to put up with his excesses. The cost of the movie is included in the admission, and it is shown every half hour.

Directions: From the Choo Choo Barn, continue east on Rt. 741 past the Strasburg Railroad until you come to Paradise Lane. Turn left onto Paradise and follow the signs to the museum (this is directly behind the Red Caboose and Restaurant where, if you are a real train buff, you can spend the night in an authentic railroad car).

Nearby Attractions: See Strasburg Steam Railroad, Railroad Museum of Pennsylvania, Hans Herr House, Eagle Gun Museum, and Mill Bridge Craft Village.

WEAVER POULTRY TOURS

Tours offered Mon.–Fri. at 9, 10 and 1. No admission fee. Rest rooms. Outlet store. Victor F. Weaver, Inc., 403 South Custer Ave., New Holland, Pa. 17557. (717) 354-4211.

When the hardy pioneers came to America in the 1600's, they brought chickens with them to supply their families with fresh eggs. Then, when famine struck in Jamestown, some hungry colonist found an equally important and heretofore unknown use for his fowl, the dinner pot. Ever since then, chicken has played an important part in the American diet, whether it be for eggs at breakfast, or fried chicken at a picnic. To meet the continuing demand for chicken, large corporations have developed which offer the consumer prepackaged frozen cooked chicken and egg products as convenience foods. The Victor F. Weaver Corporation is one of these.

Tours of the manufacturing plant start with a twelve-minute slide-tape show which depicts the history of the chicken and of the Weaver Corporation. Starting 37 years ago as a Mom and Pop operation which produced 200 fried chickens a week, the corporation has mushroomed into a plant which processes over 100,000 cooked chickens a day. Weaver Products, such as Weaver's frozen Dutch Fried Chicken, Chicken Rondeles, Liquid Egg products, white meat chicken rolls and chicken franks, can now be found in stores from Bangor, Maine to Miami, Florida.

Although the Weaver Corporation oversees chicken production from the Breeder Farms to the Retail Distribution Centers, the tour focuses on two areas in the Production Center in which the already eviscerated and cut up chicken moves from the raw state to fried, frozen, and finally to packed cartons to be placed in the freezer. It is a fascinating process to watch: from the huge vats which pour the chicken onto conveyor belts, to the workers who separate the breasts from the thighs, to the frozen chicken which comes catapulting down the long chutes on its way to being packaged. Children as well as adults will enjoy this guided tour, for there is constant motion and ingenious machinery at work. When the tour is completed, free samples of a Weaver product are handed out.

If you have the time, stop at the Outlet Store which is in the large brick building along South Custer Ave. Bags of fried and frozen chicken are sold here at reduced rates because of purely aesthetic defects such as chipped batter. Also sold are the regular Weaver products along with other grocery items. A lunch counter provides sandwiches and snacks.

Directions: From W. Main Street (Rt. 23) in New Holland, take South Custer Ave. (a right turn if coming from the direction of Lancaster). Follow South Custer to where it intersects with Orlan Street, and the plant will be on your left. Tours start at the large white building, called the Fried Chicken Production Center which is the second building you will come to (the brick building you come to first houses the outlet store).

Nearby Attractions: See New Holland Sales Stables, Phillip's Lancaster County Swiss Cheese Shop and Pork Chop Farm. While in New Holland, stop at Kauffman's Country Store for an old fashioned shopping experience. It's at the corner of Rt. 23 and Railroad Ave.

THE WEAVERTOWN ONE-ROOM SCHOOLHOUSE

Open daily 10–5. Fees: Adults, $1.00; children, 60¢. Outhouses. Weavertown One-Room Schoolhouse, 2249 Lincoln Highway East, Lancaster, Pa. 17602. (717) 768-3976.

One-room schoolhouses used to be a fact of life in Pennsylvania. Students from grades 1 through 8 would sit together in the small room and be taught their reading, writing, and arithmetic by one teacher.

Light was provided by the large windows, heat from a coal stove, and punishment by a ruler across the knuckles. Gradually, as schools were consolidated, multiple-room buildings became the norm, and most one-room schools were closed.

Today in Lancaster County, an actual one-room schoolhouse, which operated from 1877 until May of 1969, has been preserved and opened to the public. The setting is the original one with wooden desks, blackboards, large windows and coal stove. Within the classroom students sing songs, recite poetry and indulge in the typical mischievous practices of passing notes and pulling hair. While conducting her class, the teacher describes the educational system and keeps a check on the sometimes wayward students. The dress of all is common to the area. Some are dressed Amish style; others, in fancy dresses; still others in jeans and flannel shirts. What is unusual about this school is that these students and teachers, so amazingly lifelike, are really animated figures. Fine detail work in the facial expressions and postures makes it quite difficult to distinguish the real children, who may sit in one row of desks, from their animated counterparts.

Directions: The Schoolhouse is on Route 340 a few miles west of Intercourse.

Nearby Attractions: See Intercourse, Plain and Fancy Farm and Dining Room, Farmers' Markets—Bird-In-Hand, the Folk Craft Museum at Witmer, and Buggy Rides through Amish Countryside—Abe's Buggy Rides.

WHEATLAND—PRESIDENT JAMES BUCHANAN'S HOME

Tours conducted daily, April through November, from 10:00–4:30. Fees: Adults, $2.50; children (6–12), $1.75. Not recommended for small children and stairs make it difficult for handicapped. Wheatland, Marietta Ave., Lancaster, Pa. (717) 392-8721.

Pennsylvania's only President is best known for two things. He was the only bachelor to serve in the White House and was one of our most loathed Presidents for standing by helplessly during the dark days before the Civil War. Despite Buchanan's own shortcomings, the Victorian era during which he lived was truly one of the most grandiose in history both here in the United States as well as abroad. It's the memorabilia from this heady period of the mid-1800's that makes the 45-minute tour of Buchanan's handsome Georgian mansion so interesting.

Buchanan bought the 180-acre estate known as Wheatland for $6,750 in 1848 when he was still just a prosperous but politically active lawyer in Lancaster. Before reaching the White House in 1856, he served as Ambassador to Russia and England as well as a stint as Secretary of State. His international travels and tastes are reflected in the furnishing and artifacts throughout the house. There's a 200-pound fishbowl from Japan given to Buchanan by the Japanese Mikado upon America's opening of trade relations with the Far East. From the court of Queen Victoria, there's a souvenir box of wire and a message from the Queen herself sent to Buchanan upon the completion of the Transatlantic cable. And of course there are Persian rugs, Japanese woven glass wallpaper, French lace curtains, chandeliers, and Bristol glassware. In addition, there are the trophies from Buchanan's American political life, such as his 31-star campaign flag, Presidential china, and the carpet bags which were used by gentlemen of the period instead of briefcases.

After a broken engagement, Buchanan never married. His house was constantly filled, however, with nephews and nieces including his niece Harriett Lane who at age 29 served as the First Lady when Buchanan moved to the White House. Harriett also succeeded in adding the female touch to Wheatland when she lived here. There's the 100-year-old Chickering piano in the living room and elaborate mirrors in the hallways. In Harriett's bedroom, there's her Episcopal kneeling perch and a petticoat table with a mirror at the bottom to detect whether her slip was showing.

Throughout the house, there are the solid artifacts of Lancaster County heritage, such as the locally-made grandfather's clock and the peace stone inlaid in the stairwell which signifies the peace of mind that comes when the mortgage is paid off.

Tours of the house are conducted by costumed guides from the Junior League of Lancaster and special group events, such as a Victorian Christmas party can be arranged.

Directions: Take U.S. 340 West, which becomes Orange Street in Lancaster. Follow Orange Street west for about one mile and branch off to the right onto Marietta Avenue. Wheatland is about three quarters of a mile on the left along Marietta Ave.

Nearby Attractions: See Lancaster's Walking Tour, Heritage Center Museum and Rock Ford. Next door to Wheatland is the Lancaster County Historical Society, which is open Tues.–Sat., 1–5 p.m.

WRIGHT'S FERRY MANSION

Open May–Oct.: Tues., Weds., Fri., and Sat. 10–3. Fees: Adults, $2.00; students 12–17, $1.00; children 6–11, 50¢. Groups (10 or less) accompanied by guide, $1.00 per person. Wright's Ferry Mansion, 38 South Second St., Columbia, Pa. 17512. (717) 684-4325.

In the 18th century, the land west of Lancaster to the Susquehanna River was a virtual wilderness harboring wild animals, deep forests, and Indian tribes. In 1726, a remarkable woman named Susanna Wright left her comfortable life in Philadelphia to come to this area and set up a household which would soon become a center of civilization in this wilderness. A refined, well-educated Quaker, Susanna became known as the "bluestocking of the Susquehanna." She was familiar with many languages including French, Latin, Italian, and local Indian dialects. An avid reader, her shelves were filled with books from Europe, and Benjamin Franklin would often send her the latest "Best Sellers" along with little presents like a thermometer and bayberry candles. In return, he would receive presents such as local salmon and apples as well as astute advice on state matters. She was widely sought after for her medicinal knowledge on the healing power of herbs. In addition to all her other talents, she became quite a businesswoman. She was responsible for starting a silk worm industry along the Susquehanna which eventually "employed" over 1,500 silk worms and supplied material for a gown worn by the Queen at the birthday celebration of George III.

It is fitting that the mansion she had built for her in 1738 has been restored by the Louise Steinman Von Hess Foundation as a monument to her talents and ingenuity. The stone house features a layout typical of the English style of architecture of the time, but with Pennsylvania-German embellishments. A long horizontal axis forms a one-room-deep base. The two-story house with wood-shingled roof has two chimneys, pent eaves between the first and second floors, and plaster on stone exterior walls. The rooms are beautifully furnished in an authentic 18th century style. The elegant Queen Anne and William and Mary furnishings were crafted by the Philadelphia Cabinetmakers of long ago, and present a unity of style throughout the house.

Guided tours take you through the two stories of Susanna's home. The elegant furnishings are described, as well as momentous events in

Susanna's life (many of them mentioned in the marvelous letters she left behind). Some items on display belonged to her family, others are an approximation of the accessories and furnishings she would have had with her.

Directions: The mansion is located in Columbia, only a few blocks from the National Watch and Clock Museum. Take Rt. 30 west of Lancaster to Rt. 441 towards Columbia. This Rt. becomes N. Third St. Follow N. Third to Walnut Street and turn right. Go for one block, then turn left onto S. Second St. and the mansion will appear on your right.

Nearby Attractions: See National Watch and Clock Museum and Lancaster Co. Winery Tours—Nissley Vineyards (a fifteen-minute drive away).

The Gay Dutch and the Coal Miners

KEY TO MAP—AREA II (*overleaf*)

A – Adamstown Antique and Flea Markets (Renninger's, Shupp's Grove, and Black Angus)

B – Alexander Schaeffer Farm Museum and Festivals

C – Ashland Coal Mine and Steam Lokie

D – Bavarian Summer Festival at Barnesville

E – Blue Rocks

F – Boyertown Museum of Historic Vehicles and Duryea Day

G – Conrad Weiser Park

H – Cornwall Furnace

I – Mount Hope

J – Crystal Cave

K – Daniel Boone Homestead

L – Hawk Mountain

M – Hershey Park, Hershey's Chocolate World, Hershey Museum of American Life, Hershey Rose Gardens and Arboretum

N – Hopewell Village

O – Indian Echo Caverns

P – Knoebel's Groves Amusement Resort

Q – Koziar's Christmas Village

R – Kutztown Folk Festival and Reninger's No. 2

S – Bomberger's Bologna Co.

T – Palmyra Bologna Co. (Seltzer's Bologna)

U – Weaver's Bologna Plant

V – Lenhartsville One Room School and Folklife Museum

W – Mary Merritt Doll Museum and Merritt's Museum of Childhood and the Pennsylvania Dutch

X – Michter's Distillery

Y – Onyx Cave

Z – Pennsylvania Dutch Farm Museum and Festival at Kempton, and the WK&S Steam Railroad

a – Reading's Factory Outlets and Farmer's Markets

b – Reading's Pagoda, Skyline Drive, and Duryea Hill Climb

c – Roadside America

d – St. Peter's Village

e – Tulpehocken Manor Plantation

f – Zeller's Fort

g – Twin Slope Farmer's Market and Flea Market

h – Leesport Market and Auction

i – Shillington Farmer's Market

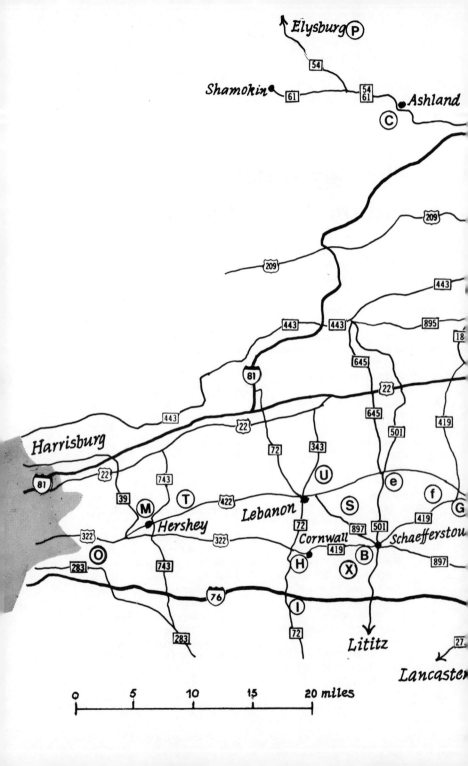

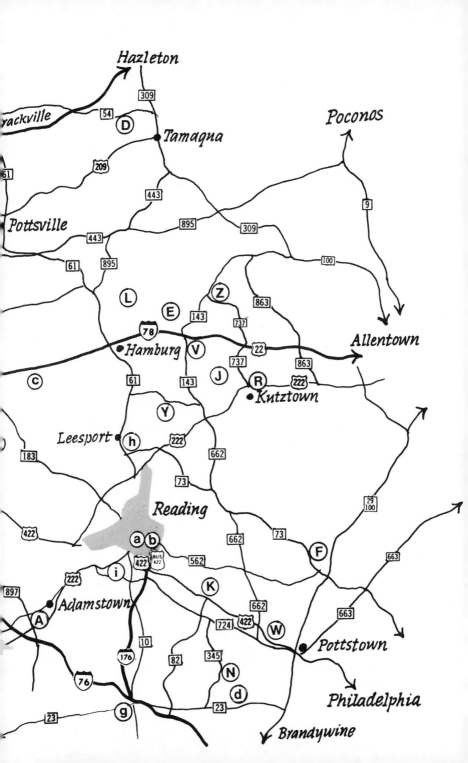

The Gay Dutch and the Coal Miners:

Hershey, Berks & Lebanon Counties, and Southern Coal Region

When most people think of the Pennsylvania Dutch, they visualize gaily painted hex signs, tulip ware pottery, industrious farmers, immaculate houses lined with neat flower gardens, and hearty home-cooked German meals. Their vision is realized in Berks County where German Lutherans have settled and preserved their culture for over 150 years. Folk Festivals, beer drinking Octoberfests, farmers' markets, museums and amusements feature the arts, crafts and folkways of these ingenious and hard-working people.

Lebanon County, which borders on both Lancaster and Berks Counties, is a meeting ground for both the Gay and Plain Dutch. However, unlike Berks and Lancaster, this region is known more for its industries, both past and present, than for its ethnic identity. Its iron furnaces contributed cannon and shot to the Continental Army; its distilleries boosted man's spirit (now as in the past); and the Lebanon Bologna Plants continue to tempt the palate with their sweet and spicy product.

Hershey and the surrounding area is unique in its appeal. It was here that the remarkable Milton Hershey built his chocolate factory and clean attractive town. Later an amusement park was added that surpasses all in the area.

The area north of these counties is the coal mining region. Many immigrants have come here throughout the years to work in the coal mines and decided to stay. This ethnic mix has created a unique culture in which you'll find coal miners with Welsh accents, small towns dominated by large churches with gold basilicas, and festivals highlighting the Polish, Irish, Ukrainian and German cultures.

THE ADAMSTOWN ANTIQUE AND FLEA MARKETS

Antiquing is a favorite pastime of visitors to the Pennsylvania Dutch area and fine antique stores abound. If you don't particularly care for trekking all over the countryside to find that butter mold you've been wanting for years, there are three large antique and flea markets all located within five miles of each other near Adamstown, Pa. All three feature plenty of free parking, food concessions, and everything conceivable, from junk to priceless antiques. There is always a lot of bargaining going on, so it is a good idea to know the approximate value of what you are looking for. One word of caution, the markets are often quite crowded and small children may be a liability (too many expensive and breakable items are within a toddler's reach).

SHUPP'S GROVE

Open Spring (starting in mid-April), Summer and Fall, every Sat. and Sun., 8–5 p.m. No admission fee. Rest rooms. Concessions. Picnics. Shupp's Grove, Adamstown, Pa. 19501. (717) 949-3656, or weekends (215) 484-9314.

This large open-air market is located on thirty acres of woodland. It has been in existence for eighteen years and is the oldest market of its kind in the area. If you have to bring your children, Shupp's Grove would be your best bet as all tables are outside and there's room to run around.

Directions: The market is one mile south of Adamstown, Pa. on Route 897. If coming from Reading on Rt. 272, turn left onto 897 at the large directional sign. Shupp's Grove is 2 miles east of the Lancaster-Reading Interchange of the Pa. Turnpike Exit 21.

ED STOUDT'S BLACK ANGUS ANTIQUE MALL

Open every Sunday 8–5 p.m. No admission fees. Rest rooms. Restaurant. Cocktail lounge. Black Angus, Rt. 272, Adamstown, Pa. 19501. (215) 484-4655.

Over 150 dealers display their wares in this clean and spacious mall. On sunny days there is an outdoor display as well. In addition to its antique shows, the Black Angus is well known for its ethnic festivals. Write for times and details.

Directions: The mall is located on Rt. 272, a few miles south of Shupp's Grove and Adamstown.

RENNINGER'S NO. 1

Open every Sunday from 8–5 p.m. No admission fee. Rest rooms. Concessions. Renninger's No. 1, Rt. 272, Adamstown, Pa. 19501. (215) 267-2177.

This is the largest of the three markets, featuring 372 individual dealers. Outdoor sections are open in the warmer months. This market appears to have the greatest selection of items, but it is also the most crowded.

If you happen to be traveling to the Kutztown area, there is another Renninger's located one mile south from the middle of town. This is Renninger's No. 2 and features 250 dealers indoors every Saturday from 9–5 p.m.

Directions: Renninger's No. 1 is located on Rt. 272, ½ mile northeast of Pa. Turnpike Exit 21, and a short ride from the Black Angus Mall.

Nearby Attractions: See Green Dragon Farmers Market.

THE ALEXANDER SCHAEFFER FARM MUSEUM AND FESTIVALS

Farm Museum open daily for visits by appointment only. Annual festivals held in May, June, July and September. Fees: Adults, $1.50; children, 25¢. Food. Rest rooms. Historic Schaefferstown, Inc., Box 1776, Schaefferstown, Pa. 17088. (717) 949-3685 or 949-3552.

"Quite a show. Keep your eye on that team!" intones the announcer, "You won't see anything like this anywhere else!" In front of him a group of horses and mules are being harnessed together to pull a road grader. Eight large draft animals will be directed across a plowed field by a single man yelling "Gee" and "Haw." Tension mounts as the sometimes unruly animals inch out of line. Finally they are all harnessed and with a "giddap" slowly make their way across the field to the shouts and encouragement of their driver. In the distance, another wagon can be seen being pulled by four magnificent palomino draft horses. Cornfields, silos, and low hills form a backdrop to this pastoral scene. Near the plowing field, a blacksmith, surrounded by curious children, busily hammers horseshoes into shape. The smell of apple butter permeates the fall air, and the sounds of a German Oom-pah Band can be heard. The Annual Harvest Fair and Horse Plowing Contest held at the Alexander Farm Museum is well under way.

The descendants of Alexander Schaeffer (who came to this area in 1738) and other founders of Schaefferstown are proud of their heritage and have determined to keep the folklore, crafts and skills of the early days alive through a series of annual festivals and seminars, the Harvest Fair held in mid-September being one of them. Each event features homemade Pennsylvania Dutch food and craft demonstrations along with the main attraction. In May, The Spinning & Weaving Frolic and Spring Folklore Festival is held. This is a lively and informative event with intent farmers shearing sheep, border collies herding and yapping at straying animals, and busy women carding, spinning and weaving the wool. It is a good opportunity to see the wool-making process from start to finish. During June, the annual Cherry Fair is held. Plenty of delicious food made from fresh cherries is served, accompanied by musical programs and craft demonstrations. In July, the annual Folklore Festival presents a look at the culture, language, crafts and religion of the early settlers through lectures, seminars and demonstrations. To end the festival season, the Harvest Festival and Horse Plowing Contest occurs in mid-September. All these festivals are well attended, and their authenticity as to craft and skill demonstrations is attested to by the attendance of local Mennonite and Amish farmers.

The site of these happenings is the buildings and grounds of the 90-acre Alexander Schaeffer Farmstead. This old farm dates from 1738 and includes a Swiss Bank House (considered an architectural rarity), a bank barn housing old farm equipment, and lovely gardens. These buildings are open for inspection during the festivals and at other times by appointment.

Directions: The Farm Museum and festival grounds are located north of Lancaster at the junctions of Rts. 419 and 897. Once in Schaefferstown, follow the directional signs.

Nearby Attractions: See Cornwall Furnace and Mount Hope and Lebanon Bologna Plant tours—Bomberger and Weaver Plants, and Michter's Distillery.

ASHLAND'S PIONEER COAL MINE AND STEAM LOKIE

Open daily May 30–Sept. 15, 10 a.m.–6 p.m. (10–8 on weekends). During May and Sept. 15 through Oct., open weekends only. Fees: Pioneer Tunnel: Adults, $2.75; under 6, free. Steam Lokie: Adults, $1.25; children, 50¢. Picnics. Playground. Rest rooms. Ashland Community Enterprises, 19th and Oak Sts., Ashland, Pa. 17921. (717) 875-3850.

In the heart of Pennsylvania's anthracite coal region lies the small town of Ashland. Here, through the efforts of civic-minded leaders, an authentic horizontal drift mine has been re-timbered and opened to the public as a tourist attraction. Known as the Pioneer Tunnel, the mine had originally been used until 1931 by the Philadelphia and Reading Coal and Iron Company.

Riding in open converted mine cars, you are taken a quarter of a mile into the bowels of Mahoney Mountain where the temperature never goes above 55 degrees (be sure to bring a sweater). For the timid, take heart. During its twenty years of operation, not one miner died in the Pioneer Tunnel and nowadays safety inspections are conducted daily. During the 45-minute tour, colorful guides, all miners themselves, provide a realistic introduction to the techniques and everyday toil of the anthracite miner. Upon disembarking from the train, you walk down the gangways (tunnels) and peer up at the confined manways through which a miner had to lug 250 pounds of gear before he could even begin picking at the unmined coal. You see the aftereffects of a process called "robbing the mine" by which the solid pillars between the individual manways are dynamited to remove remaining coal before the mine is closed. On the way out of the mine, the electric lights are turned off briefly to give you the feeling of what it's like to work in a pitch-black environment.

An added attraction is the old-fashioned narrow-gauge steam "lokie" named the "Henry Clay," which you can ride for half a mile along the side of Mahoney Mountain. Far below, the town of Ashland looks much like a miniature Christmas village with its tall-spired churches and neat row homes. Midpoint in the trip, the train stops and your guide describes another type of mining—strip mining. Across the valley you see the 150-foot walls of solid rock where giant bulldozers once carved millions of tons of coal from the rich Mammoth Vein. The old breakers (coal sorters) are still standing where young boys worked fourteen hours a day sifting coal from the slate and separating it into various grades. Immediately in front of you is a bootleg coal hole dug during the Depression by desperate miners who defied trespass laws for the heat and extra cash provided by the stolen coal.

Directions: Ashland is located on Rt. 61 about 45 minutes north of the Hamburg exit off Interstate 78.

Nearby Attractions: The New Mining Museum, recently opened by the Pennsylvania Historical and Museum Commission, is a block away. Also Fossil Hunting Tours, 1½ miles away, may be arranged at the mine.

THE BAVARIAN SUMMER FESTIVAL— OCTOBERFEST IN JULY

Held annually during the first part of July, 10 a.m. to midnight. Fees: Adults, $2.50; children 12 and under, free. Parking—$1.00. Rest rooms. Snacks. Restaurant. For tickets and further information, write: Bavarian Festival Society, Inc., Box 90-2, Kempton, Pa. 19529. (215) 756-6000 or (717) 467-2971 from June 1–July 18.

Tatooing booths, the sound of motorcycle racing, a carnival roller coaster with screaming children in it—these are some of the sights and sounds which will greet you upon entering the grounds of Lakewood Park where the Bavarian Octoberfest is held each July. You wonder if perhaps you are at the wrong place. Cotton candy? Game booths where teddy bears are assaulted by baseballs? Don't despair, the carnival atmosphere is just the preliminary attraction. Listen . . . hear the music, the oom-pah-pah of the German Band? Keep following the sound and you will find yourself at one of the two German Bier Halls where the real action is taking place. If it is early in the day, you will be able to find a seat at a table, order a filling German meal, chug a cool beer, sit back and drink in the rousing German music. There will be couples of all ages and dress dancing the polka. Young frauleins in traditional German dress and the men in their lederhosen gracefully dance by, and the whole hall is alive with the love of music, fun, and beer.

If you can manage to pry yourself away from the beer hall (where over thirty different bands will perform during the ten-day festival) there are other attractions to enjoy. These include craft demonstrations, a chance to learn a bit of German at the German language school, an International bar, where over 75 different varieties of beer are sold (a must for beer can collectors), paddle boat and speed boat rides, and the chance to see eight tons of champion Belgian horses pull a gaily-decorated beer wagon. And then, there are the numerous carnival booths and rides to entertain the whole family.

Many native Bavarians feel that if they miss an Oktoberfest they have missed a bit of living. It is a lively occasion with much celebrating and downing of beer. It provides a taste of old world fun in an attractive parklike setting. For those interested, other ethnic festivals such as the Ukrainian and Irish festivals are also held at this same location at other times during the year.

Directions: Lakewood Park is located on Rt. 54 between Mahanoy City and Tamaqua, only two miles from Exit 37E of I-81.

Nearby Attractions: The state park, Locust Lake, is located nearby. This 1,145-acre park has a family camping area and a lake for fishing.

THE BLUE ROCKS

Open daily April 1–Oct. 30. Fees: $2.00 per car with 2 people, 50¢ for each additional person. Rest rooms. Picnics. Camping. Jan & Lee Dickinson, Blue Rocks, R.D. 1, Lenhartsville, Pa. 19534. (215) 756-6366.

Mother Nature can play some awesome tricks on our planet, and, in the lovely rolling foothills of the Appalachian Mountains, is evidence of one of them. Surrounded by woods and fields is a massive bed of large boulders stretching for a half a mile and covering fifteen acres of land. These boulders, known as the Blue Rocks, were formed of Tuscarora quartzite and Silurian sandstone about 350 million years ago. During the last glacial period, some 40,000 years ago, they slowly moved downslope from Blue Mountain, about a mile to the North. Today, this rock field forms a stationary monument to the unbridled powers of nature.

Blue Rocks is a part of a 90-acre private campground located in Berks County. The daily admission fee includes climbing on the rocks, use of the picnic grounds adjacent to the boulders, rest rooms and hiking on the scenic nature trails. The campground provides the closest place to park to reach the Appalachian Trail or embark on the 1½ hour trek to the Pinnacle, the area's highest peak which commands a truly spectacular view of the Pennsylvania Dutch countryside below. For non-hikers, a road leads directly to and crosses the Blue Rocks, so you can see all without moving from your car. The campground also includes a playground, country store, hot showers, electrical hookups and easy access to local attractions.

Directions: Take Rt. 22 (east of Hamburg) to Rt. 143 North, and follow the signs to the campground.

Nearby Attractions: See Hawk Mountain, WK&S Steam Railroad, Lenhartsville One-Room School and Folk Life Museum, and the Pennsylvania Dutch Farm Festival at Kempton. For Pennsylvania Dutch cooking, try the Shartlesville or Haag's Hotel, a ten-minute drive away.

BOYERTOWN MUSEUM OF HISTORIC VEHICLES
AND DURYEA DAY

Open by appointment only (except on Duryea Day). Fees: Adults, $2.00; children 6–16, $1.00. Rest rooms. Small gift shop. Boyertown Museum of Historic Vehicles, Reading Ave. & Warwick St., P.O. Box 30, Boyertown, Pa. 19512. (215) 367-2091.

From the mid-1800's through the early 1920's, many vehicles, both horse-drawn and motorized, were built in the shops and early assembly lines of Berks County. Boyertown, Fleetwood, Hamburg, Kutztown and Reading all figured prominently in this industry. In fact, Charles Duryea, a man credited with building the world's first real automobile in 1892, constructed the majority of his cars in Reading, from 1900 to 1908. To preserve, collect, restore, study and exhibit these products of early Berks County industry, the Boyertown Museum of Historic Vehicles was established. Here, housed in a small building, can be seen many fine examples of these early modes of transportation. There is the 1902 Duryea Folding Rear Seat Phaeton, Model A Roadsters, an Electric Bus, 1928 LaSalle Convertible Coupe, and a 1912 SGV Roadster with mother-in-law seat, for starters. You will also see such curiosities as a horse-drawn funeral coach with exquisite cut-glass windows, a butcher wagon, surrey with a fringe on top, a one-horse cutter sleigh, and a 1911 Parasol Buggy. Fine examples of Early Americana are expressed through this interesting collection, which is representative of the years 1790–1937.

On the Saturday before Labor Day, rain or shine between 9 a.m. and 5 p.m., Duryea Day is held in Boyertown. Sponsored by the museum, this day commemorates the work of Mr. Duryea and other Berks County craftsmen. Antique and classic car owners from a six-state area attend this celebration and exhibit their cars. Awards are presented to antique cars in their respective classes. This festival, complete with flea market and food concessions, is held at the Boyertown Area Community Park, just a few blocks away from the museum.

Directions: If approaching Boyertown from Rt. 100, take Pa. 73 West to Boyertown. Once in the city, take a left at the fourth stop light, Warwick St. Go about a block and a half. The museum will appear on your left in back of the fire hall.

Nearby Attractions: See Pottsgrove Mansion (Area IV), Mary Merritt Museums, and Daniel Boone Homestead.

CONRAD WEISER PARK

Open year round, Tues.–Sat., 9–5 p.m.; Sun., 12–5 p.m. Closed Mondays. Grounds open 9 a.m. to 8 p.m. Hours subject to change. Rest rooms. Picnics. Conrad Weiser Park, R.D. 1, Womelsdorf, Pa. 19567. (215) 589-2934.

In the early 1700's, when Pennsylvania was more a home to the Indians than to the white man, Conrad Weiser, a German-born immigrant who lived in New York, came to the Tulpehocken Valley in search of more land. He settled here with his family in a small stone house with a single room which served as a kitchen, dining room, and sitting room. At one end of the house was a large fireplace with bake oven and upstairs was the sleeping loft. Later, another room was added as the family expanded to include 14 children. It was out of this house that Weiser performed his work as a farmer, tanner, and, most importantly, as ambassador to the Iroquois Indian Nation.

When Weiser had lived in New York, he spent an entire winter as the adopted son of an Iroquois Chief. When he brought this invaluable knowledge of Indian customs and language with him to Pennsylvania, he was much sought after for his peacemaking abilities. He and James Logan, Provincial Secretary of Pennsylvania, formed an Indian policy which kept Pennsylvania free of Indian uprisings until the French and Indian War. Weiser served as a Lt. Colonel in a Pennsylvania regiment during this war, and then, once the conflict was ended, was instrumental in reestablishing friendly relations with the Indians.

Because of his prominence as peacemaker, prosperous farmer, and later as an appointed Justice in Lancaster County, Weiser's Homestead has been turned into a museum honoring him and his accomplishments. His two-room house is restored and you can see where the Weiser family ate and slept. Simple furnishings, dating from the time period, reflect the austere lifestyle of these pioneers. There are a few of Weiser's own belongings on display. These include a money belt, silver spoon and a copy of his will. In the smaller addition to the home, tools and weapons from the late archaic period (4–5,000 years ago) are displayed. Next door is the original Weiser spring house with wooden pipe system for carrying water, and a small library of local history. These historical buildings are surrounded by a lovely 26-acre park which features a memorial area dedicated to the Honorable Fred A. Muhlenberg.

Directions: The park is on Rt. 422, a few miles east of Womelsdorf.

Nearby Attractions: See Zeller's Fort, Tulpehocken Manor Plantation, and Koziar's Christmas Village.

CORNWALL FURNACE AND MOUNT HOPE

CORNWALL FURNACE

Open all year. Daylight Saving Time: Weds.–Sat., 9–5; Sun., 12–5; Standard Time: Weds.–Sat., 10–4:30; Sun., 12–4:30. Hours subject to change. Fees: Adults, $1.00; children under 12, free. Rest rooms. Picnics. Cornwall Furnace, P.O. Box V, Cornwall, Pa. 17016. (717) 272-9711.

Peer down into the oldest and deepest open pit mine in the country. Imagine the sweat-streaked miners laboriously bringing the valuable iron ore 420 feet up the steep rock-strewn banks to the surface of the massive pit. Follow their well-beaten path to their sturdily-built stone houses lining both sides of the road. Go back in time to the 1730's to when iron ore was King and a man named Peter Grubb discovered the valuable resource in this area, opened the mine, and named it Cornwall after a town in England. Now take a step forward to 1743 when Grubb established the Cornwall Furnace. It is here he would combine the iron ore, native limestone and charcoal to produce pig iron. His product would be of great importance to the American Revolution, for his furnace was a chief producer of cannon and shot for the Continental Army. It would remain in operation until 1883, with one remodeling done in 1856.

This voyage through time can be taken at the Cornwall Furnace due to the efforts of the Pennsylvania State Historical and Museum Commission which has turned the furnace into a museum. A self-guided tour of the orientation museum and furnace provides you with an excellent quick course in the history of ironmaking, from the charging of the furnace to the foundry area at the base. The building itself, with its pointed windows and exterior of soft red and brown sandstone, is an architectural feat. Once inside, you get the feeling of being within a medieval castle. Twisting wooden stairways lead to platforms overlooking the giant water wheel which was formerly used to produce a cold air blast through a large bellows. It is an awesome sight. Throughout the tour, technological devices that laid the foundations of Pennsylvania's complex iron and steel industry are evident. In the foundry area, life-size figures enact the process of casting the munitions for the Continental Army.

Directions: Approaching from Hershey via Rt. US 322, follow the signs for Cornwall Furnace located on Rt. 419. At Cornwall, cross the railroad tracks and follow the blue signs for Cornwall Furnace.

Open Pit Mine and Miner's Village: When leaving the furnace, turn right then immediately right again. Down the road a few hundred yards, pull off the shoulder for a view into the enormous pit. A bit further down the same road is the miners' village (the houses are not open to the public).

Nearby Attractions: See Mount Hope, Alexander Schaeffer Farm Museum, Lebanon Bologna Factory Tours and Michter's Distillery.

MOUNT HOPE

Mansion hours: Mon.–Sat., 10–4:30. Call for Sunday hours. Closed Thanksgiving, Christmas, New Years and Election Day. Open Memorial Day, Fourth of July and Labor Day. Fees: $2.00 per person. Rest rooms. Special events and festivals. Mount Hope Estate and Winery, P.O. Box 685, Cornwall, Pa. 17016. (717) 665-7021.

While in the Cornwall area, you may want to stop and visit Mount Hope, the sandstone Federal Period Mansion built in 1800 by Henry Bates Grubb, grandson of Peter Grubb of Cornwall Furnace fame. Guided tours of this 32-room mansion take you through rooms decorated in Victorian splendor, from hand-painted 18 ft. ceilings to Egyptian marble fireplaces and imported crystal chandeliers. At the completion of the tour, a wine tasting is held in the Mansion's billiard room. Here you get to sample a variety of Pennsylvania wines (children are provided with grape juice). Presently, Mount Hope is importing its wines from a winery on Lake Erie, but, with the recent planting of its own vineyards, it is hoped that within four or five years the estate will be producing its own wines.

Directions: From Cornwall, take Rt. 419 west to Rt. 322. Then, exit south onto Rt. 72. Mount Hope will appear on your left just past the entrance to the Pennsylvania Turnpike (Take Exit 20 if coming from the turnpike and go south for ½ mile).

Nearby Attractions: See Cornwall Furnace, Alexander Schaeffer Farm Museum, Lebanon Bologna Tours, and Michter's Distillery.

CRYSTAL CAVE

Open every day from Washington's Birthday in February through Oct. 31st, 9–5 p.m. Weekends in summer, 9–7 p.m. In Nov., open Fri., Sat. and Sun. only. Fees: Adults, $3.50; children 6–12, $1.50. Snack bar. Rest rooms. Miniature Golf Course. Picnics. Playground. Nature trails. Crystal Cave, R.D. 3, Kutztown, Pa. 19530. (215) 683-6765.

Centuries ago, when underground streams coursed through limestone beds hollowing out rock-walled rooms and passages, the Crystal Cave was formed. It existed unknown for years until November 12, 1871, when two Pennsylvania Dutchmen, Gideon Merkel and John Gehret, discovered a crevice that opened into the rocky hill where they were working in a stone quarry. They crawled inside, but the place was pitch black, so they stopped. That evening, they told others of their find, and the next day a group of neighbors, carrying candles and coal oil lanterns, went to view this new cavern. The sights that greeted them were awe-inspiring. Hanging from the high ceilings were columns of white and rust, and along the floor rose great domes of frost-like white. There were subterranean passages that led off into unknown reaches, and the walls of the cave were studded with millions of diamond-like crystals. The place was a fairyland, enchanting and at the same time, forbidding.

News of their discovery traveled fast, and many came to see the wonders of this underground cave. As the years passed, access to the cave was improved so that all could enjoy its beauty. Now, colorful lights highlight such unusual formations as the prairie dogs and the bridal veil formation. There are graded walkways with hand rails, and concrete steps which lead to the higher reaches of the cave. Guides lead tours lasting 35 minutes through the passages and explain the various formations, such as the stalagmites and stalactites, which are still growing as a result of the mineral-carrying water which seeps through the cave's ceiling. The main chamber of the cave, called the Crystal Ballroom, has been used in times past for square dances and parties. The mineral deposits sparkle in the light like diamond-like crystals. The cave has been civilized, or has it? There are still some mysteries left, hidden corners and passages too small to wiggle through, and, standing in the deepest section of the cave (125 feet below the surface) with the lights turned out, the awe-inspiring fear of the unknown can still be experienced.

Directions: The cave is located between Allentown and Reading in the hills surrounding Kutztown. Take Rt. 222 to the Virginville Exit, then follow signs to the cave. If coming from Rt. 22 (I-78), turn South at Krumsville onto Rt. 737 and follow directional signs.

Nearby Attractions: See Onyx Cave, Lenhartsville One-Room School and Folklife Museum, Kutztown Folk Festival, and Rodale Organic Gardening & Research Center (see Lehigh County—Area III).

THE DANIEL BOONE HOMESTEAD

Open weekdays except Monday, Daylight Saving Time: 9–5 p.m., Sunday, 12–5 p.m. Standard Time: 10–4:30, Sunday, 12–4:30. Closed certain holidays. Hours subject to change. Fees: Adults, $1.00; children, free. Rest rooms. Picnics. Daniel Boone Homestead, R.D. 2, Box 162, Birdsboro, Pa. 19508. (212) 582-4900.

When one hears the name of Daniel Boone, one thinks of pioneers, Kentucky, Indians and the unchartered wilderness—not of Berks

County, Pennsylvania. But it was here where Daniel Boone was born in 1734. At that time Berks County was a primitive wilderness—the woods teemed with wild animals, and the nearest neighbors were miles away. The Boone family lived in this area for twenty years, leaving for North Carolina when Daniel was sixteen. It was in these Pennsylvania woods that Daniel Boone acquired the skills that would earn him the reputation of one of the most intrepid and best known of the American Pioneers.

The original foundation of the Boone's log cabin still remains, although the log house was replaced by the present two-story stone structure some time in the late 18th century. Guided tours include a look at this foundation, which also serves as a cellar complete with food storage area, a fresh spring to provide refrigeration and water, and a small wooden bathtub which was used on rare occasions. The interior of the upper portions of the restored house is furnished to create a vivid picture of 18th century rural life. The furniture is often primitive—trundle beds with straw mattresses, a trestle table, straight-backed chairs . . . Decorations are utilitarian—teas and herbs hanging from the ceilings, a hornet's nest resting on a cabinet, iron kitchen utensils lining the mantel of the huge walk-in fireplace. One downstairs room is completely given over to looms, spinning wheels and implements of the weaver's trade, for this was how the Boones made their livelihood. It is hard to believe, but the original two-room cabin with loft and cellar served as workshop and home for the Boone parents and their eleven children.

Although the guided tour includes only the Boone house, there are other things to see and do here. The Visitor's Center houses exhibits depicting Daniel Boone's life during and after his Pennsylvania sojourn. Artifacts of his life as well as that of the early pioneers are on display in the center. Animal food may be purchased for feeding the horses and chickens kept in the large bank barn on the property. There is also a Blacksmith Shop which is frequently manned during the summer months, smoke house, and scenic picnic areas. During the year there are occasional craft demonstrations, and scheduled flintlock shoots. Write ahead for times and dates.

Directions: The Homestead is located off Rt. 422 southeast of Reading near Baumstown. There are directional signs on Rt. 422.

Nearby Attractions: See Hopewell Village, St. Peters Village, Pottsgrove, Mary Merritt Doll Museum and Museum of Early American Life.

HAWK MOUNTAIN

Sanctuary open daily from 8 a.m. to 5 p.m. Fees: Adults, $1.50; children, 75¢. Picnics. Fresh water and rest rooms near the headquarters. Small book store. Hawk Mountain Sanctuary, Rt. 2, Kempton, Pa. 19529. (215) 756-6961.

Each autumn when low pressure systems advancing across the northern Appalachian regions start birds on their southward migration, the area around Hawk Mountain comes alive with large numbers of migrating hawks and eagles. Total counts for the last 35 years have averaged more than 15,000 birds of prey a season. Once targets for avid hunters, these migrating birds are now given safe passage through this mountain area by the Hawk Mountain Sanctuary, a privately maintained wildlife refuge established in 1934. It was the first sanctuary in the world to offer such protection. Encompassing over 2,000 acres of rugged mountain terrain, this refuge provides not only a sanctuary for the birds, but an exciting opportunity for bird watchers and those who love the outdoors to hike along scenic nature trails that lead upwards to a panoramic view of the surrounding countryside.

A visit to Hawk Mountain starts at the Sanctuary Headquarters, a unique building that features a large subterranean museum displaying birds of prey in flight. This series of exhibits explains hawk migration, what types of birds to be on the lookout for, and the history of the sanctuary. From here you may begin your hike up the mountain. For the less enthusiastic hiker, a short, gently ascending path to South Lookout may be taken. From this overlook some of the migrating birds may be seen, although the view from the "North Lookout" is much more spectacular. The trail to the North Lookout is more rugged, for there are a number of rocky areas to be scaled. However, most amateur hikers should have no difficulty with this 45-minute hike (one way) as the trail is not overly steep or dangerous. The lookout is a massive outcropping of Tuscarora sandstone which provides a magnificent 70-mile view of the surrounding countryside. Perched on top of these huge boulders, you can view at close hand the migrating birds. In the fall, the colorful leaves and crisp wind add to the rugged beauty of the area.

What you will see at Hawk Mountain largely depends on the time of year you visit. In September, there are Ospreys, Bald Eagles, and Broad-winged Hawks. October brings the greatest variety of Hawks.

The cold winds of November bring the Red-tailed Hawks and Golden Eagles. In the spring, a few hawks and warblers pass by, their migration reaching a climax in early May. Whatever time of year you choose, there is always something to be enjoyed.

When visiting the sanctuary, it is wise to dress warmly, especially in the autumn. While temperatures may appear warm down in the valley, the lookouts can get quite chilly with the constant blowing of the wind. Also, don't forget to bring a pair of binoculars.

Directions: Hawk Mountain is located off Interstate 78 (Rt. 22) near Kempton, Pa. Approach roads to the Sanctuary are Pa. Routes 895 to the west and 143 to the east. The rural road that leads to the mountain is well-marked with directional signs.

Nearby Attractions: See Pennsylvania Dutch Farm Festival at Kempton, Lenhartsville One-Room School and Folklife Museum, and WK&S Steam Railroad.

HERSHEY, PENNSYLVANIA

HERSHEY'S CHOCOLATE WORLD

Open Mon.–Sat., 9–5 p.m., Sun. 12–5 p.m. year round. No admission fee. Rest rooms. Gift shop. Food concessions. Hershey Information Center, Hershey, Pa. 17033. (717) 534-3005.

In the year 1903, a man with a dream and the imagination to make it come true came to Derry Township in the fertile Lebanon Valley of South Central Pennsylvania. The man was Milton Hershey and his dream was to build a chocolate factory in the middle of this farm country and then create a town near it based on humanitarian principles. Many thought his dream would be a failure. He proved them wrong. Hershey became one of the first successful planned communities. Here were no depressing rows of worker's houses but rather individual homes surrounded by trees and lawns. The business existed for the workers rather than the other way around. Contented workers help make for a successful business, and Hershey's was. Today it has become one of the largest cocoa and chocolate manufacturing plants in the world and is famous for such delectable products as Hershey's Cocoa, Hershey's Milk Chocolate Bars, Hershey's Kisses and Reese's Peanut Butter Cups.

Although the chocolate factory itself is not open to the public, the tour of Hershey's Chocolate World presents an entertaining look at the chocolate-making process from the African cocoa tree plantations to the milk barns on Pennsylvania Dutch Farms. Riding in automated cars, you travel through exhibits which simulate the process used in the actual Hershey Chocolate Factory located on the other side of town. You can see the miniature equipment turning cocoa beans, milk and sugar into chocolate bars, and are taken through the roasting oven where the beans are being heated to just the right temperature before being shattered and ground. The trip takes you step-by-step from cocoa bean to finished product and the animated scenes with life-like machines make it a truly enjoyable experience that even small children will appreciate. At the tour's completion, there are gift shops, an historical display and an unusual indoor garden which features live cocoa trees.

Directions: Chocolate World is located at the entrance to Hershey Park (see this entry for directions).

HERSHEY MUSEUM OF AMERICAN LIFE

Open year round: Tues.–Sun. 10 a.m.–5 p.m. and 10–6 during summer. Fees: Adults, $2.00 ($1.75 for groups of 10 or more); children (5–18), $1.00; school groups, 75¢; under 5 free. Rest rooms. Gift shop. Hershey Museum of American Life, One Chocolate Avenue, Hershey, Pa. 17033. (717) 534-3439.

Jesus raises his arms in blessing as the twelve Apostles circle in front. The scales of Justice then rise to signal the coming of Peter, but Peter turns away in denial as the cock crows. When Judas approaches, Satan peers down ominously from several vantage points. When Judas fails to face him, Christ turns toward Satan who retreats before his wrath. No, it's not a scene from the Passion Play, but the show which takes place 15 minutes before every hour on the face of the 7-foot, 114-year-old Apostolic Clock, which is one of the highlights at the Hershey Museum of American Life. It took a local Strasburg man eleven years to build the clock, which is remarkable in its animation and intricacy.

Immediately following the clock drama, there's a live demonstration of various types of musical simulators. The delicate tones of the Swiss and Regina Music Boxes are contrasted with the cacophonous sounds of the hurdy-gurdy and 1830 German Band Clock. This is followed by recordings played on the Edison cylinder and Victor disc phonographs. By now it's almost time for the 10-minute slide tape show entitled "One Day in Early Pennsylvania" which depicts the rigors of early colonial life and begins 15 minutes after every hour.

Three distinct types of collections are effectively blended together to form the museum. First, there's the attractively-displayed objects of local Pennsylvania German heritage such as the handmade Dutch furniture, needlework, rag rugs, pottery, tinware, fractur writing, and printed Bibles. Included in this section is a larger collection of the fine early American blown glass produced by Henry Stiegel, the noted craftsman from nearby Manheim, Pa. Next are the displays focusing on later periods of American life including a variety of fire wagons and other horse-drawn vehicles, a fully-furnished Victorian bedroom, toys like the ones your grandfather used to play with, and clothes and weaponry from different periods of American history. There's even the massive crystal torchere (lamp) from the mansion of Milton Hershey, the Museum's founder. Finally, there's an extensive collection of Eskimo and American Indian artifacts. Special exhibits are also frequently featured.

Directions: The Museum is located at the entrance to Hershey Park (see this entry for complete directions).

HERSHEY ROSE GARDENS AND ARBORETUM

Open daily 9–7 p.m. April 15–Nov. 1. Fees: Adults, $1.50; children 5 and over, 50¢. Gift shop. Rest rooms. Hershey Information Center, Hershey, Pa. 17033. (717) 534-3005.

Enjoy a pleasant walk through the Hershey Rose Gardens, a 23-acre picturesque oasis of blooming flowers situated high on a hill overlooking the town of Hershey. Each season the gardens feature over 200,000 roses, 30,000 tulips, and countless chrysanthemums. A lovely time to come is early June because of the variety of roses in bloom then. There are benches to sit on and relax while enjoying the view; chipmunks, ducks and swans to entertain the little ones; and flower-lined alleyways which lead to an assortment of ponds and gardens including an English Formal Garden and a Japanese one.

Directions: The gardens are located near Hershey Park, and a third of a mile south of the Hotel Hershey. There are signs leading from Rt. 322 to the gardens.

HERSHEY PARK

Open Memorial Day to Labor Day, 10 a.m. to 10 p.m. Also open selected weekends in the spring and fall. Fees (which include all rides and amusements): Adults, $9.95; children 5–12, $8.95. Rest rooms. Restaurants. Snacks. Gift shops. Campsites nearby. Hershey Information Center, Hershey, Pa. 17033. (717) 534-3005.

Milton Hershey, the benevolent businessman who founded the town of Hershey, Pa., was a great lover of children. In 1909 he established the Milton Hershey School for orphan boys. Then, for the child in all of us, he created an amusement park which today has mushroomed into one of the finest theme parks on the east coast.

A set fee at the entrance gate entitles you to a day's worth of outstanding entertainment. Amusement rides galore will keep your senses reeling. Three roller coasters, including the thrilling Sooperdooper Looper which literally turns you upside down, will challenge the most fearless. The Coal Cracker Flume Ride, a milder type of roller coaster on water, will send you hydroplaning in a boat at the rate of thirty-five miles an hour. For a tamer high, the Kissing Tower will take you 360 feet into the air for a panoramic view of the town and lush surrounding countryside. There's an endless variety of sophisticated rides that will appeal to all ages and degrees of derring-do. Special amusements with height restrictions have even been set aside for the younger set. Toddlers just out of diapers drive bumper cars, and ride on miniature airplanes—all the while thumbing their noses at their older siblings who for once are just "too big" to ride.

There's much to do at Hershey apart from the rides. The Park has been tastefully designed into a mini-world of the American past and our European forebears. At the park's entrance is Tudor Square, a 17th century English setting complete with charming shops, cobblestone streets, and shopkeepers dressed in period costume. There's a Pennsylvania Dutch area where crafts are demonstrated and home-style delectables are served. In another section is the Rhineland, a quaint 18th century German village of courtyards, attractive shops with steeply-pitched wood shingle roofs, and bright splashes of native color decorating the costumes of the young hosts and hostesses.

For the animal lover, a complete section of the park has been given over to a zoo which features plant and animal life from throughout North America. It is open 10:30 a.m. to dusk and contains both indoor and specially landscaped outdoor exhibits. At the nearby Aquatheatre, dolphins perform at regular intervals delighting young and old with their antics.

Entertainment abounds in the park. There are plays, concerts and dance exhibitions going on throughout the day and you can usually time yourself to see all of them. They provide a nice respite from the noise and excitement of the amusement rides.

Directions: Hershey is located about 15 miles east of Harrisburg on Route 322. It is easily reached by car from the North and East (Interstate 81 and 78), from the South (Interstate 83), and from the East or West via the Pennsylvania Turnpike.

Nearby Attractions: See Indian Echo Caverns, Cornwall Furnace and Mount Hope, and Lebanon Bologna Plant Tours—Palmyra.

HOPEWELL VILLAGE

Open all year 9–5 p.m. Closed Jan. 1 and Dec. 25. No admission fee. Rest rooms. Picnics, camping and swimming in nearby French Creek State Park. Hopewell Village National Historic Site, R.D. #1, Box 345, Elverson, Pa. 19520. (215) 582-8773.

It's a picture postcard setting—a small village with neat white-washed buildings nestled in a valley. Cows graze in pastures with split rail fences. Chickens poke about in the barnyard. Vegetable gardens flourish between the small houses. The 1757 Valley Forge-Reading Wagon Road passes just above the town—an image of a bygone era. Dominating the setting is a handsome mansion, white walls with black shutters silhouetted against the verdant countryside.

From the late 18th to the mid-19th century, this valley setting was not so pastoral nor scenic. The air was filled with black charcoal dust and smoke which dirtied even the buildings' whitewashed walls. The village was alive with bustling workers chopping wood for charcoal, feeding the iron furnace, and making a living in a community economically dependent on making iron for America's burgeoning industrial needs.

Founded by Mark Bird in 1770, Hopewell Village with its charcoal-fired furnace provided cannon and shot for the Continental Army, and, in later times, became famous for its stoves, cookware and other cast-iron products. The village was typical of the many self-sufficient ironmaking communities that had sprung up all over Pennsylvania. These villages thrived on the iron industry until the latter half of the 1800's, when the cold-blast charcoal-burning furnaces were surpassed by more modern methods.

The cultural, economic, social and industrial life of an 18th century community is brought to life through self-guided tours of this reconstructed ironmaking village maintained by the U.S. Department of the Interior. You walk past the charcoal hearth where the collier burned acres of wood into charcoal. Nearby is a sod-covered hut where he lived while keeping track of the wood fire. A short distance away is the coaling shed and charcoal house where the fuel was sorted and stored. The hub of the village is the mammoth furnace powered by a massive water wheel where the hot iron was forged. In the Furnace Office and Store are products bought and sold by the villagers, and a visit to the tenant houses and large Ironmaster's mansion shows the range of lifestyles of village residents. You can hear the Ironmaster's wife complaining of the dust and dirt, and the office clerk describing the complexities of bookkeeping on the audio tapes available in many of the buildings. In July and August, Living History programs of trades and crafts are presented by people in period costume.

Directions: The village is located six miles south of Birdsboro on Pa. 345, and 10 miles from the Morgantown interchange of the Pa. Turnpike via Pa. 23 East and 345 North.

Nearby Attractions: See St. Peters Village, Daniel Boone Homestead, Mary Merritt Doll Museum and Early Childhood Museum, and Pottsgrove (Area III). Adjoining Hopewell Village is French Creek State Park where you may hike, swim, camp and picnic.

INDIAN ECHO CAVERNS

Open daily 9 a.m.–7 p.m. Memorial Day to Labor Day; 10 a.m.–4 p.m. April, May, Sept. and Oct.; weekends only, March and Nov. Fees: Adults, $3.50; children 6–11, $1.75. Gift shop. Picnics. Playground. Rest rooms operable in warmer months. Indian Echo Caverns, P.O. Box 206, Hummelstown, Pa. 17036. (717) 566-8131.

Imagine being a young boy living in the vicinity of a large and relatively untamed cave. The time is 1919. The lure of the cave's underground rooms and passages is irresistable. As you crawl through the narrow passageways and into a long dark tunnel, you suddenly discover a small black box on a ledge high above the floor. When you return to the daylight and pry open the "mysterious box," you find it contains 12 moonstones, a great amethyst and a variety of coins, one of which is over 2,000 years old.

During the 50-minute tour of the Indian Echo Caverns, you'll see where the mystery box was discovered and the actual box itself with its original contents in the gift shop and museum at the completion of your visit. But, more importantly, you'll share in the excitement of those who crawled through the cave before it was civilized in 1927. As you explore its ¾ of a mile of rooms and passages for yourself, you'll gaze in amazement at the small holes and dizzying heights these early explorers climbed as they searched for unknown passages and caverns. To enhance your sense of drama and discovery, you'll also see the chamber where a cave hermit lived for 19 years (1802–1821), dying in the cave at the age of 65. The tragic story of his life and the untimely death of his sister that sent him into his self-imposed exile is the stuff that great movies are made of.

The cave not only provides the setting for a wealth of stories, but is full of some of the most beautiful formations you are likely to see in Pennsylvania. It is a veritable fairyland of caverns, lakes and tunnels all made easily accessible by graded walkways, enlarged passages and over 1,700 electric lights. There is a large variety of flowstone formations throughout the cave. "Niagara Falls," a 76-foot-high formation, is one of the most impressive. In the large Indian Ball Room (110' wide by 49' high) an entire wall of flowstone assumes recognizable shapes in the cave's lights. You'll see elephants, bears, an owl and lovebirds. Stalactites and stalagmites are in abundance. The one-million-year-old stalagmite called the "Cave Guardian" stands a silent watch over the underground chambers. A variety of colors can be seen in the Rainbow Room, which features the sparkling Diamond Cascade, and the strange but lovely world of the underground is reflected in the clear water of Crystal Lake.

The caverns are in a scenic location, across the creek from a three-million-year-old Indian Village from whence the cave got its name. There are a series of steep steps leading to the entrance, but once in the cave the going is easy. Be sure to bring a sweater as the temperature is a constant 52 degrees. It is also advisable to wear old shoes as there may be some water seepage.

Directions: The cave is 10 miles east of Harrisburg and 3 miles west of Hershey. From Route 322, take the Middletown-Hummelstown Exit. Go south (towards Middletown) for a short distance and you will see a large sign on the right directing you to the cave.

Nearby Attractions: See Hershey listings, Cornwall Furnace and Mount Hope.

KNOEBELS GROVES AMUSEMENT RESORT

Open daily Memorial Day to Labor Day with rides commencing at noon. Open Sundays in May and early September. Fees: Adults, $6.00 for all day ticket; Children, $5.00. Individual tickets for rides may also be purchased. Swimming Pool Fees: Adults, $1.50; children, $1.00. Rest rooms. Picnics (covered pavilions). Food concessions. Campsites. Knoebels Groves Amusement Resort and Campgrounds, Elysburg, Pa. 17829. (717) 672-2641.

For a change of pace and scenery, plan to spend a day at this old-fashioned resort that holds a number of delightful surprises for the entire family. First and foremost among these is the amusement park which features over thirty rides guaranteed "to thrill you, spill you, and chill you . . ." The assortment of rides come in all sizes and speeds, so that toddlers can enjoy a miniature Merry-Go-Round while their older brothers and sisters ride the mind-boggling Roto-Jet. Two highlights in this park which shouldn't be missed are the Haunted House (one of the best around), and the "Country Bear Jubilee," an animated 13-minute show featuring life-size bears who delight young and old with their country western singing.

The park's setting is a scenic one, situated at the junction of two streams, Mugsers Run and Roaring Creek. You may stroll down tree-shaded pathways that meander along the streams, cross covered bridges that span them, or watch the water-powered saw mill in operation. Throughout the day, there are demonstrations of steam power tools and of the wood shingle mill.

Be sure to bring bathing suits on your trip, for across the street from the amusement area is one of the largest swimming pools in Pennsylvania. There are over 750,000 gallons of cool refreshing stream water in this water wonderland. Children and adults will enjoy the swimming, two giant water slides, the variety of diving boards, and the South Pacific Tree House. Fountains bubble in the center of the pool which also contains a children's wading area.

Directions: From I-78 take Route 61 North. Follow 61N through Mt. Carmel, cross the bridge and continue for one mile. At the traffic light, turn right onto 54N to Elysburg. At the blinking light, turn right onto 487N (there's a large directional sign at this juncture). Continue on 487 for three miles, then bear right into Knoebels Grove.

Nearby Attractions: See the Ashland Coal Mine and Steam Lokie (a 30-minute drive away).

KOZIAR'S CHRISTMAS VILLAGE

Open July 2–Labor Day, Weds.–Sun., 8:15–10:15 p.m.; Oct.–Thanksgiving, Sat. & Sun. only, 7:30–9:30 E.D.T., and 5:30–9:30 E.S.T.; Thanksgiving–Dec. 31st, every night, 6–9 p.m. (Sat. and Sun. nights 5:30–9:00 p.m.). Fees: $1.50 per person; under 5, free. Rest rooms. Gift shop. Snacks. Koziar's Christmas Village, Rt. 183, Bernville, Pa. 19506. (215) 488-1110.

You are driving your car down a twisting country road in the middle of nowhere. The air outside is bitter cold, the night sky, pitch black, and all you can see are the broken corn stalks lining the farmer's fields. Slowly your car edges up an icy hill, and at its summit the landscape before you suddenly changes. In the valley below is a veritable fairyland of colorful lights, literally thousands of them. Their gay colors are reflected in an adjacent lake and the whole valley is aglow. Rotating windmills of color add movement to the landscape, leaving no doubt that you have finally made it to one of the world's most spectacular light displays—Koziar's Christmas Village.

Huge parking lots will accommodate your car while you take a self-guided tour of this winter wonderland. Paved walkways lead you past trees, fences, and buildings, all illuminated with Christmas lights. Strolling along to the piped-in Christmas music, you see Santa Claus in his house waiting to be visited by eager children. There are numerous displays with a Christmas theme. Glassed-in cases house scenes depicting the Night Before Christmas, Christmas Around the World, and the Nativity. Children will delight in seeing the numerous handmade nursery rhyme and storybook characters that line the walks, and will gaze with rapture at Sleeping Beauty, the Candy Shop, and Raggedy Ann's Ice Cream Parlor.

If you come to the village in December, be sure to bundle up! The majority of the displays are outside, and you will probably want to spend at least an hour looking at them. There are two gift barns in which you can warm up while purchasing Christmas decorations, handicrafts and fast food items. There is also a model train layout here that will delight all ages.

Directions: Take I-78 to Exit 7, Strausstown. Take 183 south towards Bernville. There will be signs along Route 183 directing you to the Christmas Village.

Nearby Attractions: See Roadside America, and Conrad Weiser Homestead.

THE KUTZTOWN FOLK FESTIVAL

Held yearly the last week in June and the first week in July. Fees: Adults, $5.00; children 12 and under, $2.00. Parking, $1.00. Rest rooms. Gift shops. Picnics. Snacks and dinners. The Kutztown Folk Festival, College Blvd. and Vine, Kutztown, Pa. 19530. (215) 683-8707.

One of the most popular attractions held in the Pennsylvania Dutch region is the Kutztown Folk Festival. This yearly extravaganza offers the tourist the opportunity to experience the Pennsylvania Dutch culture first–hand through craft displays, farming demonstrations, plays, hoe downs, country auctions, German band concerts, and a host of other happenings. People from all over the United States come to see such unusual activities as apple butter boiling, quilting, basket weaving, slaughtering and butchering. There is never a dull moment during this nine day festival. A mock Amish wedding and barn raising are performed. Susanna Cox is hanged for infanticide, and Regina Hartman abducted by local Indians. There are puppet shows and Pennsylvania Dutch games for the youngsters, and old-time polka bands that grownups can sit and listen to. For the curiosity seeker, there are numerous and fascinating displays and discourses on such subjects as funeral, snake and bumble bee lore.

An added highlight to this popular festival is the abundant and delectable food being offered for sale in large supper tents and stands. There is the famous Dutch funnel cake, waffles and ice cream, fritters, potato cakes, roast oxen, sausage, and many other tasty Dutch specialties. A day at the festival is not one for calorie counting. The Pennsylvania Dutch believe that "Fat is beautiful," and their cooking attests to this.

Many people come to Kutztown to buy the lovely craft items on sale. Nowhere will you find such a selection of handmade quilts, a number of them blue ribbon winners. There are handsomely painted milk cans and hex signs, framed fraktur (illustrated sayings written in script), and Sgraffito Pottery among others. You'll also discover some unusual antiques for sale.

Directions: The festival is held in the Kutztown Fairgrounds at College Blvd. and Vine Streets. From Rt. 222 (between Allentown and Reading), take the Kutztown Exit (Rt. 737 South) and follow the signs to the festival.

Nearby Attractions: See Lenhartsville One-Room School and Folklife Museum, Crystal Cave, and Rodale Organic Gardening & Research Center (see Lehigh County Area III).

LEBANON BOLOGNA FREE PLANT TOURS

When the Pennsylvania Dutch settled in the fertile Lebanon Valley in the early 1800's, they began to make a ready-to-eat semi-dry sausage-like food known today as Lebanon Bologna. This sausage was manufactured by individual farmers who developed their own delectable recipes blending a variety of meats, herbs, and spices which were then smoked using a combination of seasoned hardwoods. These recipes were closely guarded and several distinctive brands of Lebanon Bologna developed.

Today, practically all Lebanon Bologna consumed in the United States is processed at three localities in the Lebanon Valley: The Weaver, Seltzer and Bomberger Plants. These facilities offer free tours to the public. Although recipes are still closely guarded, visitors do get an excellent opportunity to see how the bologna is made. You can see the beef being precured in wooden barrels, then watch the butcher grinding the meat. In secret, the meat is then carefully blended with the spices and forced into special casings. The resulting bologna is hung by hand in old–fashioned smoke houses where it will be smoked for three to four days. The aroma of the wood smoke and spices is so enticing that by the end of the twenty-minute tour you will be eager to purchase the bologna that is for sale. In addition, you may also purchase smoked hams, smoked dried beef, mince meat and sweet bologna.

Here is a listing of the plants, their locations and hours of operation:

BOMBERGER'S BOLOGNA

Open Monday–Friday, 8–4 p.m. No fees. Bomberger's Bologna, R.D. 1, Box 940, Lebanon, Pa. 17042. (717) 272-7471.

Directions: The plant is located right off Rt. 897, on Fox Road, three miles south of Lebanon.

Nearby Attractions: See Alexander Schaeffer Farm Museum, Cornwall Furnace and Mount Hope.

PALMYRA BOLOGNA COMPANY, INC. (SELTZER'S)

Open Monday–Friday, 9–12 and 1–4. No fees. Palmyra Bologna Company, 230 North College St., Palmyra, Pa. (717) 838-6336.

Directions: The plant is located on 230 North College Ave., three blocks north of Rt. 422 in Palmyra (which is southwest of the town of Lebanon, and three miles east of Hershey)

Nearby Attractions: See Hershey, Pa.

WEAVER'S BOLOGNA PLANT

Open Monday–Friday, 9–4. No fees. Weaver's, P.O. Box 525, 15th Ave. & Weavertown Rd., Lebanon, Pa. 17042. (717) 272-5643.

Directions: From Rt. 422 in Lebanon, turn left (north) onto 15th St. and follow to where it intersects with Weavertown Road.

Nearby Attractions: See Alexander Schaeffer Farm Museum, Cornwall Furnace and Mount Hope.

THE LENHARTSVILLE ONE-ROOM SCHOOL AND FOLKLIFE MUSEUM

Open June–Aug.: Mon.–Sat., 10–5; Sun. 1–5. Open weekends in May, Sept. and Oct.: Sat., 10–5; Sun., 1–5. School groups by appointment April, May, June–Sept., Oct., Nov. Fees: Adults, $1.50; children accompanied by adult, 50¢; children without adult, 75¢. Rest rooms. Pennsylvania Dutch Folk Culture Center, Lenhartsville, Pa. 19534. (215) 562-4803 or (215) 682-7432.

History really comes alive in Lenhartsville due to the efforts of the Pennsylvania Dutch Folk Culture Society formed in 1960 to preserve the culture, dialect, and history of the Pennsylvania Dutch. This group is responsible for restoring a one-room school house and combining it with a Folklife Museum, Log House, House of Fashions, and a Genealogical and Folklore Library. Most of the more than 300 members of this society are Pennsylvania Dutch themselves, and their personal interest and involvement in the folklife museum has created an attraction where interested guides take the time to explain and illustrate how life was really lived "way back when."

On display in the museum are many household and farm implements used for the past two centuries by the Pennsylvania Dutch. Antique lovers will be intrigued by the dog-tread-power butter churn (dogs were once used instead of children on the larger dairy farms to churn the butter); the hog fiddle (a large wooden instrument played outside a new bridegroom's window along with the notorious Bull Band composed of washboard, wooden spoon, jugs, and kettle with spoon); the series of heating irons (one was even used with coal in it); the large loom used to make rag rugs; an ice plow, and other unusual items.

The highlight of this attraction, however, is the one-room school which dates from 1887 and was used until 1965. It exists in its original state with double seats, a pot-belly stove, recitation benches, and displays of homework and the "primers" used in the past. Children will enjoy ringing the school bell, sitting in the desks, and gazing at the blackboard where "Reading, Writing, and Arithmetic" were once taught to their forebears.

Two additional buildings contain the House of Fashions and a Genealogical Library. On display in the costume museum is clothing made from flax, wool, and a combination of the two called linsey-woolsey. For those interested in researching their ancestors, the genealogical library houses information pertaining to Berks, Northampton, and Lehigh Counties. This library has just recently been opened and can be visited Saturday afternoons or at other times by appointment.

Directions: Lenhartsville is located between Allentown and Hamburg less than a mile off Rt. 22 (I-78) on Rt. 143 South.

Nearby Attractions: See Pennsylvania Dutch Farm Festival at Kempton, WK&S Steam Railroad, and Onyx Cave. Lenhartsville is located on the Hex Highway (Old Rt. 22), a scenic road that leads past attractive farms with colorful barns decorated with hex signs.

MARY MERRITT DOLL MUSEUM AND MERRITT'S MUSEUM OF CHILDHOOD AND THE PENNA. DUTCH

Museums open daily 10–5 p.m., Sun. and holidays, 11–5 p.m. Closed New Year's, Christmas, Easter and Thanksgiving. Fees, which include both museums: Adults, $1.50; children 5–12, 75¢. Group rates available. Rest rooms. Gift shops. Handicapped: wheelchair available at Museum of Childhood. Some steps leading into Doll Museum. Mary Merritt Museums, R.D. 2, Douglassville, Pa. 19518. (215) 385-3809 (Doll Museum), (215) 385-3408 (Childhood Museum).

For over fifty years dolls have been Mary Merritt's passion. The museum she has established to house 1,500 of her collection of 5,000 dolls is a fascinating one considered to be among the finest and largest in the country. Doll and toy lovers will truly enjoy the time they spend here perusing the collection. Dolls dating from 1725 to 1900 are displayed in glassed-in cabinets. There are the handsomely dressed fashion dolls wearing 18th and 19th century modes of costume. Quaint dolls of the pioneers, made from cornhusks, stand alongside sophisticated Madame Jumeau dolls from France, and long lines of baby dolls in beguiling white dresses smile down from their shelves. Literally hundreds of these "little people" made from all sorts of materials and dressed in an endless variety of costumes are on exhibit.

Besides the cases containing the dolls, there are over 40 miniature period rooms which contain furnishings and dolls of the appropriate era. These are intriguing, for they are accurate down to the tiniest detail. In separate cabinets are miniatures of all types including tiny silver tea services and complete china sets. Full-size doll houses (from Mrs. Merritt's collection, which numbers over 50) and a replica of a Philadelphia Toy Shop filled with an assortment of antique toys complete the exhibit.

The adjacent Museum of Early Childhood and the Pennsylvania Dutch is an interesting conglomeration of early American artifacts collected by the Merritts. Although exhibits are not all described, many are self-explanatory. There is an extensive collection of Indian lore and metal and wood cigar store Indians. Two completely furnished rooms, done in a 1780 mode of decor, may be viewed. They are re-creations of a frontier kitchen and dining room; and bedroom with colorful quilts and braided rugs. Along one wall of the museum is a large assortment of antique pottery, china and glassware, while along another is a collection of antique children's carriages. Tin and iron toys, mechanical banks, paper weights, model trains, jewelry and butter molds round out this collection that contains a bit of everything that's old and interesting.

The gift shops at both museums deserve mentioning, for they are almost as fascinating as the museums. Here you can buy antique dolls, miniatures (both new and old), toys, original fabrics from different eras, old post cards, Indian relics and other unusual items. For doll fanciers, this place is a must!

Directions: The museums are located on Route 422, ten miles east of Reading near Douglassville.

Nearby Attractions: See Daniel Boone Homestead, Pottsgrove (Area IV), Hopewell Village, and St. Peters Village.

MICHTER'S DISTILLERY

Open daily, year round, 10–4:40 p.m. Fees: Adults, $1.00; children under 12 free. Reservations required for large groups. Rest rooms. Gift shop. Michter's Jug House, Michter's and Distillery Road, Box 387, Schaefferstown, Pa. 17088. (717) 949-6521.

If you're the type who likes to get into the "spirit" of things, Michter's, the oldest operating distillery in the United States, is the place to go. With a daily capacity of 50 barrels, Michter's is really a miniature of the massive distilleries in Kentucky or Tennessee. But it's the only U.S. distillery that still takes the time to use the traditional drop-by-drop pot still method of distillation derived from the ancient distilleries of Scotland and Ireland. The result is Michter's exceptionally aromatic and flavorful 86 Proof sour mash.

When John Shenk, a Swiss Mennonite, first set up the distillery on his farm in 1753, whisky was the chief medium of exchange in Pennsylvania, the nation's leading whisky producer until 1850. Converting excess corn and rye to whisky alleviated the difficulties in transporting bushels of grain by pack horse to distant markets. There, whisky was much in demand as a medicine as well as for its morale-boosting properties. Indeed, George Washington considered whisky a necessity for the Colonial Army and Michter's is still advertised as "the whisky that warmed the Revolution." In 1861, the Shenk family sold the distillery to Abe Bomberger who operated it until Prohibition in the 1920's.

The 45-minute guided tour of Michter's is like taking a step into the past. It begins at the old Bomberger warehouse, which now houses stacks of white oak aging barrels with Michter's "sleeping" whisky. The well-informed guide begins with the history of whisky-making in the area followed by a step-by-step description of the fermentation and distillation process. The aroma from the aging barrels and the samples of "white lightning" passed around are enough to make anyone a Michter fan. Next comes the walking tour of the various buildings that comprise Michter's modern distillery. The building that housed the old Bomberger Distillery has been restored to its 19th century appearance. It contains an operating replica of the original hand-hammered copper still—now the smallest legal distillery in America. The tour winds up at the Jug House where local farmers used to come to fill their jugs from the barrels lining the walls. Today, Michter's offers for sale bottles containing take-home samples of the distillery's output as well as an interesting assortment of unusual decanters for collectors.

Directions: The distillery, in southeast Lebanon County, is easy to find. It's located 18 miles east of Hershey, 16 miles north of Lancaster, and 6 miles from Exit 20 of the Pennsylvania Turnpike. Signs will guide you from Route 501 North through the rolling farmland to just south of Schaefferstown where Distillery Road winds up at Michter's.

Nearby Attractions: See Cornwall Furnace and Mount Hope, Lebanon Bologna Factory Tours, and the Alexander Schaeffer Farm Museum.

ONYX CAVE—A Haunting Experience

Haunting: Nightly during October from 6 p.m. to 9 p.m. Fees: $2.00. Cave open daily 9 a.m.–6 p.m., Memorial Day–Labor Day. Weekends only March, April, May, Sept., Oct., Nov., 9 a.m.–6 p.m. Fees: Adults, $3.00; children, $1.50. Rest rooms. Picnics. The Onyx Cave, R.D. 2, Box 308, Hamburg, Pa. 19526. (215) 562-4335.

When the leaves of autumn turn to rust and brown and the nights grow colder with a chill wind rattling the bare trees like so many old bones, the Onyx Cave (near Hamburg, Pa.) becomes the haunting site for ghouls, witches, and blood-lusting vampires. Dark stone chambers, lit only by hidden lights, harbor the spirits of Halloween who shriek and moan at all those brave enough to enter their subterranean kingdom. Beware of Igor, the Frankenstein monster who leads you to the cavern's door. If you escape his clutches, the ghoul with the sharpened ax will be sure to get you! Her last victim lies headless and bloody at her feet.

For those who dare to enter, a ticket to this night of fright is two dollars plus a pint of courage. The Halloween spooks settle in their cavern for the month of October, and open their cave from 6 p.m. until 9 p.m. every night of the week. The haunting lasts anywhere from ten to twenty minutes depending on how much you can take. Wear warm clothes, it is a spine-chilling experience!

During the remainder of the year (except December, January, and February when the cave is closed), Onyx Cave is spook-free and open to the public. A film on caves is offered in the Natural Rock Museum followed by cave tours, led by experienced guides, which leave every fifteen minutes. Billed as one of the longest caverns in Pennsylvania, this cave hosts such interesting formations as a pipe organ, elephant's head, turkey head, and what some believe to be the remains of a human body. One of the most intriguing formations is the Ice Jam. Geologists are hard put to explain how a solid layer of rock, confined in a narrow passage, could become so broken-up. Solid gravel walks, electric lights and wooden steps make a visit to this cave safe and enjoyable.

Directions: Onyx Cave is located off Route 662 (between Kutztown and Reading). If coming down Route 222, turn north onto 662 (the Moselem Springs Inn will be on the corner), and follow the signs for approximately four miles to the cave's entrance.

Nearby Attractions: See Lenhartsville One-Room School and Folklife Museum, Kutztown Folk Festival, and Crystal Cave.

THE PENNSYLVANIA DUTCH FARM MUSEUM AND FESTIVAL AT KEMPTON

Festival held each year the weekend after Labor Day. Fees: Adults, $2.00; children under 12, free. Parking—$1.00. Rest rooms. Snacks. Gifts. Farm Museum open weekends May–Oct., 11 a.m.–6 p.m. Fees: moderate. Rest rooms. Address and phone for both: Pennsylvania Dutch Farm Museum, Kempton, Pa. 19529. (215) 683-7130.

The sound of the fiddle can be heard over the putt-putting of over two dozen gasoline engines. Square dancers with taps on their dancing shoes are exuberantly performing on a small stage surrounded by clapping people. A goose honks in a pen nearby while curious children attempt to feed her grass. The setting is bucolic, ideal for an old-time country festival.

From horse shoeing to wheat threshing to milking cows, an education in different aspects of rural farm life is available at the Kempton Farm Festival. Through the "living history" approach, you see the way candles used to be made, sheep sheared, butter churned, and honey made. An entire field is devoted to demonstrating the tasks the old-time gasoline engines could perform on the farm, and another area is devoted to handmade craft demonstrations.

This unusual and interesting farm festival has all the appeal of a scaled-down Kutztown Folk Festival, but without the crowds. There is plenty of entertainment, good food (you can purchase all those Pennsylvania Dutch specialties like funnel cake and apple schnitz here), a large flea market filled with antiques and gifts, and a real "down home" country atmosphere.

In the middle of the festival grounds is a large red barn in which is housed a collection of tools and implements used in early farm life. There are rare old washing machines, butter-making equipment, cobblers' benches, antique butchering tools and other implements of the past. This is the Pennsylvania Dutch Farm Museum which is open during the festival and at specified times throughout the year. Adjacent to the festival grounds is the WK&S Steam Railroad where you may take a ride on an old-time steam train.

Directions: Kempton is located five miles north of Rt. 222 (between Allentown and Reading) on Route 737, and just a few miles north of Rt. 22. (Take either 143 N. to 737 and turn right, or take Exit 737 North.)

Nearby Attractions: See WK&S Steam Railroad, Lenhartsville One-Room School and Folklife Museum, Hawk Mountain and Blue Rocks.

READING'S FACTORY OUTLETS

It is a shopper's paradise, a place where bargain fever runs rampant and busloads of people scurry from store to store grabbing up the best buys in town. It's Reading, Pa., the outlet capital of the U.S.A. Literally hundreds of outlets are located here, selling everything from power tools to underwear at a reduced price.

The outlet boom began back in 1973 when two enterprising businessmen acquired abandoned mill buildings and turned them into factory outlet shopping centers. Here factory brand-name overruns and irregulars were offered for sale on a percentage basis by their manufacturers. This was the start of the famous Moss Street Shopping centers called respectively The Great Factory Store and the Reading Outlet Center. An added attraction is that there is no clothing tax in Pennsylvania.

There are four area concentrations of factory outlets within Reading. These are:

1. THE GREAT FACTORY STORE on the 1100 Block of Moss Street. There are 22 factory outlets on this block, featuring over 200 brandname products. These outlets include: Misses clothing & Sportswear, Men's Clothing, Men's Furnishings, Women's Large Sizes, Linen & Domestics, Boys' & Girls' Clothing, Jr. Clothing & Sportswear, Women's Shoes, Raincoats & Outerwear, Luggage & Handbags, Lingerie, Leather Coats, Pretzels & Snacks, Men's Shoes, Hosiery Mill, Wicker Shop, Bargain Loft and Van Heusen. The center is open Mon.–Weds., 10–6; Thurs. & Fri., 10–9; Sat., 9:30–6; Sun., 12–5. Tel. (215) 378-1681.

2. READING OUTLET CENTER, which is comprised of 14 outlets centered in the Moss Street Area. These include: ABC Linen Outlet, American Factory Shoe Outlet, B & B Jewelry Outlet, Barbizon Lingerie Factory Outlet, Big R Sporting Goods, Coat Rack, Hampshire Outlet Store, House of Leather, Judy's Closet, M & M Factory Store, Manufacturer's Outlet, Moss St. Menswear Outlet, Ship 'n Shore Ladies' Factory Outlet, and Windsor Shirt Co. Factory Outlet. Hours vary slightly from store to store, but in general they are: Mon.–Sat., 9:30–5:30; Sun., 12–5.

3. HEISTERS LANE OUTLET CENTER and nearby outlets which are all a few blocks north of the Moss St. area. These outlets include: Designers' Outlet, Flemington Fashion Outlet, Jonathan Chris Factory Outlet, Reading Dinnerware Crystal & Gift Outlet, Reading Menswear Outlet (all in one building complex); and nearby, Talbott Coat Factory Warehouse and Children's Mill Factory Outlet. Hours vary slightly from store to store, but in general they are: Mon.–Sat., 9:30–5:30; Sun., 12–5.

4. VANITY FAIR OUTLET CENTER at 8th and Hill Aves, Wyomissing. This center features five outlets in addition to the famous and large Vanity Fair store. These include: The Bachman Co., Black & Decker Power Tool Outlet, Famous Brands Jewelry Outlet, Handbags and Luggage, and Rockwell International Power Tools. Hours for these are all basically the same: Mon.–Fri., 9–9; Sat., 9–6. Tel. (215) 378-0408.

For additional information on these and many other outlets in this area, a free outlet map and pamphlet is available by writing: Reading-Berks County Pennsylvania Dutch Travel Association, Washington Towers, 50 N. 4th St., Suite # 3, Reading, Pa. 19601, or calling (215) 376-3931.

Nearby Attractions: See Reading Pagoda & Skyline Drive.

READING'S PAGODA, SKYLINE DRIVE AND DURYEA HILL CLIMB

Pagoda open daily 12–8:30 p.m. Fees: 25¢ for turnstile on top, 10¢ to use high-powered binoculars. Oriental gift shop and Hong Kong Tea Garden Snack Shop. Rest rooms. Duryea Hill Climb held second weekend in September. The Pagoda, Skyline Drive, Reading, Pa. (215) 373-5111.

A storyteller once described Reading as a Pennsylvania Dutch town with a predominately Polish population that was founded by English Quakers and is situated between two mountains—one of which (Neversink) was named by the Indians, the other named after William Penn. During the early 1900's, Reading was well known as a vacation resort due to the string of posh hotels that lined both the Neversink and Mount Penn. Unfortunately, most of these were of frame construction and have long since burnt to the ground. Luckily the most unusual one remains—a full-fledged Japanese Pagoda which was modeled after the Nagoya Castle in Japan and is outlined at night with red neon lights.

The seven-story Pagoda was built atop Mount Penn in 1908 by Mr. William Witman to help placate the local citizenry for the scars etched on the surrounding mountain by Mr. Witman's quarrying company. While it was intended as a luxury hotel, this never got off the ground since its liquor license was denied, and the Pagoda was sold to the City of Reading in 1910 for one dollar. Today, as the visitor walks through the torii gate, it's like leaving the Dutchland behind and entering the world of the ancient Orient. The stylized dolphins on the rooftop serve the purpose, according to Japanese legend, of protecting the structure from fire. Once inside, 86 steps lead through seven levels to the top. Local civic groups maintain exhibits at each level and on the top floor there's the massive Buddhist temple bell that was originally cast in Japan during 1739. There's also a scale model of Reading to help identify the city's features, such as the bandshell in City Park and Reading's rows and rows of turreted gabled townhouses, as the visitor looks through the high-powered binoculars.

The steep road that winds up Mount Penn from the City Park to the Pagoda is named Duryea Drive after Charles Duryea, the inventor of the first hill-climbing gasoline auto built in the United States. It was here that Duryea tested his cars during the early 1900's. More recently, drivers from the Sports Car Club of America compete here in the annual Duryea Hill Climb held each year on the second weekend in September. Duryea Drive leads into Skyline Drive, which runs for three miles along the top of Mount Penn. Three lookouts provide a panoramic view of the City and surrounding Pennsylvania Dutch countryside that can stretch for as far as thirty miles on a clear day. Drenkel Field, the home of a local model airplane club, is also located off Skyline Drive. On a Saturday morning, you can often see the "Flying Dutchmen" testing their custom-built model aircraft. Other nearby points of interest that can be reached by taking Hill Road off Duryea Drive, are Egelman's Park, a city-run park with picnic pavilions and a reservoir; and Stokesay Castle, a replica of an 18th Century English Castle that today serves as a fine restaurant.

Directions: Follow Rt. 422, which becomes Penn Street after you cross the Penn Street bridge into Reading. Immediately after the bridge, take a right onto 2nd Street and then left at the next block onto Franklin. Follow Franklin to 9th Street, make a left onto 9th and right onto Penn (you're merely bypassing the downtown mall area). Follow Penn Street to the first street beyond the City Park entrance and make a left onto Hill Road. Hill Road takes you along the right edge of the City Park and once you reach the first light, you'll see the beginning of Duryea Drive across the way.

Nearby Attractions: Reading's Factory Outlets.

ROADSIDE AMERICA

Open daily year round: July–Labor Day, 9–6:30 p.m. weekdays, 9–7 weekends; Sept.–June, 10–5 weekdays, 10–6 weekends. Fees: Adults, $2.00; children 6–11, 50¢. Rest rooms. Gift shop. Roadside America, Rt. 22, Shartlesville, Pa. (215) 488-6241 (from 10–5).

Resting on the summit of Mount Penn, which overlooks the city of Reading, Laurence Gieringer, 10 years old, marveled at how little the houses looked in the distance. A boy with a fertile imagination, he ran home and decided, along with his brother Paul, to build his own miniature village—one that would reflect life as it was at the time, the turn of the century. He pursued this hobby with determination, getting money to build the miniature houses by selling popcorn, shoveling snow and the like. Years passed, but his interest continued, and, in 1935 when Gieringer set up his miniature display at Christmas for his children, the Reading Eagle newspaper wrote a feature story on it. This assured its popularity for the masses. Since then, the boyhood dream of this ten-year-old has taken on an even greater reality. His unique display of a miniature America fills an entire building and people come from all over to view it. Although Geiringer died in 1963, his family continues to operate this attraction that has brought delight to all ages.

Set on a room-size platform with observation walkways encircling it, is Gieringer's miniature version of slices of American life. Model trains chug their way through mountains, tunnels and past tiny villages. Man-made waterfalls and mountains weighing over two tons form a backdrop for an old grist mill. There is a modern village which incorporates over 100 years of American architecture, and, in another area, the gay 90's are represented by a saloon, dance hall and stagecoach. Set throughout the exhibit are manual controls that enable the visitor to operate some of the equipment. Push a button and an electric trolley commences its tour about town. Push another and a water wheel starts to turn. Still another raises and lowers a coal mining elevator. Periodically, night descends on this miniature continent, and moon and stars come out. Lights come on in the hundreds of houses dotting the landscape, creating a charming nighttime scene. At daybreak, Kate Smith salutes the dawning sun with a heartfelt rendition of "God Bless America."

Directions: Take Rt. 22 to the Shartlesville Exit 8 (near Hamburg). Roadside America is directly off this exit; just follow the signs.

Nearby Attractions: See Koziar's Christmas Village.

ST. PETERS VILLAGE

Open all year. Shop hours: June–Sept., Tues.–Fri. 10:30–5:30 p.m.; Sat. 11–6; Sun. 12–6. Oct.–May, Tues.–Fri. 10:30–5; Sat. 11–6; Sun. 12–6. Restaurants. Snacks. Picnics. Rest rooms. (215) 469-9074.

In the northwest portion of Chester County is a charming restored Victorian Village. Founded over 100 years ago by the Knauer family, St. Peters Village was established to provide living quarters for the men and their families who were working in a nearby block granite quarry. The lovely location along the French Creek Falls attracted many visitors, and after the Civil War wooden bridges and boardwalks were added to make the falls accessible. When the Inn at St. Peters was constructed to house tourists, and a dance pavilion and park established to entertain them, the village became known throughout the area as Knauer's resort. Many of the gentry would come from Philadelphia to enjoy the lovely scenery and relaxed atmosphere.

Although St. Peters languished during the depression, today it has been restored to its early charm. Many of the original buildings have been turned into unique speciality shops. What was once a carriage house for guests at the Inn is now a fudge shop. A granary for the horses now acts as a display area for antiques and art objects, and the original pool hall serves as the village restaurant. Other buildings have been added over the years, but all were built in keeping with the quaint atmosphere. In them you can buy such items as quilts, handicrafts, antiques, doll house furniture, custom-made leather and sheepskin goods and much more. The old Inn still stands and serves elegant meals. Adjacent to it is the dance pavilion which, during the summer months, hosts a German Oom-pah band. Here you can dine and dance in the great outdoors while watching the nearby water cascading past.

Since French Creek has been made accessible by walkways and steps, an enjoyable pastime in the summer months is to wander about the creek, crossing the wooden bridges and rock-hopping from one massive boulder to another. It provides a refreshing break from all the shopping.

Directions: Take Rt. 422 East of Reading to Route 100. Go south on 100 to Rt. 23. Go west on 23 to Knauertown. At Knauertown, go right onto St. Peter's Road (there are directional signs) which will lead to the village.

Nearby Attractions: See Hopewell Village, Daniel Boone Homestead, and Mary Merritt Museums.

TULPEHOCKEN MANOR PLANTATION

Open all year. Guided tours from 10–5 p.m. daily and on weekends. Call ahead if possible. Fees: Adults, $2.50; children 6–12, $2.00. Group rates. Overnight lodging. Tulpehocken Manor Plantation, R.D. 2 (Rt. 422), Myerstown, Pa. 17067. (717) 866-4926.

The large Victorian mansion stands among ancient magnolia trees. Its mansard roof, spacious porches with ornate ironwork, and columned façade look incongruous in this Pennsylvania Dutch farm setting. The original house, built in 1769, was more in keeping with the German style. At that time, it was an eight-room colonial farmhouse built by Michael Ley, a captain in the Continental Army and good friend of George Washington's. In fact, George Washington was said to have visited Ley's home three times and reputedly slept in the southeast room on the second floor. It was from 1883–1885 that the house underwent its transformation from Colonial to Victorian. The house was enlarged from eight to twenty-seven rooms, embellished with Victorian decorations, and completely restored by the Urich family.

When the present owners bought the estate in 1960, they restored the house and outbuildings and opened them up to tourists for overnight accommodations and tours. The stone outbuildings located throughout the 150-acre farm include an old smoke house, 129-foot bank barn, an 18th century limestone-arched home built over a spring (a perfect example of Germanic Swiss Bank architecture) and a bakehouse.

One-hour guided tours are conducted through the 27-room mansion. Ornate Victorian lights hang from the high ceilings, seven slate mantels from Germany (hand-decorated in France and Italy) cover the old fireplaces, and wide crinoline doors of walnut and pine provide ladies with "hooped skirts" easy access to the rooms. The 18-inch-thick walls are constructed of stone quarried on the property, and the wood so beautifully used in the handcarved walnut banister and decorative trim came from the surrounding land. Pressed and cut Belgian glass windows decorate the front door which leads into the marble foyer. The wide front porch looks out to a meadow filled with Black Angus Cattle.

The furnishings within the mansion are as colorful as the house itself. The multitude of rooms (including 14 bedrooms) are all gaily decorated in Colonial and Victorian motifs. Handmade quilts cover the four-poster and high Victorian beds, knickknacks grace the tables and shelves, and a multitude of pictures hang from the walls, including some intricately hand-embroidered works. Each room you visit is full of surprises, like the claw-footed tub in the bathroom, massive gold-framed mirrors in the bedrooms, and the collection of old tools on the third floor. Two items you must not miss are the 1771 wardrobe once owned by Michael Ley and after 136 years returned to the manor, and the huge cistern located on the third floor, which was used for an indoor water supply until 1956.

Directions: The Plantation is located on Rt. 422, five miles east of Lebanon.

Nearby Attractions: See Conrad Weiser Homestead, Zeller's Fort, and Alexander Schaeffer Farm Museum & Festivals.

WK&S STEAM RAILROAD

Trolley only operates March–April: Sat. & Sun., from 1:15 to 4:30 p.m. May–June: Sat., Trolley only leaving on the hour from 1–5; Sun. Steam Train leaving on the hour from 1–5. July–August: Mon.–Fri. Berksy Trolley leaving on the hour 1–5 p.m.; Weekends, Steam Train from 1–5 p.m. Sept.–Oct.: Sat., Trolley only leaving from 1–5 p.m. Sunday, Steam Train leaving from 1–5. November: Trolley operates weekends only, from 1:15 to 4:30. Hours subject to change. Fees: Adults, $2.25; children, $1.25. Gift shop. Rest rooms. Picnics. WK&S Steam Railroad, Steam Rail Road, Box 24, Kempton, Pa. 19529. (215) 756-6469 or 395-3909.

The clickety-clack of steel wheels on a steel track is punctuated by the sounds of the mighty steam whistle. Smoke and steam drift up into the skies as you are taken for an old-time steam engine ride through the scenic Pennsylvania Dutch countryside near Kempton, Pa. For three miles you are immersed in the sights and sounds of the past. Then the train stops and you disembark for a twelve-minute stopover in the delightful small town of Wanamaker. There is even a general store where you may purchase a coke to quench your thirst. With an "All Aboard," the train engineer starts up his engine and you are taken back to Kempton, on the same tracks over which the former Reading Company Schuylkill and Lehigh branch used to run.

Your ride on the "Hawk Mountain Line" lasts about a half an hour. If you wish, you may bring along lunch and have an old–fashioned picnic at the Trackside Grove. There are tables, tall shade trees, rest rooms and a gift shop where railroad mementos may be purchased.

In addition to the steam train rides, a trolley ride is also offered over the same tracks, but at different times. All rides are round trip, leaving from Kempton rain or shine.

Directions: The railroad is located adjacent to the Pennsylvania Dutch Farm Museum in Kempton, Pa. From Rt. 22, take 737 north for five miles to Kempton. The railroad and museum will be off to your left after you go around a sharp right–hand curve in the road in Kempton.

Nearby Attractions: See Pennsylvania Dutch Farm Festival at Kempton, The Lenhartsville One-Room School and Folklife Museum, Blue Rocks, and Hawk Mountain.

ZELLER'S FORT

Open year round by appointment, 10–4 p.m. Donations accepted. The Hoffmans, Proprietors, Zeller's Fort, Rt. 1, Newmanstown, Pa. (215) 589-4301.

Don't be mislead by its name, for Zeller's Fort is not your typical frontier fort but rather an 18th century house which was used for refuge from marauding Indians during the French and Indian War. What is interesting about the structure is that it is an outstanding example of medieval German architecture. Built in 1745, the house bears a remarkable resemblance to those built in the Rhine Basin of Germany during the same time period. The steeply-pitched roof, central chimney with walk-in fireplace, small windows and unusual panelled door broken into two sections (the familiar Dutch Door); all reflect this German heritage.

This private fort is considered the oldest in Pennsylvania and has been listed on the National Register of Historic Landmarks. For history and architectural buffs, it is an interesting place to visit and compare to its restored counterpart, the Hans Herr House (another home of Medieval German construction believed to have been built by a different "guild" of craftsmen). Within the house are displays of old tools, kitchen utensils and a large assortment of antique clocks.

The Fort is located on the premises of a working farm and tours are conducted by Mr. Hoffman, the farmer and real Pennsylvania Dutchman. It's important to call in advance, for the milking of cows must take precedence over the guiding of tourists.

Directions: From either Rt. 422 or I-78 between Lebanon and Reading, take Route 419 South to Newmanstown. Go through Newmanstown and at the last intersection (the Chat-A-While Cafe will be on the corner) turn right onto Fort Zeller's Road. The house will be located at the first farm on your right.

Nearby Attractions: See Conrad Weiser Homestead, Tulpehocken Manor Plantation, and Alexander Schaeffer Farm Museum.

Lehigh County and the Pocono Region

KEY TO MAP—AREA III (*overleaf*)

A – Allentown Fair and Farmer's Market

B – Allentown's Historic Houses and Liberty Bell Shrine

C – Bethlehem: Walking tour, Moravian Museum, Goundie House, Annie S. Kemerer Museum, 18th Century Industrial Area and Bethlehem—the Christmas City

D – Bushkill Falls

E – C. F. Martin Guitar Co.

F – Camelback's Alpine and Water Slides

G – Covered Bridge Tour starting point—Lehigh County

H – Crayola Factory Tour

I – Das Awkscht Fest

J – Delaware Water Gap

K – Dorney Park and Haines Flour Mill

L – Eckley's Miner's Village

M – Hugh Moore Park

N – Industrial Museums of the Lehigh Valley—Lock Ridge Furnace

O – Industrial Museums of the Lehigh Valley—Saylor Park Cement Industry Museum

P – Jim Thorpe

Q – Leather Corner Post Hotel

R – Lehigh County Velodrome

S – Lil-Le-Hi Trout Nursery

T – Lost River Caverns

U – Magic Valley and Winona Falls

V – Quiet Valley Living Historical Farm

W – Rodale Organic Gardening and Farming Research Center

X – Trexler Lehigh Game Preserve

Y – White Water Rafting—Whitewater Challengers

Z – Whitewater Rafting—Pocono Whitewater Rafting Center

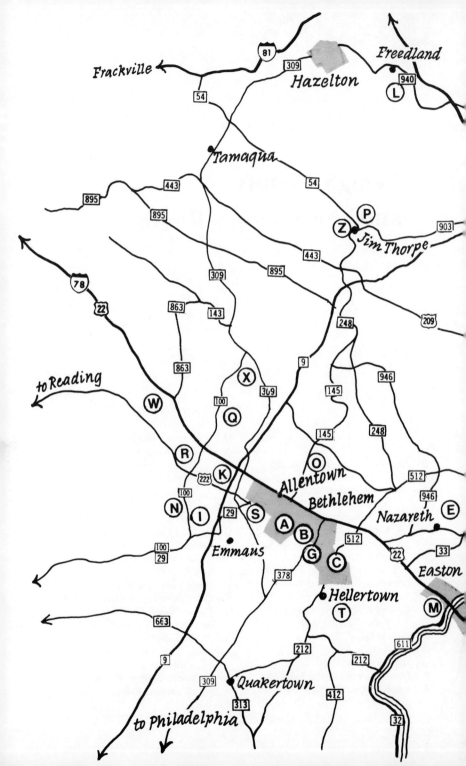

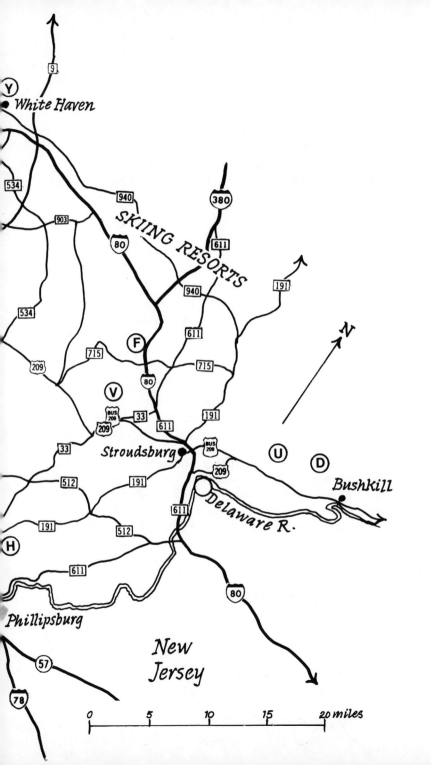

Lehigh County
and the Pocono Region

The hex signs so prevalent in Berks County continue into Lehigh, where the Hex Highway (old Route 22) leads past some of the most lavishly painted barns you are likely to see anywhere. In the western and central portions of the county, the Pennsylvania Dutch influence predominates. However, upon entering Bethlehem another ethnic influence is felt, that of the Moravians. This religious group has dominated the city and its surroundings, creating a unique culture that stresses a strong religious commitment, education, industry, and the arts. While in Allentown you hear the beat of the boom-bas, in Bethlehem you listen to a Bach Choir.

The topography of the land also changes from Berks and the more southern counties. The gently rolling farmland grows hillier until it becomes mountainous in the Pocono region. This section is full of outdoor adventures from climbing waterfalls, to whitewater rafting, to scooting down a mountain on an Alpine Slide. The Pennsylvania Germans have even infiltrated this mountain playground, making successful farms out of the fertile valley land.

THE ALLENTOWN FAIR

Held annually the last week in August. Fees: Adults, $1.50; Children under 12 free. Opening night usually free of charge. Rest rooms. Snacks and meals.

The Allentown Fair, 17th and Chew Sts., Allentown, Pa. 18104. (215) 433-7541.

Agricultural displays, 4H and FFA competition, livestock judging, auctioneers, side shows, a carnival midway with rides and a panoply of food concessions serving everything from cotton candy to Italian sausage—all the elements that make up an old-fashioned county fair are present here at Allentown's, which is considered to be one of the largest fairs held in Southeastern Pennsylvania. You can see a prize cow being curried, tilt upside-down in a terrifying carnival ride, watch an ethnic dance exhibition or hear a boom-bas jamboree. Free entertainment abounds, and, for those who like to spend their money and "take a chance," there are booths along the midway where they can risk their quarters on Lady Luck.

All the glitter and chaos of this large and popular fair really comes alive after dark when the lights cast a magical glow over all. The grandstand fills with hordes of people expectantly waiting for the biggest extravaganza this fair has to offer, the nightly live entertainment featuring well-known performers. Such high caliber entertainment as Sha Na Na, Bill Cosby, and Peaches and Herb has graced the grandstand's stage. There is an admission charge to these concerts running anywhere from $9.00 for a track seat to $5.00 for a back seat in the grandstand. Write early in August for names of performers and concert tickets.

Directions: The fairgrounds are located at 17th and Chew Sts. in downtown Allentown. Follow Rt. 222 which becomes Hamilton Blvd. to either 17th or 18th Sts. and turn left. These streets will lead you to the fairgrounds.

Nearby Attractions: See Allentown's Historic Houses, Lehigh County Covered Bridge Tour, Lil-Le-Hi Trout Hatchery, and Dorney Park.

ALLENTOWN'S HISTORIC HOUSES
AND LIBERTY BELL SHRINE

TROUT HALL

Open Tues.–Sat. 1–4 p.m. year round. Other times by appointment. No admission fee. Gift shop. Lehigh County Historical Society, Hamilton at Fifth St., Allentown, Pa. 18101. (215) 435-1074.

The stately sandstone mansion, built in 1770 by James Allen, son of William Allen, the founder of Allentown, stands much the same as it did over 200 years ago, carefully preserved by the Lehigh County Historical Society. In the 1700's, Trout Hall served as a summer home for the Allen family. Here they could retreat from the complexity of life in Philadelphia to enjoy the rural pleasures of trout fishing (from which the house got its name) and hunting. This English-German style mansion was occupied by the descendants of the Allen family until 1848, at which time it was converted to house the Allentown Seminary later to become Muhlenberg College.

Guided tours of the house lead you through rooms decorated in styles of the past two centuries. Eighteen-foot ceilings, walnut paneling, crystal chandeliers and oriental rugs all reflect a lifestyle of relative opulence. Furnishings in the house are authentic, save for one reproduction of a gaming table. One room in the back of the house has been delegated to house museum exhibits of the Historical Society's. Here you can see a rotating collection of antiques and a display of maps of old Allentown dating back to 1842. It's fascinating to see how the city expanded over the years.

Directions: Follow Rt. 222 which becomes Hamilton Blvd. into Allentown. At Fifth St. turn right then take the next left onto Walnut. Trout Hall will appear on your right at 4th and Walnut.

THE FRANK BUCHMAN HOUSE

Open Sat. and Sun. 1–4 p.m. year round. Other times by appointment. No admission fee. Lehigh County Historical Society, Old Court House, Hamilton at Fifth, Allentown, Pa. 18101. (215) 435-1074.

It is an ordinary-looking three-story brick row house in a midtown neighborhood. Built in 1892, its architecture is typically Victorian. What is so atypical is the personality and accomplishments of the extraordinary man who inhabited it and gave it the right to be included in Allentown's historic houses. That man is Dr. Frank Buchman, the founder of the Oxford Group, later to become known as Moral Re-Armament.

A tour of the Buchman house provides a look at the life of a Christian leader who was dedicated to "rebuilding the world through rebuilding the people." The tenets of his philosophy were based on honesty, purity, unselfishness and love—tenets which he and his followers used on a personal level to affect changes on a more universal one. That their efforts were successful is attested to by the number of awards and tributes Buchman received through his life. Many of these were given in gratitude for the part he and his group played in healing the relationship between the war-torn countries after World War II. On the guided tour you will see the Sword of Surrender of the World War II Japanese land armies in China, presented to Buchman by Chinese General and former Prime Minister Ho Ying-Chin. In an upstairs bedroom is a cross made of wood taken from a four-hundred-year-old camphor tree that the Mayor of Hiroshima gave to Buchman as a symbol of the atomic blast at Hiroshima. Medals and decorations from eight foreign governments are displayed, including the French Legion of Honor. There are photograph albums filled with pictures of Buchman in numerous countries visiting with important dignitaries. The house is filled with the treasures and memorabilia of a man who was able to reach millions of people through radio, books, plays, films, and an organization that by the mid-1930's was at work in over sixty countries. Although he died in 1961, his work is still being carried on by his faithful followers.

Directions: Take Rt. 222, which becomes Hamilton Blvd., into Allentown. At 11th St. turn left. The Buchman House is located in the second block of 11th St. between Linden and Turner Sts. on the right hand side. If coming from Trout Hall, take 4th St. north to Linden. Go left on Linden to 11th St. Turn right onto 11th and the house will appear on your right.

THE LIBERTY BELL SHRINE

Open Mon.–Sat. 11–4 p.m. Closed Tuesdays Oct. 16–Apr. 15. No admission fee. Small gift shop. The Liberty Bell Shrine, Zion United Church of Christ, Hamilton Mall at Church St., Allentown, Pa. 18101. (215) 821-1151.

In the fall of 1777, George Washington and his armies were faced with a major crisis. The British were descending on Philadelphia and the Americans did not have the forces to defend it. Washington and his troops retreated to Valley Forge. Meanwhile, the citizens of Philadelphia became worried that the British, running short of ammunition, would melt down the city's church bells to make more ammunition for their muskets and cannons. The most important of these bells was the one that symbolized the American fight for independence, the Liberty Bell. The Nation's Executive Council decided that these bells must be saved and arranged for their transportation to a distant settlement 55 miles away called Northampton Town, and later Allentown.

On the night of Sept. 24, 1777, a group of young patriots secretly hauled the bells out of Philadelphia and hid them under the floor of Allentown's old Zion Reformed Church. The bells remained here until the following June, when they were returned to Philadelphia. The famous Liberty Bell had been saved from a certain melt-down.

Today a shrine marks the area where the Liberty Bell was secreted. Guides relate the story of its perilous journey and pepper their accounts with fascinating historical anecdotes. On display is an exact replica of the Liberty Bell, one of only fifty-three replicas cast to mark the U.S. Savings Bond Drive of 1950. The bell weighs 2,080 pounds. Along one wall of the shrine is a 46-foot oil painting depicting in six scenes the important events occurring in the Allentown area during the War for Independence. Also on display are flags, colonial artifacts and relics.

Directions: Come into Allentown on Rt. 222, which becomes Hamilton Blvd. The church is located between 7th and 6th Streets on Hamilton Blvd. Just before the church, turn right into the alley. There is a small parking lot in the rear of the church.

THE TROXELL-STECKEL HOUSE

Open Sat. and Sun. 1–4 p.m., June–Oct. Other times by appointment. No admission fee. Rest rooms. Lehigh County Historical Society, Hamilton at Fifth St., Allentown, Pa. 18104. (215) 435-1074.

This lovely old stone farm house with its red shutters and German medieval architecture was originally built in 1755–1756 by Peter Troxell, an immigrant of Swiss and German origins. It stands as a monument to the hard-working families who settled in the Pennsylvania wilderness in hopes of carving out a future for themselves and their descendants in the new world.

Guided tours take you inside this sturdy structure where the rooms are furnished simply in the style of the pioneer family. Rope beds, straw mattresses, chamber pots, rag rugs and hope chests grace the upstairs bedrooms while on display downstairs are implements needed to survive the wilderness life, and period furnishings. There are butter churns, handmade baskets, apple butter kettles and slipware pottery, among others. And, of course, there is the all-important family Bible with its safe located on the wall for fire protection. The house itself boasts beamed ceilings, two massive fireplaces, arched windows, timbered walls and wide-plank wooden floors. Carved into the mortar over the portal of the front door is a German saying which, translated, reads: "God protect this house and all therein and lead their souls to Heaven's chamber."

Near the house is a red barn decorated with hex signs. On display are old sleighs and buggies, covered wagons, blacksmith tools, old plows, and a variety of leatherwork, including harnesses and saddles. The stone for the barn's foundation and for the house itself was quarried from a site across the street.

Directions: The Troxell-Steckel House is located in Egypt, a few miles north of Allentown. From Rt. 22 (I-78) take the exit for MacArthur Rd. (Rt. 145) North. Go for approximately four miles to Rt. 329 (Main St. in Egypt). Turn left onto 329 and continue to Reliance St. Turn left and follow Reliance to the house, which will appear on your right.

THE GEORGE TAYLOR HOUSE

Open 1–4 p.m., Tues.–Sat., June–Sept. Other times by appointment. No admission fee. Rest rooms. Gift shop. Lehigh County Historical Society, Hamilton at 5th Sts., Allentown, Pa. 18101. (215) 435-1074.

Along the banks of the Lehigh River stands an elegant stone mansion. Its architecture reflects the influence of the Italian Villa style popular with the English country gentry during the 18th century. It was built by a man who would take a stand against the English and play a part in the fight for American independence. That man was George Taylor, one of Pennsylvania's representatives to the Second Continental Congress who signed the Declaration of Independence. That his summer mansion would eventually be listed as a National Historic Landmark is not surprising, for in addition to being his residence, it was later owned in 1790 by Colonel David Deshler, a man of great wealth who aided the Revolutionary cause with substantial loans and contributions.

The interior of the house is furnished elegantly in the manner of its original 18th century appearance. A description and date is provided for each piece of furniture. Rich paneling, pedimented door-heads, and fine wood trim reflect the refined tastes of its owners. Surrounding the house is a scenic park which features a formal walled garden and terrace with flag pole. Nearby, the combination summer kitchen and ice house (cooled by a spring located beneath the bake oven) may be visited.

Directions: This home is located in Catasauqua, a few miles north of Allentown. Take Rt. 22 (I-78) to the 4th St. Exit. Go north on 4th St. to Bridge St. Turn right (east) onto Bridge. You will cross a large bridge and then a ½ block farther a smaller one. Take the first right after the small bridge onto Lehigh St. Go south for one block and go left onto Poplar. After one block, the mansion will appear on your left, between Front and Poplar Streets.

Nearby Attractions: Since these historical houses are open primarily in the afternoon, you may want to fit in another type of tour in the morning. See: Covered Bridge Tours-Lehigh County, Trexler-Lehigh Game Preserve, Lil-Le-Hi Trout Hatchery, Dorney Park, Leather Corner Post Hotel, and Haines Mill.

BETHLEHEM, PENNSYLVANIA: WALKING TOUR, MORAVIAN MUSEUM, GOUNDIE HOUSE, ANNIE S. KEMERER MUSEUM, EIGHTEENTH CENTURY INDUSTRIAL AREA AND BETHLEHEM: THE CHRISTMAS CITY

––––––

Bethlehem Area Chamber of Commerce Visitor's Bureau, 11 West Market St., Bethlehem, Pa. 18018—for festival times and dates.

To those unfamiliar with Bethlehem, the city's name evokes two somewhat conflicting pictures. On one hand is the religious connotation of the name as the birthplace of Christ; on the other, the materialistic image of a thriving industrial community headed by Bethlehem Steel. In fact, this unusual city combines both the spiritual and materialistic aspects of life to the benefit of all. This is due in large part to its essentially Moravian background.

The Moravians came to the Bethlehem area during the 18th century. They brought with them a rich spiritual, cultural, and industrial heritage which they put to good use in the New World. According to a carefully-drawn plan based on European church-centered towns, they first built strong Germanic structures out of stone and wood to serve as communal dormitories and group centers for their church members.

In the five-story medieval log building known as the Gemein House they worked at their crafts and developed a thriving center of commerce. When all were housed, they constructed a Tannery down the hill by the creek as the starting point of their soon-to-be-expanded industry.

Through all their endeavors, the Moravians worked as a religious community that stressed the absolute authority of the Bible, a disciplined Christian life, and a simplicity of worship. However, this did not preclude them from indulging in worthwhile business enterprises, for the Moravians accepted business as a legitimate way of participating in life. In 1845, they gave up both their mandate to govern Bethlehem and their claim to exclusive control of the land around it to make way for industrial interests to set up their factories on the south side of town. Although the Moravians tended to live and work in their already-established northern section of town, they regarded the southern half as an industrialized colony and source of wealth.

Today the rich culture that these people brought to the area and the industries they fostered still flourish. They are widely known for their exquisite needlework and crafts, excellent educational institutions, superior musical abilities, and strong sense of religious and historical identity. Their heritage has been preserved through historical museums; annual festivals such as Historic Bethlehem Folk Festival (June), The Bach Festival (May), A Day In Historic Bethlehem (Oct.), Christmas celebrations and the Shad Fest (May); and an ongoing sense of religious community.

WALKING TOUR OF HISTORIC BETHLEHEM

Maps available at Bethlehem Area Chamber of Commerce Visitor's Bureau, 11 West Market St., Bethlehem, Pa. 18018. (215) 868-1513 or 867-3788. Markers posted at all significant points. Guided tours available through the Central Moravian Church by appointment only, Weekdays 10–4. Fees: Adults, $2.00; children, 50¢. Moravian Tours c/o Central Moravian Church Office, Bethlehem, Pa. 18018. (215) 866-5661 or 867-0173.

To take a walking tour of historic Bethlehem is like taking a walk back in time to the late 1700's when Moravian missionaries settled here and built a planned community that emphasized the subordination of personal wants and needs to the overall good of the community. Large stone buildings with sloping roofs and two stories of dormers still line Church St. as they did back then. Used two hundred years ago as communal dormitories for church members, they now serve as schools and apartment houses and serve a vital function in the Moravian Church life. The unique log building known as the Gemein House (see write-up) that served as a communal center still stands intact as well as the tannery and spring house down the hill in the ''Industrial Area'' (see write-up).

As you leisurely stroll for an hour or more down the scenic streets and through flower-lined courtyards you'll visit 26 sites, most of them constructed by Moravians over 230 years ago. Along Market Street is the peaceful old God's Acre, a small cemetery in which the graves of the town's founders rest alongside those of Indians and Blacks from the West Indies. It is rumored that Cooper's "Last of the Mohicans," known as Chingachgook is buried here. Down New Street and located near the cemetery is the interesting Annie S. Kemerer Museum (see write-up) which is housed in a gracious old Bethlehem Townhouse. You'll also see the 1746 Bell House, which served as the first permanent residence for married couples; the 1768 Widow's House; the 1748 Brethren's House; the Central Church; and the 1801 Schnitz House where dried apples were prepared. During festival days, the old Apothecary Museum which features medicinal tools from the past, is open. All stops are described by placards. Whether you decide to take this walk with a tour guide or by yourself, you'll come away with a greater understanding of, and appreciation for, the part the Moravians played in our nation's history.

Directions: The Vistior's Center (from which maps may be obtained) is located at 11 West Market Street. From Rt. 22, take the Bethlehem Exit 378 South. From 378, take Center City Exit 3. At the first stop sign, turn right onto East Union Blvd. At the next stop sign, turn right onto West Union Blvd. At the second light, turn right onto N. New St. Go for about four blocks, then turn right onto Market St. The Visitor's Center will be on your left.

Nearby Attractions: See Lost River Caverns.

THE GEMEIN HOUSE—MORAVIAN MUSEUM

Open Tues.–Sat., 1–4 p.m. Closed during January. Fees: Adults, $1.00; students, 50¢. The Moravian Museum, 66 W. Church St., Bethlehem, Pa. 18018. (215) 867-0173.

This amazing five-story medieval log house is the second structure to be built by Moravians in Bethlehem, and is considered to be the largest log dwelling still in existence in the United States. It needed to be large, for the top floors were used as dormitories housing up to fifty people at one time; its second floor contained a chapel which was the earliest place of Moravian worship in America; and the bottom floors were used as workshops for various crafts people. The Gemein Haus was the focal point for the Moravian community for many years, and it is only recently that it was converted into a museum housing early Moravian religious and secular artifacts.

Volunteer guides from the Moravian Church lead tours through several floors of this fascinating building. The structure has changed little over the past 200 years. It was built entirely without nails using wood from the nearby forests and mud plaster. The whitewashed walls, plain wood floors, and rough-hewn doors with hand-wrought ironware form the perfect backdrop for the museum exhibits.

Many aspects of early Moravian life will be revealed as you take your tour of the museum. You'll see a typical kitchen with a ten-plate cast-iron stove, handmade tinware and pottery, copper kettles and an assortment of kitchen utensils. Throughout the rooms are samples of fine Moravian sewing including three-dimensional pictures and intricate needlework. Their emphasis on education is revealed through a replica of a classroom complete with authentic schoolmaster's desk, a long working table with slate tablets and wood benches, and a blackboard. Upstairs is the original chapel where the early Moravians worshipped. It is still in use for wedding ceremonies. In an adjacent room are religious articles that play a part in their ceremonies. You'll learn of their beliefs and much talked about "Love Feast," a spiritual song fest where buns and coffee are served. Another room is furnished as it might have been when Count Zinzandorf, patron of the Moravians who was instrumental in bringing them to the New World, stayed here. Many of his belongings are displayed, including a walking stick and watch fob. Other rooms house musical instruments, old tools, a collection of dolls, and samples of Moravian furniture. Throughout the tour, your guide will explain what you are seeing and how it fit in with the early settlement in Pennsylvania.

Directions: The Gemein Haus is on Church Street, which runs perpendicular to New and Main Streets and parallel to Market St. It is next door to the Central Moravian Church, which is on the corner of Church and Main Streets.

THE JOHN SEBASTIAN GOUNDIE HOUSE

Open Mon.–Sat. 10–4. Extended hours during Christmas Season. Gift shop. John Sebastian Goundie House, 501 Main St., Bethlehem, Pa. 18018. (215) 691-5300.

The Federal style 1810 Goundie House is considered to be the first townhouse in Bethlehem to be built entirely of brick. It was constructed for Mr. Goundie, a well-known businessman and leader in the Moravian Community. At one time, he was in charge of the Single Brethren's Brewery, and in 1810 opened his own down the hill from his house.

The inside of the Goundie home is composed of two parlors on the south side, and a kitchen and dining room on the north. The upstairs area is believed to have contained four bedrooms. Historic Bethlehem Inc. has been involved in restoring this lovely old dwelling, and presently the northern rooms have been completed and are open to the public. The dining room exemplifies the Federal style of architecture and features fine furniture of mahogany and cherry (dating from the late Federal–early Empire periods). The kitchen reflects a simple German style with a beehive bake oven (still to be restored). In one parlor is housed the Historic Bethlehem Inc.'s Gift Shop which features a wide selection of handicrafts. Future restoration plans include adding gardens and porch in the rear area of the house and restoring the parlors and upstairs bedrooms.

Directions: The Goundie House is located on Main St. near the Hotel Bethlehem. From the Visitor's Center on Market Street, turn left and follow Market until it intersects with Main. Turn right onto Main and the house will be a few doors up on the opposite side of the street.

THE ANNIE S. KEMERER MUSEUM

Open Mon.–Fri. 1–4 p.m. and second and fourth Sundays, 2–4 p.m. Closed holidays and during January. Fees: Donations accepted. Gift shop. Annie S. Kemerer Museum, 427 North New St., Bethlehem, Pa. 18018. (215) 868-6868.

Dark, plump and pretty is how Annie S. Kemerer is described: a retiring woman with an insatiable love for antiques and the wherewithall to purchase them. When she died in 1951 at the age of 85, she bequeathed her large antique collection to Bethlehem and the Lehigh Valley as the nucleus of a museum collection with the "hope that this generation and the generations of the future will find the contents of the museum interesting and instructive and thereby be encouraged to emulate the fine qualities of their ancestors."

Miss Kemerer's hope has not been in vain, for her fine collection, now housed in a lovely old Bethlehem townhouse, presents an instructive look at the elegance of the past two centuries. Well-versed guides lead you through the various rooms, all decorated primarily with Miss Kemerer's belongings. Philadelphia Chippendale, Hepplewhite, Sheridan, these are only a few of the names mentioned as you walk through the elegantly-furnished rooms. Exquisite oriental rugs decorate the wood floors, and the windows are modeled after Monticello, with tie-back curtains and cornices. Locally-made Grandfather Clocks and Moravian hand-embroidered pictures reflect Bethlehem's past, while china from the world over, boasting such names as Dresden, Limoges and Wedgewood, is tastefully displayed in glassed-in cabinets.

While the downstairs rooms are decorated much as a home would be, the upstairs features a number of interesting galleries. Two rooms are furnished as Victorian parlors with ornate carpets and rich red and gold wallpaper. Intricate needlework done by Miss Kemerer is evident in the numerous pillows and pictures. Opposite the Victorian rooms are two others. One of these is dedicated to Bethlehem's German and Moravian past and features some early Pennsylvania Dutch Fraktur work, woven coverlets from the 1800's, a well preserved dower chest and other items of local interest. The second room, used as a modern art gallery, displays changing collections of local, national, and international artists. A hallway connecting the rooms is entirely devoted to Miss Kemerer's impressive collection of Bohemian glass. The collection is considered to be one of the finest in the country, and consists of both American and Venetian art glass.

Directions: The museum is located on N. New St. just beyond the Moravian Cemetery called God's Acre, and around the corner from the Visitor's Center.

THE EIGHTEENTH CENTURY INDUSTRIAL AREA

Buildings open Sat. 10–4 p.m., other times by appointment. Closed January. Fees: Adults, $1.25; children, 75¢. Rest rooms in spring house. Gift Counter. Historic Bethlehem, Inc., 516 Main St., Bethlehem, Pa. 18018. (215) 868-6311.

Down the hill from the elegant Hotel Bethlehem on Main Street is a green park dominated by a large limestone building and several smaller ones. The area is divided by a stream which provided the fresh water needed to enable these buildings to play an integral part in the early industry of the Moravians. To the right of the path coming down the hill from the hotel is the Luchenbach Flour Mill. Built in 1869 on the foundations of Bethlehem's second grist mill, which burned down in that same year, the mill was in continuous operation until 1952. It was here that local farmers would have their important grain crops ground into fine flour and meal. The entire building is to be restored by Historic Bethlehem, Inc., and presently its outer walls stand as a reminder of the important milling process that once occurred here.

Across the path from the mill stands the massive building known as The Tannery which was constructed in 1761 by the early Moravians. The building housed a thriving tanning industry that annually processed over 3,000 animal hides, turning them into leather for use in clothes, shoes, harnesses, and machine parts. Today the Tannery has been restored and the entire process is explained from the soaking of hides in a solution of lime and water to the final preparation of the leather. On the ground floor of the building, a large room holds the vats in which these hides were soaked. From wooden walkways you can see these huge receptacles that held the skins for up to six months at a time. Other rooms contain equipment used in the process as well as explanatory notes.

Historic Bethlehem Inc. has used the Tannery Building to both interpret the art of leather making to the public and to house a museum displaying early Moravian crafts, trades and industries. The museum presents its subject in an interesting manner. Besides the traditional displays of early artifacts, there are actual working models of two of the earlier industries on the third floor. With a flick of the finger you'll see a miniature of the 1765 Old Mill come to life. Lights come on, a water wheel turns, and the pistons go up and down starting the milling operation. At one time, linseed oil milling was one of the most profitable of businesses. The other model is of the 1762 Waterworks which still exists in the Industrial Area and has been fully restored to working order. You'll see water turning the wheel that pumped water to the dwellings up the hill—starting the first municipal waterworks to be established in the Colonies. After you see this miniature in operation, you'll want to visit its actual counterpart only a short walk away.

A new addition to the Tannery is the Discovery Room which is housed on the second floor. The joint venture of Historic Bethlehem and The Junior League of the Lehigh Valley, the Discovery Room provides children with a "hands on" approach to history. Here they can touch and explore items relating to the museum's collection. There are old clothes to try on, discovery boxes filled with objects to be guessed at, Indian sign language to learn, artifacts to be felt and experiences to be shared. It is requested that only a few children come at one time and these be accompanied by a chaperone.

An enjoyable time to visit the Industrial Area is during June when the Historic Bethlehem Folk Festival is held here. The event interprets early Moravian craft and culture through a panoply of craft demonstrations, concerts, lectures and scrumptious food and beverages.

Directions: The area is located on the right side of Main St. if coming from the Hotel Bethlehem, and is to the immediate right of the entrance to the Hill to Hill Bridge. If coming from the Visitor's Center, turn left onto Market and proceed to Main and turn left again. See "Bethlehem, Pa." for full directions to the city.

BETHLEHEM, THE CHRISTMAS CITY NIGHTLIGHT TOUR AND CHRISTMAS PUTZ

Bus tours available Dec. 1–Dec. 31st at 5, 6 and 7 p.m. Fees: Adults, $3.00; children, $1.50. Reservations recommended. Bethlehem Of Pennsylvania Visitor's Bureau, 11 West Market St., Bethlehem, Pa. 18018. (215) 868-1513 or 867-3788.

On December 24, 1741, a small group of Moravians who had recently settled in eastern Pennsylvania were seated together in a cabin singing Christmas hymns. As they were singing a favorite one "Not Jerusalem, But Bethlehem," their acknowledged leader, Count Zinzandorf, suggested that this hymn seemed to be directed to them in particular. The group agreed and decided to name their settlement Bethlehem after the song that had spoken so clearly to them.

Many years have passed since then, and the settlement has grown into a large city. However, Bethlehem has never forgotten its Moravian heritage, its Biblical name, and the multiple significance of the Christmas season. The month of December is one filled with songfests, Christmas plays, candlelight receptions, Lanternlight Walking

Tours, Christmas Pageants and other festive activities. Two of the most popular are the Christmas Night Light Tours and the Moravian Community Putz.

All over the city, from the centuries old buildings in the historic area, to the downtown stores, to the top of South Mountain, the trees, windows, doorways and bridges are aglow with shining white lights during the holiday season. The traditional Moravian Star hangs in doorways, and white candles light up windows. A mountaintop star, 91 feet high and 26 feet in diameter, glimmers in the distance.

So that visitors can see the Christmas display in its entirety, one-hour Night Light Bus Tours are available. Each tour is accompanied by a guide dressed in authentic Moravian attire who provides a running commentary on the history of the town and the sights of the city. The tour will take you from the Visitor's Center to City Center Plaza with its large Nativity Scene and four Advent candles, through the historic area of town, and to the top of South Mountain. Here you enter Bethlehem Steel's Homer Research Laboratory complex for a panoramic view of the Lehigh Valley aglow with the Christmas lights. Afterwards, you descend the mountain, cross the Lehigh River, and end your tour at Bethlehem's Plaza Mall.

Directions: Bus tours commence at the Visitor's Center, 11 West Market St. (see Bethlehem main entry for full directions).

THE MORAVIAN COMMUNITY PUTZ

Putz open for viewing 4–8:30 p.m. Dec. 6–31st. Closed Dec. 24 & 25. No fees, but donations accepted. Christian Education Building of the Central Moravian Church. (215) 866-5661 or 867-0173.

Housed in a small auditorium of the Central Moravian Church is a charming Moravian Putz. Both the story of the Nativity and founding of Bethlehem are told through the use of narration and the intricately carved wooden figures and scenery of which the Putz is composed. It is a larger version of the many hand-carved Nativity scenes the Moravians are fond of having in their own homes, and is yearly constructed by whole families participating. Many of the wooden figures came originally from Germany, while other decorations, such as the moss for the landscape, are gathered yearly.

Directions: The auditorium of the Central Moravian Church is located on the other side of God's Little Acre (the Moravian Cemetery) from the Visitor's Bureau (see Bethlehem entry for directions to Visitor's Center).

BUSHKILL FALLS, THE NIAGARA OF PENNSYLVANIA

Open April 1–Nov., 8 a.m. to dusk. Fees: Adults, $2.50; children, 75¢. Rest rooms. Snacks. Gift shop. Bushkill Falls, Harry M. Stevens, Inc., Rt. 209, Bushkill, Pa. 18324. (717) 588-6682.

An early chronicler once wrote that Bushkill Falls was regarded as the "extreme limit of civilization in this direction, all beyond being a howling wilderness . . ." This aura of the wild and untamed is still felt, although now there are wooden walkways and bridges crossing the steep and magnificent waterfalls. The dusky forest surrounds the paths, and often the only sounds are those of rushing water and leaves rustling in the wind. Dark moss-covered boulders line the stream's bed, accenting the white water cascading past.

Bushkill Falls is a lovely natural haven, made accessible to the public by the Peters family who first opened the falls in 1904. Starting with a single path and a swinging bridge over the head of the main falls, the Peters have now constructed a network of overlooks and hiking trails that will appeal to even the most avid of hikers. There is the Bridal Veil Falls Trail, an exhilarating one-mile hike (lasting one to one-and-a-half hours) that leads you around the main, lower gorge and Bridal Veil waterfalls. The scenery is breathtaking and well worth the walk. A more popular route that the average walker might enjoy takes about 45 minutes, involves some climbing, and leads you along both sides of the main falls. The short hike which does not involve any uphill climbing takes 15 minutes and leads to an overlook of the main falls.

In addition to the falls, there are other things to see and do at Bushkill. At the entrance to the nature path there is an excellent wildlife exhibit featuring wild animals that are native to the Pocono Mountains. Created by noted taxidermist Parker Riday, the exhibit portrays each animal in a startlingly lifelike setting. If you like to fish, try your hand at the Twin Lakes (at the entrance to the Park). No fishing license is required, and the lakes are stocked with bass, pickerel and bluegills. Paddleboats and rowboats may be rented for a leisurely paddle about these scenic ponds. Picnic grounds are available as well as an ice cream parlor, fudge kitchen, snack bar, and cookie stand. There is a woodcraft shop and art gallery through which you may browse while your children happily play on the swings and slide conveniently located nearby, and a miniature golf course for family enjoyment.

Directions: From Interstate 78, take Route 33 North. Continue on Rt. 33 until Exit 52, Route 209 North. Turn at the blinker light off Rt. 209 in Bushkill (this is well marked) onto Bushkill Falls Road.

Nearby Attractions: See Magic Valley & Winona Five Falls, and Delaware Water Gap.

THE C.F. MARTIN GUITAR COMPANY

Tours conducted daily Mon.–Fri. at 10:30 am. and 1:15 p.m. Closed weekends and holidays. Tours not appropriate for small children. Reservations not necessary except for large groups. No admission fees. Rest rooms. Shop. The C.F. Martin Guitar Company, 510 Sycamore St., Nazareth, Pa. 18064. (215) 759-2837.

For almost 140 years the Martin Guitar Company has been manufacturing quality guitars, ukulele's and mandolins. Today it is the only guitar company in the world where skilled craftsmen continue to build these instruments primarily by hand, which accounts in part for the company's outstanding reputation. From the initial cutting of the wood to the moment when a guitar is vacuum packed in a protective package takes upwards of three-and-a-half months. There are many steps in its journey to completion, and if the guitar is found to be the least bit flawed at the final inspection station, it is sawed in two. Imperfection is not tolerated.

Guided tours lasting about an hour cover all phases of guitar manufacturing. You see the craftsmen with their drawing knives carving the neck of the guitar. Others work the hydraulic presses which put the flowing curves into the sides of the instrument. In the inlay section, bits of abalone are painstakingly inlaid, a process involving up to three-and-a-half days of concentrated work. When a guitar reaches the Lacquer Department, six individual coats are carefully applied to each instrument with sanding being done between every two coats. Once it is lacquered and strung, it is ready to be vacuum packed and shipped to waiting customers and stores. An interesting highlight at

the tour's completion is a glimpse at the Repair Department. The guitars belonging to well-loved celebrities are often sent here for repairs.
Many of them are quite elaborately decorated with bits of abalone,
silver and pearl. When your tour is over, you are free to browse in the
adjacent small museum which houses a collection of Martin instruments constructed throughout the last century and a half, and visit the
gift shop.

Directions: The factory is located in the town of Nazareth. Take Rt. 22 (I-78)
to Rt. 191 North (the last Bethlehem exit). At the main stop light in Nazareth
(two gas stations and two diners will be on the corners) turn right onto Easton
Road. At the second light, turn left onto Broad Street. Stay on Broad for about
a mile and you will see a park on your left. Shortly after this you will take a
right turn at Sisco's Diner onto Sycamore Street. Go one block and the factory
will be on your right.

Nearby Attractions: See Hugh Moore Park and Crayola Factory Tours.

CAMELBACK'S ALPINE AND WATER SLIDES

Alpine Slide open May 17–June 15; Weekends and Memorial Day 10–5:30 p.m.,
June 21–Sept. 1: Daily 10–5:30 with night sliding available June 27–Aug.
30, Fri. and Sat. to 10 p.m. Fall: Weekends and holidays only, 10–5:30. Fees:
Adult single ride tickets, $3.00; junior (7–12) single ride tickets, $2.50. 6 and
under must be accompanied by adult and pay full junior fare. Water slide open
daily June 21–Sept. 1 and weekends May 17 on, weather permitting. Fees:
75¢ per ride. Cafeteria. Bar. Picnics. Rest rooms. Gift shop. Small playground. Hiking trails. Outdoor flea market. Camelback Ski Area, Tannersville, Pa. 18372. (717) 629-1661.

The chair lift slowly takes you 3,265 feet up to the top of Camelback Mountain—all 3,265 feet of which you will have to come back
down, sooner or later. From your scenic vantage point, you can see
tiny toboggans catapulting down asbestos and concrete chutes. Screams
of fear and delight can be heard as the sleds careen around steep curves
and shoot down the sharp inclines. Tension builds as you leave the
chairlift, grab your six-year-old and fiberglass sled and walk to the
Starting Point. Your heart beats faster, blood fills your head, as you
read the sign saying there's a 632-foot vertical drop to the slope, to
go slowly around the curves, and to beware of the 10-foot jump half-
way down the slope. At this point, you're ready to quit, call it a day,
swallow your pride and walk down the mountain, but your six-year-
old won't let you. The track attendant says, "Take the track on your
right, it's slower, for beginners. No need to worry, pull back on the

stick to go slower, push forward to speed up." "Okay," you say and prepare to meet your maker. With six year old between your legs and stick pulled back as far as it will go, you inch your sled around the first perilous curve. It isn't so bad. The six-year-old says to go faster. You ease up a bit and take the second curve at the speed of a fast walk. It's all downhill from here, and with the fanatic glee of a Mario Andretti you bravely push the stick to a neutral position to negotiate the 10-foot jump that ends up feeling like a "Thank you Ma'am" in the road. From here on out the slope isn't quite so steep and you finish triumphantly, stick pushed forward to full throttle and spirits heightened by your exhilarating ride down Camelback Mountain.

On a hot summer day you can also enjoy another wetter but equally thrilling ride. The 300-foot-long water slide that dips and curves down a hill to a small swimming pool offers fun and splashes for all ages. People come shooting down the slippery fiberglass in all positions—on their bellies, backs, forwards and backwards. Their downward speed is accelerated by a steady stream of 80-degree water. Unlike the Alpine Slide, however, you use your own legs to get to the top of this one.

Once you tire of all the sliding, you may relax and sun bathe on the sundeck, go for a relaxing hike, or have a picnic on the grounds. The resort has facilities for all ages, and even grandparents will enjoy the slides and scenery.

Directions: Take Rt. 22 (I-78) to Rt. 33 North (near Easton). Follow Rt. 33 to Rt. 80 West. Follow Rt. 80 to Tannersville Exit (45) Pa. Rt. 715 north towards Tannersville. After a few miles, turn left at the directional sign to the slide (a church and cemetery will be at this juncture). Follow the brown directional signs to Camelback. One word of caution, once you turn left at the church, bear left and follow the smaller road, don't get back on Rt. 80 which bears off to the right.

Nearby Attractions: See Quiet Valley Living Historical Farm. Two miles from Camelback is Big Pocono State Park. The mountaintop park provides scenic views of the ski slope and valley below. For winter activities, see Skiing In The Poconos.

COVERED BRIDGE TOURS—LEHIGH COUNTY

A sure sign that you're traveling through the Pennsylvania Dutch country is the sight of a covered bridge. These structures abound throughout Southeastern and Mideastern sections of Pennsylvania, which explains why the state is known as the "Covered Bridge Capital of the World." Many of the wooden bridges were built by local people much in the way of a Barn Raising, where all joined together to get the structure finished; others were built by mill owners to provide easy access to customers living across the stream. Whatever the method, the bridges became an integral part of everyday life. They provided shelter for travelers during a rain storm or during the heat of a summer's day. Sweethearts, looking for secluded places to kiss, would often court in the hidden areas of the bridges, hence the name "the kissing bridges." The structures also served as a type of billboard upon which local merchants would advertise their wares. Most importantly, they provided a means to cross a river. That their life expectancy is a long one is not surprising, for the reason they were covered was to protect the floors and underpinnings from the ravages of inclement weather.

One of the best ways to see the scenic back roads of the countryside is to take a Covered Bridge Tour. The tours included here (see also Bucks County Covered Bridge Tour) were mapped out by the respective tourist bureaus and lead you up hill and down, along tree–lined streams, through covered bridges, down country lanes surrounded by verdant farmland, and into some of the most beautiful scenery you are likely to see anywhere.

Although only Lehigh and Bucks County covered bridges are included in this book, Lancaster County has its own share of them. These are scattered throughout the area and no cohesive tour of them has been established. If you are interested in seeing some of them, a book entitled *Seeing Lancaster County's Covered Bridges* by Gipe Caruthers (© 1974) is available at area book stores.

THE LEHIGH COUNTY COVERED BRIDGE TOUR

For detailed map and brochure, write Allentown-Lehigh County Tourist and Convention Bureau, 462 Walnut Street, Box 665, Allentown, Pa. 18105. (215) 821-1151. Alternate bus route available, as bridges not built to accommodate them. Call (215) 437-9661.

Of the two tours listed, this is by far the best-marked and the most compact. Discreet directional signs are posted at every turn so there is little likelihood of getting lost. The tour includes six covered bridges and passes by many points of interest in and around Allentown. Each year on Memorial Day weekend a Covered Bridge Festival featuring arts, crafts, good food and entertainment is held at selected bridge sites.

The best place to commence your tour is at Center Square at 7th and Hamilton Blvd. in Allentown (if you come into Allentown on Rt. 222, this becomes Hamilton Blvd.). Turn right (south) onto 7th Street and go two blocks to Union, turn left for half a block, then turn right onto Lehigh Street. Proceed on Lehigh Street to the traffic light, then bear right. Continue on Lehigh past traffic lights at 8th and 10th, then just past a softball field (Bicentennial Park), turn right onto Lehigh Pkwy. South. Cross S. Jefferson Street at stop sign and enter Little Lehigh Pkwy. Bogert's Bridge is on your left at a stop sign at the end of the park.

1. Bogert's Bridge was built in 1841 and spans the Little Lehigh River. It is a 145-foot-long structure which features the Burr truss. There is parking available next to the bridge if you wish to walk across it and meander along the banks of the river. This is a part of the Allentown Park System.

    Upon leaving Bogert's Bridge, turn left at the stop sign and then take the first right onto Hatchery Road. This passes by the Lil-Le-Hi Trout Hatchery (see write-up) and continues to Rt. 29 (Cedar Crest Blvd.) at the top of the hill. Turn right and follow Cedar Crest past Rt. 309, Rt. 222 and Rt. 22 Interchanges. Cross Walbert Ave. then Main Blvd. (at the top of a steep hill). Take the next left onto Iron Bridge Road, which is before the concrete bridge at the bottom of the hill. Proceed to Guth's Bridge and turn right through the bridge.

2. Guth's Bridge is a single-span bridge of 140 feet which crosses the Jordan Creek. It was built in 1858 and boasts a double wood floor and stone abutments.

    After crossing this bridge, take an immediate left onto River Road. This will lead you to Wehr's Bridge which will be on your left. You may either turn right at the bridge, then left onto Parkland Terrace Road and continue on your tour, or, turn left, cross the bridge, and park on the right in the designated area.

3. Wehr's Bridge was built in the same year as Bogert's Bridge, which makes these two the oldest in the county. It spans the Jordan Creek, is 120 feet long, and features a double wooden floor and stone abutments. The area around the bridge is quite scenic with a small dam with waterfalls, and has been turned into a local

park. There is playground equipment as well as picnic areas. Locals may often be seen fishing here.

From Parkland Terrace Road continue to Rt. 309 and turn right. At the blinking light in Orefield, turn left onto Kernsville Road and proceed for one mile to Jordan Rd. (the first road on the right beyond the iron bridge) and turn right. Follow Jordan Rd. to Rex's Bridge and drive through it.

4. Rex's Bridge is the longest covered bridge in Lehigh County, measuring 150 feet. The bridge was built in 1858, features stone abutments and a double wood floor, and crosses the Jordan Creek.

Continue on Jordan Road for one mile to a 'Y' in the road. Instead of bearing left on Jordan, you may travel straight on the gravel road to Geiger's Bridge.

5. Geiger's Bridge was also built in 1858 and is one of the five that span the Jordan Creek. It is a one-span bridge, 120 feet long, that has the double wood floor and stone abutments.

Return to Jordan Rd. by taking a hard right onto it. Proceed up the hill for 0.2 mile to where the tour continues on a dirt road, then downhill and onto a macadam road where the tour bears right. Continue past the entrance to the Trexler-Lehigh Game Preserve (see write-up) and through Schlicher's Bridge.

6. Schlicher's Bridge is the shortest bridge on the tour, measuring only 108 feet in length. It was built in 1882 and is a one-span structure constructed with the Burr truss.

After crossing this bridge, continue to Rt. 309 and turn right. This is a major route with exits for Rt. 22, Rt. 222 (Hamilton Blvd. to the east, towards Reading to the west) and Rt. 29 (Cedar Crest Blvd.).

Nearby Attractions: See Dorney Park, Haines Mill, Lil-Le-Hi Trout Hatchery, Trexler-Lehigh Game Preserve, Allentown's Historic Houses, and Leather Corner Post Hotel.

CRAYOLA FACTORY TOURS

Advance reservations required for free factory tour offered 3–4 times weekly, usually on weekday mornings. Groups welcome. Each tour limited to 30 people. Children under 6 not admitted. Waiting list is usually shortest in the summer. Binney and Smith, Church Road, Easton, Pa. 18042. (215) 253-6271.

The most colorful plant visit in the Pennsylvania Dutch region is the 40-minute tour through the Crayola Factory in Easton, Pa. The

Lehigh Valley plant is one of several operated throughout the world by Binney & Smith, Inc. which not only produces 95% of the world's crayons, but also makes magic markers, pencils, chalk, paint brushes, card games, and a variety of other school and art supplies. Since many of the guides are retired workers from the factory, you'll get a chance to see the production process up close and talk to the workers at each station. Children especially will enjoy the visit and are given a complimentary box of crayons at the end.

The tour begins in the receiving department where stacks of raw materials such as the pigments produced from dyes at a separate plant in downtown Easton stand alongside various types of end products produced at the plant. The next stop is the hot wax rolling machines where richly colored vats of hot wax are heated to 250 degrees Fahrenheit. As the workers pull tray after tray from the machines, the crayons appear as if by magic. These are then dumped in a kaleidoscope of colors onto a moving conveyor belt which takes them to the automatic labeler. Here they are labeled at the astounding rate of 80,000 crayons per day. Every conceivable size and shape of crayons are automatically packed into boxes of 8, 16, or 64 units which are in turn loaded in groups of 24 boxes into cartons by the bundling machine. Now they are ready for delivery to schools and stores throughout the world. The tour also shows how Crayola magic markers are made from felt containing water soluble ink being pressed into plastic casings.

Directions: Take I-78 to Exit 33 North near Easton. Follow 33 north about five miles to the Stockertown Exit which becomes Rt. 191 North. Follow Rt. 191 a short distance and make a right onto Sullivan Trail. Go 1 mile on Sullivan Trail and make a left onto Church Road. The Crayola Factory is about ⅓ mile down Church Road on the left-hand side.

Nearby Attractions: See Hugh Moore Park and C.F. Martin Guitar Company.

DAS AWKSCHT FESCHT

Held the first weekend in August, Sat. 8 a.m.–10 p.m. (approx.), Sun. 9–4 p.m. Fees: Adults, $2.00; children 12 and under, $1.00; parking, $1.00. Rest rooms. Food. Flea market. Picnics. Macungie Memorial Park, Macungie, Pa. 18062. (215) 437-5534.

Flashy Duesenbergs straight out of the Jazz Age; beautifully restored Model T Fords; the stylish Pierce Arrows, a movie star's delight; and a host of other cars dating from 1901 to 1959 make their way slowly down the streets of Macungie, Pennsylvania to the Memorial Park where over a thousand of them will be judged over a two-day period. The antique classic cars will be pampered, polished and put on display for the countless visitors who annually come to this car show which is considered to be one of the biggest and the best in the country. One day of the festival is set aside for individual antique and classic car shows while the second day is devoted to special car club and sports car shows. Saturday afternoon is an ideal time to come, for then the finest of the old-time cars, the award winners, will parade around the park demonstrating their virtuosity.

Car buffs will be in heaven during this festival. Not only will they see the beautifully restored cars, they can browse the large antique car flea market and find any of those car parts they might need to complete their own restorations. In addition to the parts, they can also find owner's manuals for a variety of cars on sale. There are all kinds of automobile memorabilia on display, and adults as well as children will be tempted to buy the model cars and trucks.

For the less enthusiastic, there is plenty to do aside from looking at cars. There are at least two large tents filled with working artists and craftspersons. Here you can find exquisitely painted hex signs and milk cans, quilts, metalcraft, ceramics, jewelry, and a host of different objects. In the Memorial Hall and Park Pavilion are antique shows and sales. For the children, there is a mini-circus with clowns, magic acts and petting zoo; a playground; and the Macungie Swimming Pool which is located in the center of the festival ground. Entertainment is available throughout the day at the bandshell, which features such groups as the Macungie Band, country and western singers and barbershop quartets. The foods available at this festival are almost as popular as the cars. At the cafeteria, such Pennsylvania Dutch delectables as chicken pot pie, potato filling, chicken corn soup, and beet eggs may be purchased. These are all prepared from scratch by the local people and follow age-old recipes. The ever popular funnel cake, and ice cream and waffles are available at the food concessions.

Directions: Macungie Memorial Park is located off Rt. 100, about 5 miles south of the intersection of Rt. 222 and Rt. 100, and 12 miles southeast of Allentown.

Nearby Attractions: See Lehigh County Velodrome, Dorney Park, Haines Mill, and Industrial Museums of the Lehigh Valley-Lockridge Furnace.

THE DELAWARE WATER GAP
NATIONAL RECREATION AREA

Kittatinny Point Information Center (in New Jersey) open daily 9–5 p.m. On weekends and in July and August hours are extended from 8 a.m. to 7 p.m. Trail guides, maps and information on entire park. Picnics. Rest rooms. A-V Program. (201) 496-4458. For general maps and brochures write Delaware Water Gap National Recreation Area, Bushkill, Pa. 18324.

Consisting of 70,000 acres along both the Pennsylvania and New Jersey sides of the Delaware River, the Delaware Water Gap National Recreation Area offers a multitude of recreational opportunities and special attractions. Foremost among these is the Gap itself, a distinct notch, more than a mile wide, cut through the Kittatinny Ridge by the Delaware River. It is believed that the river was here before the mountains, and as they were formed by underground pressure slowly folding the earth's crust, the river was able to cut through the rock layers faster than the folds being created across its path. There are three overlooks at which the gap may be observed. These are located on the Pennsylvania side of the river south of Stroudsburg on Route 611 (there are parking areas practically on the river's bank). At Overlook No. 2 (the second one you will see coming south on Rt. 611) a park ranger is on duty daily from 9–5 during July and August to explain the geology of the area.

Getting to know the park, which extends into both Pennsylvania and New Jersey, takes more than just a few visits as there are a variety of activities to enjoy with the hues of the different seasons lending their accents. To gain a greater understanding of what the area has to offer, it is suggested that you first visit the Kittatinny Point Information Center. Park rangers are on duty here to answer your questions and a slide show is presented on the area.

For the outdoor enthusiast, there is much to be enjoyed within the park's boundaries. Canoeing on the Delaware River is quite popular. From July 1st through Labor Day daily canoe trips led by park naturalists may be taken. For those of you who don't own your own canoe, they may be rented from area suppliers (who also provide for the launching and pickup). Information on these is available at the Kittatinny Point Information Station. Hiking trails to suit all levels of walkers are available from short 15-minute walks to a twenty-mile stretch of the Appalachian Trail. Each weekend in July and August, naturalists lead walks to some of the most scenic areas of the park. These include a two-hour hike to Mount Minsi, and a ½-mile walk to Dingman's Falls. At Milford and Smithfield Beaches swimming is permitted, and during the summer months lifeguards are on duty. Both beaches include comfort stations, parking lots, and picnic and boat launching facilities. Rock climbing is found around the Water Gap itself and there is good climbing for both the novice and experienced climber. For the fisherman in the family, pike, walleye, bass, perch, bluegill, shad, catfish and brown trout may be caught in the river, the lakes and streams throughout the park. Fishing licenses are required. It should be noted that camping is not permitted in the park, but there are numerous private campgrounds located nearby.

Directions: The Kittatinny Point Information Center is located at Kittatinny Point, New Jersey, between Interstate 80 and the river, at the last exit before the toll bridge.

Within the perimeter of the park are three special attractions which deserve separate attention. One of these is located in Pennsylvania, the other two on the New Jersey side of the river.

SLATEFORD FARM

Open daily July 1st through Labor Day, 9 a.m. to 5:30 p.m. No admission fees. Rest rooms. (717) 897-5545.

After you have travelled down scenic Route 611 and taken in the magnificent scenery surrounding the Delaware Water Gap, visit this partially restored farm site located at the foot of Mount Minsi. A winding trail that leads through woods and over small bridges will lead you from the parking lot to the 19th century farm which was also the site for one of the first slate quarries in the area. Costumed National Park Service employees provide tours of the farm house (furnished in 19th century pieces) and grounds, and provide an interesting commentary on the history of the farm and adjacent slate quarry. Although you may not visit the quarry itself (which is reputedly loaded with Copperheads), the guides will describe the techniques of quarrying slate and demonstrate how it is split to make shingles.

Directions: If driving south on Rt. 611, turn right on National Park Drive (which intersects with 611 a few miles south of Overlook No. 3), and follow this to the parking lots.

MILLBROOK VILLAGE (NEW JERSEY)

Open July through Labor Day, 9 a.m. to 5:30 p.m. Rest rooms. No admission fees. (211) 841-9558.

Millbrook Village, a small farming town which had reached its heyday in 1870–1885 and then declined after the 1900's, has been rebuilt and assembled by the National Park Service to represent the many farming communities which used to play such an important part in our country's rural life. Today, park service employees dressed in period costume demonstrate in the reconstructed buildings the various handcrafts practiced by their forebears. There is spinning, blacksmithing, weaving and a variety of other tasks performed. There are also several buildings open for inspection, including a general store and hotel. Each fall a festival is held which features crafts, entertainment and country cooking.

Directions: The village is located on the New Jersey side of the Delaware River. From the Kittatinny Point Information Center travel north on River Road and the village will appear at the intersection of River Rd. and Old Mine Road.

PETERS VALLEY CRAFT VILLAGE (NEW JERSEY)

Open daily except Monday, April through December, 10 a.m. to 5:30 p.m. Studios open from 10 a.m. to 4 p.m. Store and gallery. Rest rooms. Call Kittatinny Point for information: (201) 496-4458.

In 1970, a non-profit organization, Peters Valley Craftsmen, Inc., founded with the cooperation of the National Park Service this charming craft village situated in the buildings of an early 19th century farm village. Here this small community of craftspeople produce a variety of handicrafts using natural materials such as wood, clay, fibers, iron and fine metals. Craft courses as well as demonstrations are offered at these studios. The craft items are often for sale at the local gallery, and, if you come after 1:00 p.m., you can have the crafts interpreted for you by the craftspeople themselves. A two-day Craft Fair is held here each summer.

Directions: The village is located in Northwest New Jersey just south of the Dingman's Ferry Toll Bridge. Just after crossing the bridge, turn right and follow the road to Peters Valley.

DORNEY PARK

Open Tues.–Sun., noon–10 p.m., late May through Labor Day; Weekends only, Late April–Late May. Closed Mondays except holidays. Fees: No entrance fees, but a book of 55 ride tickets costs $5.00. Parking fee, 50¢. Group rates available. Rest rooms. Picnics (grounds, but no rides, open at 9 a.m.). Concessions. Restaurant. Dorney Park, 3830 Dorney Park Rd., Allentown, Pa. 18104. (215) 395-3724.

Since 1884, people have been coming to this old-fashioned amusement resort, whether just for an evening when all the lights cast a romantic glow over the area, or for an entire day. The park is attractively situated among tall trees and babbling streams. Ponds are filled with ducks and surrounded by colorful lights. The smell of cotton candy drifts by, combined with the heady odor of beer and sauerkraut from the adjacent Bavarian Inn. Entertainers perform at the Band Shell, their controlled music at variance with the general cacophony of the amusement rides and their devotees. It's a crowded and colorful melange of sights, sounds, and smells that will delight old and young alike.

At the heart of Dorney Park are the amusement rides. People come back time and again for the thrills and variety of rides provided. There are three roller coasters, including one for small children; a gut-chilling ride for grownups; and, for the most fearless, the Flying Dutchman, a spindly framework upon which individual cars zoom up and down. There are bumper cars, train and boat rides, merry-go-rounds, The Whip, Sky Ride, and a whole set of kiddie rides. For horror aficionados, there's the "Bucket of Blood" and "Journey to the Center of the Earth." For the gambler, there are game stands, the Penny Arcade, and Skeeball. For the animal lover, there is a petting zoo and sea lions. And, for hot rodders, there is stock car racing every Saturday and on holidays. There is also a Roller Skating Rink, which on Saturday nights throughout the year, converts into a Texas style nightclub with mechanical bull riding and live country music.

Directions: Dorney Park is located about one mile west of Allentown. As you approach Allentown along Rt. 222, you will see the park on your left. Turn left here onto Hillview Rd. then bear right onto Dorney Park Road.

Nearby Attractions: See Haines Mill, Lil-Le-Hi Trout Hatchery, Allentown's Historic Houses, Leather Corner Post Hotel, and Covered Bridge Tours–Lehigh County.

ECKLEY'S MINER'S VILLAGE

Visitors' Center open year round, Tues.–Sat., 9–5 p.m.; Sun. 12–5 p.m.
Walking tours available April–Oct. only, Tues.–Sat., 10–4 p.m., Sun. 12–5.
Hours subject to change. Fees: Adults, $1.00; children under 12, free. Rest
rooms. Gift shop. Picnics. Handicapped: Visitors' Center accessible to wheelchairs, but not the houses on the walking tour. (717) 636-2070.

Gnarled and stunted trees blackened by coal dust cling tenuously
to a barren landscape. An isolated village, dominated by a large coal
breaker, stands in the midst of this desolation. Simple wooden buildings, interspersed with churches, a company store, mule barn and doctor's office, look much as they did during the 1800's when they were
inhabited by the ethnic mosaic of immigrants who comprised the work
force of the anthracite mining industry. It is due to the efforts of the
Pennsylvania Historic and Museum Commission that this mining
"patch" has been preserved as a living history museum which reveals
the way of life that has dominated the anthracite coal region for the
past 140 years.

A visit to Eckley provides a fascinating look at the life of the
coal miner during the 19th century. In the large Visitor's Center (recently constructed to house the educational exhibits), is a museum
which presents all facets of the miner's life through an excellent arrangement of photographs and exhibits. Large pictures of young boys,
their faces blackened by coal dust, tell the sad story of child labor (in
1901, only 2 percent of all children in the anthracite region graduated
from high school). Miniature coffins, constructed for the many infants
who died from communicable diseases, stand in a corner. A whole
section of a room is devoted to illustrating the day-by-day toil of the
miner's family, from washday on Monday to the Sunday day of rest.
Each exhibit is accompanied by photographs, items used in the daily
life (such as antique washing machines, coal stoves and irons), and
peppered with the personal comments of the miners' families themselves. Interesting details that make history come alive are included in
all the displays, from the layout of a typical miner's house to the
surgical instruments used by the company doctor.

An added highlight to a visit are the 45-minute guided tours of
the village. These are available during the warmer months and include
a visit to the Roman Catholic Church and a typical miner's house.

Many of the buildings are still inhabited by the miners and their families, so only a select few are open to the public. During the tours, the guide relates the history and life of the people who lived in a town run and owned by the mining concerns. Most of the buildings are original ones, save for the few (including the massive coal breaker) that were constructed by Paramount Studios when they filmed the movie, "The Molly Maguires," here.

Directions: The Village is located 45 miles north of Allentown in the Pocono Mountains. Take the Pennsylvania Turnpike to Exit 35, Route 80 West. Follow Rt. 80 to Rt. 940 West. Follow 940 to Eckley (there will be a left–hand turn, marked by directional signs, shortly after passing through the town of Drifton).

Nearby Attractions: See Whitewater Rafting on the Lehigh River–Whitewater Challengers; and, about a 30-minute drive away, Jim Thorpe.

HAINES FLOUR MILL

Open March–Nov., Sat. and Sun. from 1–4 p.m. Other times by appointment. No admission charge. Rest rooms. Picnics. Dr. Mahlon H. Hellerich, Archivist. Lehigh County Courthouse, Fifth and Hamilton Sts., Allentown, Pa. 18101. (215) 820-3282.

Open to the public since 1974, Haines Flour Mill, "home of Gilt Edge Flour," stands as an example of the many mills that played such an important part in Pennsylvania's agricultural history. Here the farmers would bring their corn and wheat to be ground into grain and flour. In the months of July and August, it was not uncommon for wagons and trucks to wait in line for hours to obtain the service these mills provided. Here also the farmers sold their grain for cash and bought feed for their livestock and flour for their families.

The guided tour of Haines Mill gives an historical perspective to the life of the farmer of bygone days. You walk where the busy miller received the grain, weighed it on the platform scale, and then emptied it into the hopper. You can see the ingenious machinery work, powered primarily by the water that flows in Cedar Creek, and can watch the intricate system of pulleys, wheels and belts work without the use of modern energy sources. The guide explains in detail the intricacies involved in running a successful milling operation and the daily challenges facing the miller.

An added highlight to the tour is a slide presentation which is given on modern agriculture in the Lehigh Valley. From past to present, a tour of Haines Mill provides an overall picture of farming in Pennsylvania.

Directions: The mill is located in Dorneyville, which is a mile east of Allentown along Rt. 222. If going east on 222, turn left onto Lower Main Blvd. which is just before the Dorneyville Light (The Music Factory and Perkins will be on your right). Follow Lower Main for 0.6 miles and the Mill will be on your right across from the entrance to Dorney Park.

Nearby Attractions: See Dorney Park, Allentown's Historic Houses, Industrial Museums of the Lehigh Valley-Lockridge Furnace, Covered Bridge Tours-Lehigh County, Das Awkscht Fest, Leather Corner Post Hotel, and Lehigh County Velodrome.

THE HUGH MOORE PARK—
CANAL MUSEUM AND BOAT RIDE

Park open year round. Canal Museum Hours: Mon.–Sat., 10–4 p.m., Sun., 1–5. Fees: Adults, 75¢; children, 25¢. Boat rides: Available Memorial Day Weekend through Labor Day, departing at 11 a.m., 1, 2:30 and 4 p.m. Weds.–Sat. and 1, 2:30 and 4 p.m. Sun. In Sept., boat departs at 1, 2:30 and 4 p.m. Sat. and Sun. only. Fees: Adults, $2.50; children, $1.25. Group rates available. Rest rooms. Picnics. Hugh Moore Park, P.O. Box 877, Easton, Pa. 18042. (215) 258-7155.

For a day's worth of recreational and educational activities for the entire family, pack a picnic lunch and head for the Hugh Moore Park. Purchased in 1962 by the city of Easton, this park consists of over 250 acres of land along the Lehigh Canal, as well as slackwater pools created by the Easton Dam and Chain Dam. The Canal traverses the length of the park and includes a cable suspension bridge, eight locks (three of them operable), and other canal structures. Industrial ruins exist within the park as well as a Canal Museum and restored Locktender's House.

The ideal spot to commence your visit to the Park is at the Canal Museum (on Rt. 611 one mile south of U.S. 22). Here are exhibits on canals, a mini-theater presentation on the history of transportation and the important part played by canal boats, and artifacts from this era. From the museum you can view the juncture of the Delaware and Lehigh Rivers and the Easton Dam which is the last dam for the Lehigh Canal. Here also is the beginning of the Delaware Canal (Guard

Lock #24) and the stone arch entrance to the Morris Canal on the Jersey side.

After gaining an understanding of the canal life and history, drive your car to the section of the park where the canal boat rides are offered (the Glendon area park entrance off Glendon Ave.). Here you can experience the lifestyle of those bygone days as you sit in deck chairs on board the Josiah White, a mule-drawn canal boat. Your "captain" relates the history of the canal and peppers his account with interesting details in the life of the boatmen. Your trip can last up to an hour depending on the disposition of the mule.

Once the boat ride is over, a variety of activities will await you. At the Glendon area you can have a picnic, rent paddleboats and canoes, or hike down the scenic towpath. This trail extends from the Canal Museum to the Locktender's House and retraces the route followed by the Canal Mules as they pulled the boats along Section 8 of the Lehigh Canal. An alternative route is to hike the River Trail which parallels the Towpath Trail but is along the Lehigh River. For those of you with bikes, these paths are flat and level—ideal for biking.

The Locktender's House near the picnic area has been restored and is open for viewing. The first floor has been turned into a museum and illustrates how a Locktender and his family might have lived in the 1890's. The view of the Chain Dam from the house is a breathtaking one.

Directions: Hugh Moore Park is located 16 miles east of Allentown. Take Rt. 22 (I-78) to Easton. Exit on Route 611 South. Be sure to turn left at the traffic light immediately following this exit, and continue on 611 South to the Canal Museum.

Nearby Attractions: See Crayola Factory Tour and C.F. Martin Guitar Factory.

INDUSTRIAL MUSEUMS IN THE LEHIGH VALLEY

***

LOCK RIDGE FURNACE

Park open daily 8 a.m.–10 p.m. Museum open Sat. and Sun. 1–4, March–Nov. Other hours by appointment. Free admission. Handicapped: packed dirt and concrete walkways, museum exhibit on one floor. Rest rooms (some steps). Covered picnic pavilion. Dr. Hellerich, Archivist. Lehigh County Courthouse, 5th & Hamilton Sts., Allentown, Pa. 18101. (215) 820-3282.

The massive stone buildings of Lock Ridge Furnace, some with only a few walls standing, resemble the ruins of an ancient civilization. They belong to another time—a time when iron was king and the anthracite iron industry in Pennsylvania was an important source of commerce. During the period from 1860 to 1920 pig iron was manufactured here, using anthracite coal as fuel, which was then oxidized by a hot blast pumped into the furnace by a steam engine. Domestic iron ore, limestone and other ingredients were then added to the process.

Due to the efforts of the Lehigh County Historical Society and dedicated citizens, this authentic iron furnace has been partially restored, and you may take a self-guided tour through the various buildings and exhibits. In the old Engine Room and Cast House are permanent exhibits displaying the earliest methods of iron making. There is a slide show depicting the history and manufacture of pig iron, and a guide is present who will describe the various items you will be seeing. Brick floors, stone walls and foundations are all that's left of many of the sites, each of which is numbered. Twenty-eight points of interest are scattered throughout the park and connected by scenic paths. These include the brick Weighmaster's House, a narrow gauge railroad track, Furnace Room, and meandering stream among others. The furnace buildings are surrounded by a green and lovely park. Bring a picnic lunch and spend a pleasant afternoon.

Directions: Take Rt. 22 (I-78) to just outside of Fogelsville (near Allentown). Go south on Rt. 100. Follow signs to Alburtis. From Main St. in Alburtis, go left onto Franklin Street. The park entrance will appear on your left.

Nearby Attractions: See Allentown's Historic Houses and Liberty Bell Shrine, Covered Bridge Tours-Lehigh County, Das Awkscht Fest, Leather Corner Post Hotel, Lehigh County Velodrome, and Rodale Organic Gardening & Research Farm.

SAYLOR PARK CEMENT INDUSTRY MUSEUM

Open 1–4 p.m., Sat. and Sun., March–Nov. Other hours by appointment. Free admission. Handicapped: exhibits all on one floor. Rest rooms. Dr. Hellerich, Archivist, Lehigh County Court House, Fifth & Hamilton Sts., Allentown, Pa. 18101. (215) 820-3282.

Silhouetted against an azure sky are a series of massive vertical brick kilns. They stand in perpetuity as a monument to the ingenuity and tenacity of an exceptional man, David O. Saylor, known as the Father of the Portland Cement Industry. A man with vision, Saylor realized that the availability of valuable limestone deposits plus the proximity to railroads and local markets made the Lehigh Valley an ideal area for developing a cement industry. So, in 1866 he organized the Coplay Cement Industry taking advantage of the valuable limestone that could be quarried in nearby Coplay. Shortly after, he developed a process for manufacturing a cement that would be more durable than the natural cement being made at the time. It would be called Portland cement. However, the improved cement required more complete combustion at higher temperatures, something the dome kilns then being used could not accomplish. The answer was the vertical brick kiln with chambers for creating, burning and cooling the material—a kiln which could also be in continuous production except when being repaired.

From 1892–1893 eleven of these kilns were built and used at Coplay until 1904, when they were replaced by the rotary kiln. It is these vertical kilns which have been preserved as a museum through the joint efforts of the cement industry and Lehigh County. Surrounding them are a series of concrete stands displaying information about Saylor and the cement industry. Inside is housed the museum exhibits. Through photographs and a motion picture, the process of cement manufacturing and its interesting history are depicted. When you finish browsing through the museum, take a drive further down Second Street (away from town) and you will see the buildings that house a modern-day cement industry—the Whitehall Cement Plant.

Directions: Take Rt. 22 (I-78) to Allentown. Take the 7th Street (MacArthur Rd.) exit north. Follow 7th Street until you come to Lehigh Street. Go left onto Lehigh and follow it into Coplay. Then take a left onto 2nd Street and the museum will shortly appear on your right.

Nearby Attractions: See Allentown's Historic Houses and Liberty Bell Shrine, Covered Bridge Tours-Lehigh County, and Trexler-Lehigh Game Preserve.

JIM THORPE, THE SWITZERLAND OF PENNSYLVANIA

New Jersey Central Railroad Station and Tourist Welcoming Center: Open year round, Mon.–Fri., 9–4 p.m. Asa Packer Mansion: Open May–Oct., 12–5, closed Mondays. Fees: Moderate. Harry Packer Mansion: Open May–Oct.

Sunday afternoons only. Fees: Moderate. Restaurants. Stores. Rest rooms. Parks with picnic tables. Carbon County Tourist Promotion Agency, Box 90, Jim Thorpe, Pa. 18229. (717) 325-3673.

Jim Thorpe, named after the famous Indian track star born nearby, is a picturesque little village that lies nestled between two towering mountains. Built along the Lehigh River almost two centuries ago, this town, then called Mauch Chunk, was a bustling pioneer coal mining community. It is here that the valuable coal would be brought for shipment by canal boat and railroad to the port city of Philadelphia. Many of the original buildings still stand, and even today a walking tour through this quaint town is reminiscent of the turbulent yet glorious days when coal was king.

The place to begin your tour is at the Tourist Welcoming Center in the restored New Jersey Central Railroad Station. This lies on the right side of Hazard Square just as you enter town. Here you can get a map of the area and browse through the museum that has on display items of importance to both the history of the town and the coal mining industry. In the summer months, usually on a Sunday, 2–3-mile train rides may be taken starting at the station (write or call for details).

Armed with your map and a good pair of walking shoes, you can then go visit the more than 25 buildings, parks, and cemeteries that reflect the life of this town that has become known as the Switzerland of Pennsylvania. As you stroll the winding streets, you will see St. Mark's Episcopal Church on Race Street, a lovely old church of rural Gothic design built in 1869. Inside can be seen windows of Tiffany glass, a wrought iron elevator, and furnishings of gold, marble and brass. Farther down Race Street stands Stone Row. These homes were literally built into the steep sides of the mountain slope. Stone that was carved away from the mountain to accommodate the structures was then used in building them. They stand much the same way they did in 1840, when they were built. Around the bend of the road is the Old Capitol Theatre. This has been restored by the Mauch Chunk Historical Society to the original Opera House and boasts a lovely vaulted hand-painted ceiling.

After seeing the Opera House, come back down Broadway, turn left at Hazard Square, and follow the road to the Asa Packer and Harry Packer Mansions which overlook the town. Both are open to the public at selected times and are fascinating to visit. The Asa Packer Mansion, home of the founder of Lehigh University and the Lehigh Valley Railroad, is a 20-room Victorian house that is a showplace for the wealth and treasures of a bygone era. Guided tours, lasting close to an hour, take you through authentically furnished rooms with hand-carved wood-panelled walls. There are original paintings, exquisite stained glass windows, and fine furniture. The view from the windows is breathtaking. The neighboring Harry Packer Mansion is still under restoration, but here also you can see the intricate wood panelling, painted ceilings, cut glass windows and other decorative techniques found in the homes of the wealthy. After finishing the house tours, sit on benches and relax in the nearby park and let your children cavort on the assorted playground equipment.

When you've had enough of walking, get in your car and proceed down Broadway for a look at the Carbon County Jail. This grim fortress was the location of a series of hangings following the 1876 Trials of the Molly Macguires, the forerunners of our modern day labor unions. The film, "The Molly Macguires," was filmed on location in Jim Thorpe, as was the CBS program, "You Can't Go Home Again." Although the jail is generally not open to the public, you can try to make an appointment to see it by calling the local sheriff at (717) 325-2821.

If you continue down Broadway for about two miles, you will come to Flagstaff Park. This is an ideal spot for a picnic and a spectacular view of the town in the valley. The park is 1,400 feet above the town and is fittingly called "The Rooftop of the World." Here you can see the three sections of Jim Thorpe and the meandering Lehigh River which cuts its way through the opposing mountains. On a distant slope is evidence of a fairly recent coal mining operation—a visual reminder of the history and livelihood of the unique town of Jim Thorpe.

Directions: Take the Pennsylvania Turnpike Exit 34—Rt. 209 South. Follow 209 South for approximately 6 miles to Jim Thorpe.

Nearby Attractions: See Whitewater Rafting on the Lehigh River: The Pocono Whitewater Rafting Center; Beltzville Dam, a park with picnic facilities and swimming area is nearby, located off of Route 209 North.

THE LEATHER CORNER POST HOTEL—
BOOM–BAS AT THEIR BEST

Boom–bas featured from 9 p.m.–2 a.m. Tues., Fri. and Sat. nights. No cover charge. Restaurant. Rest rooms. Leather Corner Post Hotel, R.D. 2, Orefield, Pa. 18069. (215) 395-1782.

It looks like a typical country bar complete with red neon lights and a "Bud on Tap" sign. In the bar room is a TV, dart board and large rectangular bar. Locals sit on the stools drinking beer and eating sandwiches. It's early on a Saturday night and the only things that seem a bit peculiar are a sign on the wall that says: "It's better to beat your boom-bas than your wife," and a number of what look like pogo sticks hanging on the wall. Grab a seat, order a stiff drink, and brace yourself, for at the witching hour of 9 o'clock the action starts. An innocuous looking man saunters over to the juke box and pushes a few buttons. With a loud fanfare, the William Tell Overture comes on. Said man then walks over to the walls with the pogo sticks and grabs one. Young lovelies, dressed in black pants and cowboy hats follow his example and soon all available space is taken up. It becomes evident that those weren't pogo sticks on the walls. Each one seems to be a one man percussion stick, each player a virtuoso exhibiting his or her musical skill on a popular instrument of German origin, the Boom-bas. Sleigh bells jingle, tambourines sound, cymbals clash and cow bells clang—the Boom-bas Jamboree is in progress.

Boom-bas are said to have had their origin in Germany. In the "old country" they were quite elaborate, often boasting two drums, three cowbells and three horns, all attached to a pole that goes up and down like a pogo stick. The American counterpart is more simple, although the complexity of the custom made instruments varies with the desires and capabilities of their owners. Most come equipped with sleigh bells, wood blocks, bass string, cymbals, and cow bells. These are played by striking them with a drum stick and bouncing the instrument up and down on the floor. They are often decorated with beer tap handles and Pennsylvania Dutch folk designs on the tambourines.

The action at the Leather Corner Post Hotel continues until the wee hours of the morning. The boom-bas players are usually local people, amateurs, who enjoy performing for others. It is quite an experience watching each player keeping beat with the juke box (which supplies all types of music from country to disco, to polkas and classical pieces). Most boom-bas are privately owned and jealously guarded, but, if you are fortunate, some kindly soul will let you try your hand (check with the bartender, sometimes there are unclaimed boom-bas you can play). It's a great instrument for the beginning musician and for a brief time you can become immersed in a Pennsylvania Dutch pastime that is rarely performed outside of this area.

Directions: Take 309 north to Allentown. Pass exits for Rt. 22. About a mile or two beyond these, you will come to a yellow blinking light and a sign that says, "left to Claussville." Turn left at the light onto Kernsville Rd. and continue on this road for three miles. The hotel will be on your right.

Nearby Attractions: See Covered Bridge Tours-Lehigh County, Trexler-Lehigh Game Preserve, Allentown's Historic Houses, Dorney Amusement Park, Haines Mill, and Lil-Le-Hi Trout Hatchery.

THE LEHIGH COUNTY VELODROME

Open during bike racing season, May through Labor Day. Track open for use by public most afternoons with no admission fee. Races scheduled every Tuesday and Friday night beginning at 7:30. Programs can last up to four hours. Fees: Standing room along track, $1.00; Reserved seats, $2.00. Sr. citizens, ½ price. Rest rooms. Concessions. Handicapped: wheelchairs make ideal track seats, but cushions may be needed, the link fence is high and may obstruct the view. Lehigh County Velodrome, Management Office, 217 Main St., Emmaus, Pa. 18049. (215) 965-6930.

During the early years of the 20th century, bike racing was in its heyday. Over 100 tracks existed in the U.S. and entire towns would shut down for the day to attend a local race. At one point, this sport was more popular than baseball, with huge crowds filling places like Madison Square Garden to watch the skilled racers compete. With the advent of the Great Depression, the automobile and World War II, interest in the sport waned, and by the 1950's only two tracks remained in the U.S.

Today there is a renewed interest in this exciting sport, and the two tracks have expanded to thirteen. Foremost among these is the Lehigh County Velodrome which has been in operation for eight years. Begun in 1974 by Bob and Ardath Rodale, the track is now a county facility which presents a summer season of bike racing that is unmatched in its excitement, competition and fan appeal. The 333-meter track with its lightning-fast cement surface is banked at 28 degrees, and to watch the bikers racing past on this steep incline is breathtaking. On this track you will see Olympic hopefuls, top-ranked professionals, and the up-and-coming amateurs racing at almost unbelievable speeds.

If you are one of those unfamiliar with the sport, you won't be for long. Knowledgeable commentators describe what is going on, and keep you informed of all the strategies, tactics, and skills required of this sometimes grueling sport. There are a variety of races demanding different skills of the riders. Races such as the Miss And Out, an exciting elimination race where the last rider of each lap is withdrawn from the race; the individual and team pursuits, where single riders or teams of riders start at opposite sides of the track and pursue each other for a prescribed distance; and the Kilometer Time Trial, a race where one man is pitted against the clock for 1,000 meters—provide a night's worth of stimulating entertainment.

The Tuesday night races are scheduled for the up-and-coming racers who have yet to prove their mettle. Friday nights are reserved for the best male and female, amateur and professional bike racing talent. During the racing season, professional coaching and racing development programs are sponsored by local business. These programs, free of charge with all equipment provided, teach bike safety, maintenance and the fundamentals of riding.

Directions: The Velodrome is located at Trexlertown, 6 miles west of Allentown, Pa., and one block west of the intersection of Routes 100 and 222, with entrances to the parking lots from either 222 or Mosser Road.

Nearby Attractions: See Rodale Organic Gardening and Research Farm, Allentown's Historic Houses, Covered Bridge Tours-Lehigh County, Industrial Museums-Lockridge Furnace, and Das Awkscht Fest.

THE LIL-LE-HI TROUT NURSERY

Open year round 9 a.m. until dusk. No admission fees. Handicapped: paved walkways around pools. Benches. Rest rooms (some steps). Picnics across the street. Hiking Trails. Fish Hatchery Rd., Allentown, Pa. 18104.

Situated along the banks of the Little Lehigh Creek is a co-operative trout nursery which is one of the largest in Pennsylvania. It raises over 20,000 trout annually and is a popular spot for children and adults to visit. Brown, Rainbow and Brook Trout are brought here from state hatcheries as fingerlings and are raised to maturity. They are then released in the local creeks and rivers as fair game for the ardent fisherman.

For a dime, you can buy a bag of approved fish food from the hatch house at the nursery, and feed the thousands of fish of all sizes in the different ponds. There is one stone-lined pool filled with the biggest trout you are likely to see anywhere. Children will squeal with delight as they watch the schools of fish thrashing about on the water's surface as they race to get the fish pellets, and the adults can sit on the park benches and dream of what a good meal these fish will some-day make.

For those with strong stomachs and a curiosity about the inner workings of nature, stop in the hatch house and take a close look at the large bottles lining the wall opposite the door. These are filled with formaldehyde and preserved in them are a fetus of a fawn and a snake among other things.

A half a mile from the hatchery is a FISH FOR FUN stream. Here you can practice fly fishing without a license. Across the road from the hatchery are some lovely picnic areas along the creek, and, for hikers, the hatchery boasts three nature trails. Maps of these are available at the Hatch House.

Directions: The nursery is located on the outskirts of Allentown. From Rt. 222, take Cedar Crest Blvd. (Rt. 29) South. Go past the light at the Allentown Sacred Heart Hospital, then take the next left onto Fish Hatchery Road. The nursery will appear on your left. If you are taking the Lehigh County Covered Bridge Tour, you will be approaching the nursery from the opposite direction on Fish Hatchery Road.

Nearby Attractions: See Covered Bridge Tours-Lehigh County, Dorney Park, Haines Flour Mill, Allentown's Historical Houses, Leather Corner Post Hotel and the Trexler-Lehigh Game Preserve.

THE LOST RIVER CAVERNS

Open year round, 9 a.m. to 8 p.m. except Christmas and New Year's. Fees: Adults, $4.00; children, $2.00. Rest rooms. Gift shop. Picnic area and trailer camp. Lost River Caverns, Box 103, Hellertown, Pa. 18055. (215) 838-8767.

The entrance to the Lost River Caverns is flanked by great chunks of petrified wood. A door opens into a large room, one whole wall of which is a tropical garden with waterfall. Goldfish swim lazily in a pool beneath it, while the large heads of stuffed animals gaze gloomily from an adjacent wall. Cases housing an antique rifle and pistol collection and a variety of fossils complete the upstairs exhibit. A concrete ramp leads down to a lower level with counters filled with rocks and minerals. Gem stones glitter in small compartments and lapidary equipment fills an entire corner of the area. This delightful hodgepodge of museum exhibits, souvenir and lapidary shop, and tropical gardens surrounds the lone door that leads into the main drawing card of this attraction, the Lost River Caverns. ·

In 1883, limestone quarry workers discovered this natural limestone cave, and in 1929 it was opened to the public by the Gilman family. Concrete walkways and iron rails make this underground world easily accessible. Guides leading tours lasting about thirty minutes lead you through the ¼ mile of rooms and passageways. Being a "live" cave, there are often water deposits in it, so wear old shoes and clothes. Some of the things you will be seeing are the Crystal Chapel, where weddings are often held, a room with a 60-foot-high ceiling formed by a long ago cave-in and supported by a two-ton boulder, and the New Room, a fairly recent extension to the cavern. Leading to this is a 13-foot-long concrete bridge that crosses the underground stream that gave the cave its name. One hundred feet below the earth's surface, this six-foot-deep stream of crystal-clear spring water flows through the cave at the rate of two million gallons a year. In the New Room the stream disappears through a crevice in the wall, and even though dye has been added to the water to trace its destination, it has never been discovered. Throughout the cave interesting formations may be seen such as the 300-pound piece of flowstone called the "Ear of Corn." For children, an entire cave tour may be arranged around these peculiar formations and what familiar objects they resemble such as, a slice of bacon, the rear end of a horse, and two parakeets in a nest. Once the tour is over, you are free to wander about the museum and use the nearby picnic grounds.

Directions: Take Route 22 (I-78) to Bethlehem. Take the Rt. 378 exit towards Bethlehem. Follow 378 then turn left onto Route 412 South shortly after the Expressway ends. Follow 412 to Hellertown (just a few miles south of Bethlehem). In Hellertown, turn left onto Penn Street, then bear left onto Durham Street. The entrance to the cave will appear on your right.

Nearby Attractions: See Bethlehem Historic Area Attractions.

MAGIC VALLEY AND WINONA FALLS

Park open May 26–June 29 daily from 10 a.m. to 7 p.m. Weekends 10–8.
Closed Mondays. From June 30–Sept. 4, daily 10–9; Weekends, 10–10. Sept.
8–Oct. 15, open weekends only. Fees: (this includes admission to the waterfalls) Adults, $6.25; children 4–11, $5.25. Rest rooms. Cafeteria. Snacks.
Gift shops. Magic Valley, U.S. Rt. 209, Bushkill, Pa. 18324. (717) 588-
9411.

"Bird Brain, bet you can't beat him!" reads the sign over the
chicken in the glassed-in cage. You pay your quarter, the chicken
pecks the X and now it's your turn. You carefully punch the center
O. The chicken covers with his X. Before you know it, he has you—
either place you put your O he can make tic-tac-toe. More corn for
the chicken. You wander down to the games pavilion where a group
of teenagers are playing "Whack a Mole." You try a few whacks,
but you aren't as aggressive as the others. There goes another quarter.
Now for "roll 'a ball," that exciting horse race where you roll your
ball into holes marked "walk," "trot," and "run." You're lucky this
time, rolling runs continually. One stuffed animal for the gentleman.
You walk away happy, and continue to explore this wonderland known
as Magic Valley.

There's plenty to do in this amusement park amid the forest. A
high and scary-looking roller coaster named appropriately, "The
Screamin' Demon," hurtles down its steep and circular tracks. The
Yo-Yo, a crazy swing arrangement, goes around in circles thirty feet
off the ground; the antique cars putt-putt down shady lanes, an entertaining ride for the more timid. Little children are content with the
merry-go-round and kiddie rides built just for them, and music lovers
are delighted to listen to the folk singer strumming from a perch atop
one of the buildings. An authentic craft fair is held continuously
throughout the day. Pottery making, blacksmithing, broom-making,
wood carving, leather sewing and a host of other crafts may be observed.

When all and sundry weary of the thirty amusement rides and
singing and craft shows, another surprise awaits them, the beautiful
Winona Five Falls. The entrance to these is in the rear of the park.
It's amazing how quickly the hub-bub and noise of the amusement
park can be left behind for the peace and quiet of a natural abode.

Well-marked paths lead along the five distinctive waterfalls which tumble over 175 feet of scenic Pocono woodland. Wooden foot bridges cross the rushing stream, affording a close look at the waterfalls. The hike lasts about forty minutes, give or take those refreshing rest stops at scenic overlooks. It's a good idea to wear sneakers and not to take the baby in its stroller (there are countless wooden steps leading up the sides of the falls).

Directions: Park located off Rt. 209 in the Pocono Mountains. From Rt. 22 (I-78) take Rt. 33 north (this exit is just before Easton). Follow Rt. 33 to 80 East. Continue on Rt. 80 to Exit 52, Rt. 209 North. Follow 209 to Bushkill. Here you will see the sign for Magic Valley which directs you to take a left towards Saw Creek. Follow this road to the park.

Nearby Attractions: See Bushkill Falls and Delaware Water Gap National Recreation Area.

QUIET VALLEY LIVING HISTORICAL FARM

Open weekends with continuous tours Sat., 9:30 a.m.–5:30 p.m. Sunday, 1–5 p.m. (last tour starting at 4), from June 20 to Labor Day, rain or shine. Group tours by appointment May 1–June 20. Harvest Festival-Columbus Day weekend. Fees: Adults, $3.00; children, $1.50. Rest rooms (primitive). Gift shop. Picnics. Sue and Gary Oiler, Managers, Box 2495, R.D. 2, Stroudsburg, Pa. 18360. (717) 992-6161.

"Them was hard years when me and my family moved to this here valley. Ma and Pa were tired of all that religious persecution in Germany, so they packed up us young'uns, boarded a boat, and brought us here to the promised land, Pennsylvania. It wasn't easy, many died on that fearsome sea, and when we got here, why we had to spend that first shivery winter holed up like bears in this dark earth floor kitchen. Wouldn't want to see them days again."

Dressed in the garb of a young colonial girl, a braided blue-eyed teenager holds her audience spellbound while she describes the trials and tribulations of her life on a farm in the late 1700's. She is a part of a dedicated volunteer community, the Historical Farm Association, a non-profit educational institution devoted to developing and maintaining a humble and authentic Pennsylvania-Dutch homestead called the Quiet Valley Farm Museum.

As you make your way from building to building (there are fourteen of them, some original, some reconstructed), costumed guides playing the roles of family members who have inhabited the farm, share with you the humble manner in which they live. Through the technique of living theatre, a play unfolds revealing the hardships and pleasures of a long-ago lifestyle. If it's a Saturday, Grandmother is outside at the bake oven busily baking a week's worth of bread. You get to sample it, fresh from the oven and smothered with homemade butter. In the Granddaddy House, two sisters are busy carding and spinning the wool. A sheepskin hangs on the wall of the cabin, a reminder of the ugly-tempered ram who terrorized the children. A spinster Aunt, industriously cleaning the old bank kitchen, describes how cooking, preserving foods, and cleaning were done in the old days, while the proud mother of the family shows off her "new" kitchen with its iron stove. In the back parlor, a reluctant daughter practices her music lessons on the family's harpsichord.

A visit to Quiet Valley can last from one-and-one-half to two hours. Even small children will enjoy a visit. This is storytelling at its best, and the variety of domestic animals who punctuate each talk with their squeals and grunts provide an added appeal. Craft demonstrations, such as soap making, wool dyeing (dyes are made from local plants such as goldenrod and onion skins), broom and pitchfork making, and butter churning, are presented at the tour's commencement, providing you with a unique opportunity to see how everyday items taken for granted today were painstakingly handmade in the past.

Directions: Quiet Valley is located five miles west of Stroudsburg, Pa., off Business Route 209. From Rt. 22 (Interstate 78) take 33 North. Follow this to 209 North (there will be a large directional sign for the farm). Take a left onto Shafers School House Road, then left again at the stop sign onto South Business 209. Continue following the signs to the farm.

Nearby Attractions: See Camelback's Alpine Slide.

THE RODALE ORGANIC GARDENING & FARMING RESEARCH CENTER

Open May–October. Tours conducted at 9:30 a.m., 11:00 a.m. and 1:00 p.m. Reservations required for large groups. If alone, 1:00 is the best time to come since groups are usually taken through in the morning. No admission charge. Rest rooms. Rodale Organic Gardening Farm, Maxatawny, Pa. (215) 435-9281.

Directional signs lead you to a small red school house seemingly placed in the middle of nowhere. There are no traditional desks inside, no obvious signs of our formal educational system except, perhaps, for the wooden benches and movie screen. An unassuming guide in halter top and blue jeans announces to all that the slide show is about to commence. Grab your pencils and notepads, for what you are about to embark upon is a fascinating and enlightening look into the dynamic relationship between man and nature.

The slide show promotes the philosophy of a unique group of people, the Rodale Organization. Started in the 1930's by J. I. Rodale, a forward-thinking man who discovered a real need for agricultural research, this organization has mushroomed into a well-known research group that publishes such popular magazines as *Organic Gardening* and *Prevention*. The emphasis in all their work is on a harmonious non-exploitive relationship with nature. Their goals are ambitious. They would like to see diversification in food crops, an independence from chemical insecticides and fertilizers, a maintenance of current life styles without depletion of resources, and the discovery of alternative energy sources, among other things. The individual, they feel, is the key to the success of their philosophy and programs, and it is to the individual (whether he be a farmer or city dweller with a small backyard garden) that their education and research primarily is directed.

While the slide show promotes these ideals, the Organic Gardening Farm is the proving grounds for them. Over 25 acres are devoted to extensive research programs in the areas of home gardening, family food preparation, new crops, organic gardening techniques, fish farming and nutrition. On your guided tour of this farm, you'll discover useful hints to overcome gardening problems such as: planting French Marigolds next to your vegetables to repel the Japanese beetle, using the French intensive method to grow an extraordinary quantity of vegetables in a limited space, and building simple solar growing frames for a winter crop of produce. Alternative food crops, such as raising amaranth as a major grain and fish farming in small backyard pools are being studied. Experiments are also being conducted on integrated ecological gardens in which nutrients are derived from all components, such as the waste from the fish pool fertilizing the gardens.

A tour of the farm is not only educational, but is also pleasing to the eye. The 305 acres are located in the rolling Pennsylvania Dutch countryside near Maxatawny, Pa. Bright flowers and neat herb gardens brighten the landscape and the rustling fields of corn (farmed organically by a Mennonite farmer) add a pastoral flavor. The guided tour lasts for an hour but you are welcome to browse for as long as you wish.

Directions: The Rodale Farm is located about 8 miles west of Allentown. Take Route 22 to Grim Road (there's a directional sign at this juncture). Go north on Grim and follow the signs to the one-room school house. Further information can be obtained by calling (215) 435-9281.

Nearby Attractions: See Lehigh County Velodrome, the Crystal Cave (Berks County) Area II, and Kutztown Folk Festival (Berks) Area II.

SKIING IN THE POCONOS

When winter holds you in its icy grip and you start to go stir crazy, bundle up, jump in your car and head for the Pocono Mountains for a day's worth of skiing. The crisp outdoors, bright white snow and scenic landscape are a sure cure for those winter blahs, and there is enough variety and number of ski slopes to keep you coming back again and again. An added bonus is that most ski areas manufacture their own snow, so that skiing is available all winter long.

The following is a list of the major ski areas in Southeastern Pennsylvania. Please keep in mind that hours and fees can change and it is highly recommended that you call in advance.

BIG BOULDER: Open daily, nightly Tues.–Sat. Lifts: 1–J, 6–C. Vertical drop: 475 feet. Snow making. Ski school. Rentals. Nursery. Babysitters. Basic weekend fee: $13–A, $11–J. Big Boulder, Lake Harmony, Pa. 18624. (717) 722-0101. 5 miles from Blakeslee Exit 43, I-80 via 115 and 903.

BUCK HILL: Open daily. Lifts: P-2. Vertical Drop: 320 feet. Snow making. Ski school. Rentals. Cross country. Basic weekend fee: $7.75-A, $5.00-J. Buck Hill, Buck Hill Falls, Pa. 18323. (717) 595-7441, Ext. 130. 8 miles from Mt. Pocono, 15 miles from Stroudsburg off Exit 52 on I-80.

CAMELBACK: Open daily and nights. Lifts: 6-C, 2-T, 1-J. Vertical drop: 800 feet. Snow making. Ski school. Rentals. Nursery. Basic weekend fee: $14.00. Box 168, Tannersville, Pa. 18372. (717) 629-1661. N.W. of Stroudsburg off I-80, Exit 45.

CHADDS PEAK: Open daily and nights. Lifts: 1-P, 3-R, Vertical drop: 284 feet. Snow making. Ski school. Rentals. Nursery. Basic weekend fee: $10.00-A, $9.00-J. P.O. Box 154, Chadds Ford, Pa. 19317. (215) 388-7421. U.S. Rt. 1, 4 miles west of Rt. 202.

DOE MOUNTAIN: Open daily and Mon.–Sat. nights. Lifts: 3-C, 1-T, 1-R. Vertical drop: 500 feet. Snow making. Ski school. Rentals. Basic weekend fee: $12-A, $11-J. R.D. 1, Macungie, Pa. 18062. (215) 682-7109. 15 miles S.W. of Allentown off Rts. 29 & 100.

ELK MOUNTAIN: Open daily and Mon.–Sat. nights. Lifts: 5-C. Vertical drop: 1,000 feet. Snow making. Ski school. Rentals. Basic weekend fee: $12. R.D. 1, P.O. Box 258, Uniondale, Pa. 18470. (717) 679-2611. 9 miles east of I-81.

FERNWOOD: Open daily. Lifts: 2-T, 1-R. Vertical drop: 300 feet. Snow making. Ski school. Rentals. Cross Country. Basic weekend fee: $10.50-A, $8.00-J. Fernwood, Bushkill, Pa. 18324. (717) 588-6661. 8 miles N. of I-80, Exit 52.

HAHN MOUNTAIN: Open daily, Mon.–Sat. nights. Lifts: 1-C, 1-T, 1-R. Vertical drop: 500 feet. Snow making. Ski school. Rentals. Basic weekend fee: $12-A, $10-J. R.D. 2, Kempton, Pa. 19529. Rt. 22 at Lenhartsville.

HANLEY'S HAPPY HILL: Open Sat., Sun., and holidays, daytime only. Lifts: R-2. Vertical drop: 200 feet. Rentals. Cross country. Basic weekend fee: $8.00. Laporte Ave., Eagles Mere, Pa. 17731. (717) 525-3461. Rte. 42, N.E. of Williamsport.

JACK FROST: Open daily. Lifts: 5-C, 1-J. Vertical drop: 500 feet. Snow making. Ski school. Rentals. Nursery. Basic weekend fee: $13-A, $11-J. Box 37-A-1, White Haven, Pa. 18661. (717) 443-8425. 3 miles W. of Blakeslee off Rte. 940.

LITTLE GAP: Open weekdays 3–10 p.m., Sat. 8:30 a.m. to 10 p.m., Sun. 8:30 a.m. to 8 p.m. Lifts: 1-C, 1-T. Vertical drop: 270 feet. Snow making. Ski school. Rentals. Basic weekend fee: $12-A, $10-J. P.O. Box 201, Palmerton, Pa. 18071. 5 miles east of Palmerton, 30 min. north of Allentown.

MASTHOPE SKI AREA: Open daily. Lifts: 1-C, 1-J. Vertical drop: 650 feet. Snow making. Ski school. Rentals. Cross country. Basic weekend fee: $11-A, $9-J. Masthope, Lackawaxen, Pa. 18435. (717) 685-7101. Near Hawley.

MT. AIRY LODGE: Open daily. Lifts: 2-C. Vertical drop: 240 feet. Snow making. Ski school. Rentals. Cross country. Babysitters. Mt. Pocono, Pa. 18344. (717) 839-8811 Ext. 7088. Off Rt. 611, 3 miles south of Mt. Pocono.

MOUNT TONE: Open Fri.–Sun., days, Wed., Fri., and Sat. nights. Lifts: 1-C, 1-T, 2-R. Vertical drop: 450 feet. Snow making. Ski school. Rentals. Cross country. Basic weekend fee: $8.00. Lake Como, Pa. 18437. (717) 798-2707. 2 miles from Rt. 247.

NORTH MOUNTAIN: Open Sat., Sun., holidays, daytime only. Lifts: 1-J, 1-P. Vertical drop: 250 feet. Snow making. Rentals. Basic weekend fee: $7.50-A, $5.00-J. R.D. 1, Muncy Valley, Pa. 17758. (717) 482-2541. 2 miles N. of Muncy Valley on Rte. 220.

POCONO MANOR: Open daily. Lifts: 1-J, 1-T. Vertical drop: 250 feet. Snow making. Ski school. Rentals. Cross country. Babysitters. Basic weekend fee: $8.00. Pocono Manor, Pa. 18349. (717) 839-7111. 15 miles N.W. of Stroudsburg off Rte. 611.

SAW CREEK: Open Wed.–Mon. daytime only. Lifts: C-1. Vertical drop: 300 feet. Snow making. Ski school. Rentals. Basic weekend fee: $8-A, $6-J. Bushkill, Pa. 18324. Off Rte. 209.

SHAWNEE MOUNTAIN: Open daily. Lifts: 4-C. Vertical drop: 700 feet. Snow making. Ski school. Rentals. Cross country. Nursery. Babysitters. Basic weekend fee: $14-A, $11-J. Shawnee-on-Delaware, Pa. 18356. (717) 421-7231. Exit 52, Marshalls Creek, off I-80.

SKI LIBERTY: Open daily and nightly. Lifts: 3-C, 1-J. Vertical drop: 575 feet. Snow making. Ski school. Rentals. Nursery. Basic weekend fee: $14.00. Box D, Fairfield, Pa. 17320. (717) 642-8282. Rt. 116, 8 miles S.W. of Gettysburg.

SKI ROUNDTOP: Open daily and nightly. Lifts: 5-C, 2-J. Vertical drop: 550 feet. Snow making. Ski school. Rentals. Nursery. Babysitters. Basic weekend fee: $14.00. R.D. 1, Lewisberry, Pa. 17339. (717) 432-9631. Between Harrisburg and York.

SPLIT ROCK SKI AREA: Open daily, Wed. and Fri. nights. Lifts: 1-T. Vertical drop: 200 feet. Snow making. Ski school. Rentals. Cross country. Babysitters. Basic weekend fee: $8-A, $7-J. Lake Harmony, Pa. 18624. (717) 722-9111. Exit 42 off I-80 on Rte. 940.

SPRING MOUNTAIN: Open daily and nightly. Lifts: 3-C, 2-R. Vertical drop: 475 feet. Snow making. Ski school. Rentals. Nursery. Basic weekend fee: $11. Box 42, Spring Mount, Pa. 19478. (215) 287-7900. 30 miles N. of Phila. off Rte. 29 & 73 near Schwenksville.

TAMIMENT: Open daily. Lifts: 1-C. Vertical drop: 125 feet. Snow making. Ski school. Rentals. Cross country. Nursery. Basic weekend fee: $8.00. Tamiment, Pa. 18371. (717) 588-6652. Off U.S. 209.

TANGLEWOOD: Open daily, Wed.–Sat. nights. Lifts: 1-C, 2-T, 1-J. Vertical drop: 415 feet. Snow making. Ski school. Rentals. Cross country. Nursery. Babysitters. Basic weekend fee: $11-A, $9-J. Box 56, Tafton, Pa. 18464. (717) 226-9500. Rte. 390 at Lake Wallenpaupack.

TIMBER HILL: Open daily and nightly. Lifts: 2-T, 1-P. Vertical drop: 450 feet. Snow making. Ski school. Rentals. Basic weekend fee: $9-A, $7-J. Canadensis, Pa. 18325. (717) 595-7475. On Rt. 447, 10 miles N. of East Stroudsburg, 5 miles South of Canadensis.

THE TREXLER-LEHIGH COUNTY GAME PRESERVE

Open daily Memorial Day weekend to Labor Day, 10 a.m.–6 p.m. Open May, Sept. and Oct. Sundays only 10 a.m. to dusk. Fees: Adults, $1.00; children, 50¢. Parking, $1.00. Rest rooms. Snacks. Picnics. Handicapped: Benches, paved walkways, some hills. Trexler Lehigh County Game Preserve, Rt. 1, Schnecksville, Pa. 18078. (215) 799-4171.

Would you like to pet a llama? Feed a fallow deer an ice cream cone, or watch a wild bobcat snarling at you through a glassed-in cage? All this and more awaits you on your visit to the Trexler-Lehigh County Game Preserve which was founded in 1909 by General Harry Trexler as a sanctuary for the preservation of various wildlife species.

There's an aura of an untamed wilderness in these steep and scenic hills above the town of Schnecksville. Palomino horses, buffalo, white-tailed deer and elk roam the pastures lining the curving road. The golden grass and sparse trees of the foothills provide a magnificent backdrop for the wild animals.

Set in the center of 1,500 acres of rolling countryside is a 28-acre fenced-in zoo where native and exotic animals from the world over are housed in small paddocks. You may wander through this area and observe the animals in their more-or-less natural habitat. Certain areas have been set aside for petting and feeding the animals. Ice cream cones and grain feed may be purchased on the grounds for this purpose. Goats, sheep, chickens, llamas, pigs, donkeys—all vie for your attention and food! Even the shy deer will come up to the fence for a treat, and the massive camels are a real sight to behold as they snuffle up the food with their enormous lips.

Near the entrance to the zoo is a Nature Study building which houses an interesting collection of stuffed birds and mounted butterflies. On weekends, conservation and nature films are shown here.

As you leave the preserve, you will ford a shallow stream. On either side of it are shaded picnic tables, providing the perfect place for a leisurely lunch. The children will enjoy wading in the water, skipping stones across its surface, and trying to capture the elusive minnows in their hands. Hiking, outdoor photography and bird watching are other activities enjoyed here.

Directions: Take Rt. 22 (I-78) to just west of Allentown. Take Rt. 309 north for 5.6 miles to Schnecksville. Turn left at the directional sign pointing to the Game Preserve. Drive 2 miles to the entrance on left.

Nearby Attractions: See Covered Bridge Tours-Lehigh County (this tour goes right by the Game Preserve), the Lil-Le-Hi Trout Hatchery which also is on the covered Bridge Tour, and Industrial Museums of the Lehigh Valley-Saylor Cement Industry.

WHITEWATER RAFTING ON THE LEHIGH RIVER

Whitewater rushes past huge boulders at the rate of 800 cubic feet per second. Inflated rafts, holding up to six people, bob up and down through the river's whirls and eddies. The air is alive with the sounds of splashing water, laughs, and screams as these adventurous souls maneuver their rafts around large boulders, down small waterfalls and over to the smooth surface of an eddy. They are embarked on an extraordinary adventure full of thrills and excitement, a whitewater rafting trip down the scenic Lehigh River.

Although the Lehigh is not as challenging as the notorious Snake River, it is no quiet mountain stream. All who wish to take a raft trip must wear a life jacket, know how to swim, and be over ten years old. Groups of rafts are guided down the river by professionals in a lead raft and by aides in two kayaks who paddle upstream and down, marking the current and riding shotgun. Beyond that, the rafters are on their own. All are given brief instructions in paddling and safety techniques, then launched on their downriver trip. Having a raft flip over is rare. Getting hung up on a rock is probable. Getting wet is inevitable!

The time of year in which the trip is taken is of some importance. Generally, before May 1st the water is cold, and a wet suit (which rents approximately $10 for a two piece, $5 for just the top), will be needed. The river is also higher at this time, and a trip will be faster and more exciting. For these spring (and fall) trips, wear a windbreaker over wool, wool ski hat, and fabric-lined kitchen gloves. Tennis shoes are required at all times, as well as a dry change of clothes. In the warmer months, T-shirts, shorts, bathing suits, cut-offs and windbreaker are appropriate. You will usually be asked to bring your own lunch, although some of the tours will pack one for you (check in advance). All other equipment, such as life jackets, paddles, rafts, and waterproof equipment are provided by the tour.

Whitewater Challengers: Rafting tours leave daily March 1–June 30, and mid-Sept. through mid-Nov. Trips also held on scheduled water release dates, 3rd Sat. of July and August. On weekends, trips offered for half-day down upper (12½ miles) or lower (18 miles) gorge of Lehigh River, or combination of the two (a two day trip of 30 miles). Fees: Half-day trip, $24-weekday; $28, Saturday. Group discounts. Reservations required. Whitewater Challengers, Star Route 6A1, White Haven, Pa. 18661. (717) 443-9532.

Directions: White Haven is located on Rt. 437 just north of its intersection with I80 West (Exit 35 of Pennsylvania Turnpike).

Nearby Attractions: See Eckley Miner's Village.

The Pocono Whitewater Rafting Center: Tours leave daily March 1–June 30, and mid-Sept. through mid-Nov. Trips also held on scheduled water release dates, 3rd Sat. of July and August. Offers day-long trips through southern Lehigh River Gorge ending at Jim Thorpe. Fees: $24.00 weekday; $28.00 Saturday. Reservations required. Pocono Whitewater Rafting Center, Rt. 903 (Box 44), Jim Thorpe, Pa. 18229. (717) 325-4097.

Directions: Jim Thorpe is located on Rt. 209 South (Exit 34 of the Pennsylvania Turnpike).

Nearby Attractions: See Jim Thorpe.

Land of the Quakers— Bucks, Montgomery and Chester Counties

KEY TO MAP—AREA IV (*overleaf*)

A – Audubon Wildlife Sanctuary and Mill Grove

B – Brandywine Battlefield and Christian Sanderson Museum

C – Brandywine River Museum

D – Brinton 1704 House

E – Washington Crossing State Park and starting point for Bucks County Covered Bridge Tour

F – Bucks County Vineyards and Winery

G – Buckingham Valley Vineyard and Winery

H – Burpee's Fordhook Farm's August Garden Tour

I – Elmwood Park Zoo

J – Green Hills

K – Hillendale Museum

L – Historic Fallsington

M – Longwood Gardens

N – Mercer Mile

O – Morgan Log House

P – National Shrine of Our Lady of Czestochowa

Q – Nockamixon State Park

R – New Hope: Bucks Co. Playhouse, Parry Mansion, New Hope & Ivyland R.R., Mule-drawn Barge Rides

S – Newlin Mill Park

T – Peddler's Village

U – Peter Wentz Farmstead

V – Pennsbury

W – Pottsgrove

X – Sesame Place

Y – Swiss Pines

Z – Valley Forge Park

a – Buckingham Farmer's Market

b – Quakertown Farmer's Market

Area IV

Land of the Quakers— Bucks, Montgomery and Chester Counties

While other counties in Southeast Pennsylvania are predominantly Pennsylvania Dutch, the area around Philadelphia became a haven for the Quakers. William Penn settled in Bucks County and proceeded to divide his immense holdings among other Quakers in the area. Many of the immigrants came from England and the influence of the English Quakers is evident even today. As you drive through the region, you'll discover English-style manor houses alongside their more stolid Dutch counterparts, and Quaker Meeting houses supplementing the usual Lutheran Church.

Today the area is not only a Quaker stronghold, for the scenic rolling land with its streams, forests and fields has become famous as a center for the arts. New Hope has been an artist colony for years, attracting both the rich and famous. Chadds Ford has been immortalized by the works of the Brandywine River School of Art, including most notably those of the Wyeth Family. Valley Forge is famous for John James Audubon who once lived and worked here, while Pearl Buck made her final home in Bucks County. It is worthwhile to not only visit these attractions, but also to drive through the lovely countryside that inspired them.

AUDUBON WILDLIFE SANCTUARY AND MILL GROVE

Open daily Tues.–Sun., 10–5 p.m. Closed Mondays except legal holidays. Closed New Year's, Thanksgiving and Christmas. No admission fee. Rest rooms. Hiking trails. Curator, Audubon Wildlife Sanctuary, Audubon, Pa. 19407. (717) 666-5593.

Along the wooded banks of Perkiomen Creek stands Mill Grove, the stately stone mansion that was John James Audubon's first home in America. The mansion is surrounded by the woods and fields in which the noted naturalist hunted, observed, collected and sketched the local wildlife. Although only a young man when he lived here, Audubon experienced in his two years at Mill Grove the early stirrings of what would become an overwhelming fascination for the natural world, a fascination which would eventually lead him to become one of the foremost naturalists of his time. During his life (1785–1851), Audubon became famous for his accurate portrayals of nature. A quality of aliveness became a trademark of his work, and each subject was depicted in a realistic setting. One of his best known accomplishments is his *Birds of America,* paintings of North American birds which are remarkable in their lifelike color and style.

In 1951, Mill Grove and its accompanying sanctuary were purchased by Montgomery County and subsequently opened to the public. Six miles of wooded trails wind through the sanctuary and along the banks of the Perkiomen Creek. Many species of birds may be viewed eating at the various feeding stations and nesting among the shrubs and trees. Trail maps available at the mansion guide visitors uphill and down, over wooden bridges, down to the old Ecton Copper Mine where the mine dumps and chimney may still be seen, and along old logging roads. Hiking these scenic trails provides a sense of the natural beauty which inspired Audubon.

Mill Grove is also open to the public for self-guided tours during the daytime. Original Audubon prints line the walls, and in one room the magnificent engraved elephant folio of *Birds of America* is on display. Throughout the home, murals painted by noted artist George M. Harding depict the story of Audubon's life and studies. Stuffed specimens of squirrels, birds and other mammals are displayed and the attic has been restored as a studio and taxidermy room, re-creating Audubon's working quarters while he lived here. Some rooms are completely furnished in the style of the early 19th century, while others serve as display areas for interesting collections of arrowheads, Audubon's mementos, birds' eggs, and lovely china birds and animals.

Directions: Audubon is located two miles from Valley Forge. From Exit 24 of the East-West Extension of the Pa. Turnpike, follow Route 363 North (which becomes Trooper Road) to Audubon Road. Turn left onto Audubon Road and follow this to the entrance of the sanctuary.

Nearby Attractions: See Valley Forge, The Elmwood Park Zoo, and Swiss Pines.

BRANDYWINE BATTLEFIELD PARK

Park and Visitors Center open daily year round except certain holidays. Park— 9:00 a.m. to dusk; Visitors Center—9:00 a.m. (noon on Sundays) to 4:30 p.m. Historic buildings open daily June through September from 9:00 a.m. (noon on Sundays) to 5:00 p.m., weekends only October through May. Free admission. Picnic areas. Rest rooms. Gift shop in Visitors Center. Visitors Center easily accessible to handicapped but not historic buildings. Brandywine Battlefield State Park, P.O. Box 202, Chadds Ford, Pa. 19317. (215) 459-3342.

Don't be surprised if you're in the Brandywine area some September 11th and see British cavalry charging up a hill or George Washington posing majestically. It's just the annual reenactment by the local historical society of the confrontation that took place in 1777 at Brandywine Battlefield Park, one of the few battlefield memorials commemorating a partial defeat. The Brandywine Battle was the culmination of British General Howe's attempt to divide the colonies and trap the Continental Congress in Philadelphia. During the summer of 1777, Howe sailed his army of 15,000 men from New York to Head of the Elk, Maryland and then marched northward, taking the Revolutionary War onto Pennsylvania soil for the first time. The 14,000-man American Army under General Washington had marched south in anticipation of Howe's seaward movement and had dug in on the east side of Brandywine Creek near Chadds Ford. Unfortunately, Washington was plagued during the battle itself with faulty intelligence reports and allowed the main component of the British force to outflank him and force the Continental Army to retreat back to Chester. Nevertheless, the Americans had fought hard and well and prevented Howe from achieving his ultimate objective—total defeat of the Continental Army and cause.

The rolling 50-acre Brandywine Battlefield Park includes a modern Visitor's Center, the Quaker farmhouses used as headquarters by Washington and General Lafayette, and various areas set aside for picnics and general recreation. The Visitor's Center features a 20-minute slide-tape on the background and strategy of the battle as well as dioramas and exhibits showing scenes and artifacts from the battle and the surrounding Quaker countryside in which it took place. The headquarters used by General Lafayette is the restored and authentically-furnished Quaker farmhouse of Gideon Gilpin, originally built in 1698. It's rumored that Lafayette treated his wound from the battle under the 1650 Sycamore tree which shades the house. Surrounding the house is a variety of outbuildings including a bakehouse, roothouse, barn, carriage house, and shed holding a real Conestoga wagon.

The three-story farmhouse used by General Washington had burned down and was rebuilt by the State in 1949. It is also authentically furnished. On weekends, volunteers can often be seen weaving on the various-sized looms found on the top floor of the house. Be sure to peer in the icehouse at the rear of the main house, where a wax Hessian soldier is still trapped as prisoner. Christian Sanderson, a local historian who provided much of the impetus for making Brandywine a battlefield monument, lived in the original Washington Headquarters house from 1906 to 1922.

Directions: The Battlefield is located southwest of Philadelphia on Rt. 1 about 1 mile west of the intersection of Rts. 202 & 1 near Chadds Ford, Pa.

Nearby Attractions: See Christian Sanderson Museum, The Brinton 1704 House, The Brandywine River Museum, Longwood Gardens, Newlin Mill Park, and Hillendale Museum.

THE BRANDYWINE RIVER MUSEUM

Museum open daily except Christmas from 9:30 to 4:30 p.m. Fees: Adults, $1.75; children 6–12, $1.00. Guided tours by reservation. Rest room. Gift shop. Brandywine River Museum, Chadds Ford, Pa. 19317. (215) 459-1900.

John Chadd House open June–August, 12–5 p.m. Fees: Adults, $1.00; children under 12, 50¢.

Along the treelined banks of the Brandywine River stands a lovely, centuries-old grist mill. Its charm carefully preserved, this mill has been restored and converted into a modern museum with a dramatic tower of glass and brick. Inside are galleries with hand-hewn beams, pine floors, and white-plastered walls; a fitting backdrop for the paintings displayed. This museum is the showcase of the Brandywine Conservancy, which is dedicated to housing and preserving for the years to come the art and illustrations emanating from the Brandywine School of Art. This school had its beginnings in the summer of 1897 when Howard Pyle, the famous book illustrator, taught a course in illustration at Drexel University in Philadelphia. The course, which proved to be a great success, was expanded, and by 1900 Pyle brought his most gifted students to Brandywine to form an outstanding group of artists.

On the walls of the grist mill hang paintings by Andrew Wyeth, his father, N. C. Wyeth, his son James, and other members of the talented family. Book lovers in particular will enjoy viewing the colorful illustrations N. C. Wyeth produced for such classics as *Treasure Island, Kidnapped,* and *The Black Arrow.* Other famous artists of the region include Maxfield Parrish, Howard Pyle and Harvey Dunn. Their works are well represented within the museum. Some fascinating items in the history of illustration, such as old covers from *Harper's Magazine* and *The Saturday Evening Post,* are also displayed. Throughout the year a rotating special collection is featured.

If you have the time, take a hike along the Brandywine River Trail, which starts in back of the museum and continues for a mile along the banks of the river. It is a lovely well-marked trail over elevated walkways and through marshland and swamps to the restored Chadd House. This stone building, erected in 1726, was the home of John Chadd, a farmer, ferryman, and Tavern Keeper for whom Chadds Ford was named. The adjacent two-story springhouse was a one-room school house in the nineteenth century.

Directions: The Museum is located along U.S. Rt. 1, 28 miles from Philadelphia, in Chadds Ford, Pa.

Nearby Attractions: See Brandywine Battlefield, Brinton 1704 House, The Christian-Sanderson Museum, Longwood Gardens, Hillendale Museum and Newlin Mill Park.

THE BRINTON 1704 HOUSE

Open May–Oct. 31, Tues., Thurs., and Sat., 1–4 p.m. Closed holidays. Groups by appointment only. Fees: Adults, $1.00. Rest room. The Brinton Family Association, Inc., R.D. 5, Oakland Rd., West Chester, Pa. 19380. (215) 692-4800.

As you approach the Brinton 1704 House from the treelined gravel driveway, it's almost as if you are taken back in time and place to Medieval England. Leaded casement windows, a steeply-pitched wood-shingled roof covering a narrow stone building one room deep, and a small adjacent herb garden—all seem reminiscent of an earlier age. Indeed they are, for when William Brinton Jr., the son of an English Quaker who immigrated to the U.S., built this house in 1704, he based its construction on his recollections of medieval English architecture. The front door leads into a fairly large room known as the "hall." Adjacent to this is a downstairs guest parlor and bedroom. There are three upstairs bedrooms and a large kitchen in the basement. Throughout the house, doors are situated opposite doors, windows opposite windows, a style typical of an English manor house. Closets are found in all the bedrooms—an anomaly to this time period, for none of the German homes built in the 18th century contain such "luxuries." The house's interior walls are covered with either whitewashed plaster or wood, reflecting the simplicity and quiet elegance of an educated Quaker family.

When William Brinton died in 1751, detailed inventories of the house's furnishings were taken. These provided his descendants with an authentic basis upon which to furnish the restored house. The Brinton Family Association has travelled extensively to locate antiques which accurately fit the inventories, and most of the rooms are furnished as they were in the 1700's. What is especially interesting is the downstairs kitchen and dining area. The long wood table is set with bone-handled knives and wooden trenchers (plates). The children have their own small table set with pewter ware. In a large open-fronted dresser are displays of pewter and pottery donated by members of the Brinton family. A dough table with wooden butter-washing bowl stands in a corner, while opposite it is the large walk-in fireplace which features an unusual beehive oven that is completely contained within the house walls.

Directions: The house is located near the Kennett Square area of Pa. If coming from Kennett Square, take Rt. 1 north to Rt. 100. Go north on Rt. 100 to Brinton Bridge Road and turn right. Follow this to Dilworthtown and at the main intersection turn right onto Oakland. The house will appear shortly on your left.

Nearby Attractions: See The Christian Sanderson Museum, Brandywine Battlefield, The Brandywine River Museum, Newlin Mill Park, Longwood Gardens, and Hillendale Museum. If you have time, there is a charming old country store in Dilworthtown at the main intersection. It features an old-time counter with antique cash register and numerous handicrafts attractively displayed throughout its three rooms.

THE BUCKS COUNTY COVERED BRIDGE TOUR

(A full description of covered bridges may be had by reading Covered Bridge Tours-Lehigh County write-up.)

For detailed map and brochure, write the Bucks County Historical Tourist Commission, One Oxford Valley, Langhorne, Pa. 19047. (215) 752-2203.

Of the 36 bridges that were built in Bucks County, only 13 now remain. These were all built with a lattice-type construction developed in 1820 by a New Englander, Ithiel Town. There are no arches or beams in these bridges, but rather an overlapping series of triangles that could support a bridge of up to 200 feet in length. If you have time, examine one of these bridges up close. The unusual criss-crossing of woodwork held together with pegs is fascinating to see.

The tour itself meanders through the resplendent Bucks County countryside, which is famous for its homes and farms of the wealthy. You'll see unusual houses made from converted barns, fieldstone mansions, old farm houses, neat pastures bordered by white fences and filled with blue-blooded thoroughbreds, and quaint towns. The tour is a long one and covers most of the county. You may want to cut it in half by visiting bridges 1–6 and then returning to New Hope or Washington Crossing by taking the scenic River Road (Rt. 32) south. One word of caution: some of the road signs may be down. If so, the distances given in the tour are fairly accurate and should enable you to find the correct turn.

The ideal spot to commence the tour is at the Memorial Building at Washington Crossing State Park (located on Route 32 south of New Hope and north of Yardly). From here proceed north on Rt. 32 for 4.4

miles to Lurgan Road. Turn left and go 1.5 miles to Van Sant Rd.
Turn right and go 0.6 miles to:

1. Van Sant Bridge which was built in 1875 and is 86 feet long. It is
   near Bowman's Hill and was often called Beaver Dam Bridge. It
   crosses Pidcock Creek.

After crossing the bridge, continue for one mile to Aquetong Road. Turn
left and go for 5 miles to Upper York Road. Turn right and then take an
immediate left and go 2.8 miles to Carversville (a lovely village which has
been included in the National Register of Historic Places). At the center of
the village turn left, go for one block, then turn right onto Pipersville Road
(which becomes Wismer Road, then Carversville Road). Go 4.6 miles to:

2. Loux Bridge, which is 60 feet long, making it the second shortest
   in the county. It is built of hemlock and presents a lovely picture
   with its adjacent waterfall and farmhouse.

Continue through the bridge and for 0.5 miles to a dead end. Turn right
onto Dark Hollow Road and go 1 mile to Covered Bridge Road. Turn right
and go 0.6 miles to:

3. Cabin Run Bridge which crosses Cabin Run Creek and was built
   in 1871 by David Sutton. It is 82 feet long.

After seeing the bridge, turn around, return to Dark Hollow Road and
continue straight ahead. On the right you will see Stover-Myers Mill which
was built in 1871, and the nearby John Stover House. Both are restored and
open to the public June through August. Continue on Dark Hollow Road for
3.2 miles, then turn left on Cafferty Road (if the sign is missing, there is a
B.F. Goodrich sign on one corner, and a sign to the airport on the other). Go
for 0.8 miles to:

4. Frankenfield Bridge, which is 130 feet long and crosses Tinicum
   Creek two miles upstream from where the creek empties into the
   Delaware River.

Continue for 0.2 miles to Hollow Horn Road, turn right, and go 1.3 miles
to Headquarters Road. Turn right, then go 0.9 miles to Geigel Hill Road. Turn
left and go 0.2 miles to:

5. Erwinna Bridge, which crosses Lodi Creek and is the shortest covered bridge, being only 56 feet long. Built in 1832, it is a good
   example of lattice-type construction.

Turn around and return to Geigel Hill Road 0.4 miles to River Road (Rt.
32). Go for 1.7 miles on River Road, then turn left on Uhlerstown Road. Go
0.3 miles to:

6. Uhlerstown Bridge, which was built of oak in 1832. It is the only covered bridge which crosses the Delaware Division of the Pennsylvania Canal, which parallels the Delaware River. A unique aspect to this bridge is the windows in it, which afford the traveler a view of the scenery.

Return to River Road, turn left and go 8.0 miles to Rt. 611. Go north on 611 for 1.8 miles, then turn left on Rt. 212 and go 3.5 miles to Haupt's Bridge Road. Turn right for 0.7 miles to:

7. Haupt's Bridge, which spans Durham Creek near the Durham Furnace. It was built in 1872 and is sometimes known as Witte's Bridge.

Return to Rt. 212, turn right and go 4.0 miles to Slifer Valley Road. Turn left and go 1.3 miles to:

8. Knecht's Bridge, which was built of hemlock in 1873 and measures 110 feet long.

Return to Rt. 212, turn left and go through Pleasant Valley for 1.1 miles. Then, bear left on Old Bethlehem Road and go 5.6 miles to Mountain View Rd. Turn right, go 1.4 miles to Sterner Mill Road. Turn right, then take the next immediate right and go one mile to Covered Bridge Road. Turn right and go 0.5 miles to:

9. Sheard's Mill Bridge which is 130 feet long, was built in 1873, and crosses Tohickon Creek at the mill near Thatcher. It is often referred to as Thatcher's Bridge.

Return to Mountain View Road, turn right, and go 0.9 miles to Rt. 313. Turn left, go 1.7 miles, turn right at the Texaco Station and go 1.8 miles on 5th St. to Blooming Glen Rd. Turn left to:

10. Mood's Bridge which was built in 1872, rebuilt in 1962, and crosses the northeast branch of the Perkiomen Creek. The bridge is 120 feet long.

Return to 5th Street, turn left, and go 1.4 miles to Walnut Street. Turn left and go 2 blocks to Lenape Park to:

11. South Perkasie Bridge, which is the only bridge on the tour that does not cross water. It used to span the Pleasant Spring Creek, but was condemned a number of years ago. Due to the efforts of the Perkasie Historical Society, the bridge was moved to the park and has been preserved for posterity. Here you can walk through the bridge and see up close the detailed work involved in its construction. The bridge was built of oak and pine and is 93 feet long.

Return to 5th Street, turn right, and go 3.2 miles to Rt. 313. Turn right and go 6.9 miles, then turn right on Ferry Road at the Fountainville traffic light. Go 3.2 miles on Ferry Road, then turn left on Old Iron Hill Rd. Go 0.5 miles to:

12. Pine Valley Bridge, which is 81 feet long, built in 1842 of white pine and hemlock, and crosses the Pine Run Creek.

Cross the bridge and go 5 miles to Rt. 202. At the stop sign turn left and continue on Rt. 202 for 6.8 miles to Rt. 413. Turn right and go 5.2 miles, then bear right on Rt. 232 South. Go 1.9 miles, then turn left on Swamp Road. Go 1.9 miles to a small road on the right. Park in the designated area and walk the path leading you to:

13. Schofield Ford Bridge which is the county's longest bridge, measuring 150 feet in length. It is located within Tyler State Park and crosses the Neshaminy Creek.

Return to Swamp Road and continue for 1.6 miles to Rt. 413. Turn left and go 0.9 miles, then turn left on Rt. 532. Go 5.8 miles to Washington Crossing State Park, then turn left on Rt. 32 North and return to the starting point.

Nearby Attractions: See Washington Crossing State Park, New Hope and its attractions, Bucks County Wineries, and Peddler's Village.

BUCKS COUNTY WINERIES

BUCKS COUNTRY VINEYARDS AND WINERY

Open all year: Mon.–Fri., 11–5 p.m.; Sat. & Hol., 10–6 p.m.; Sun., 12–6 p.m. Fees: No fees on weekdays. Weekends and holidays: Adults, $1.00; under 21, free. Reservations required for large groups. Wine and cheese parties may be arranged. Wine and gift shop. Museum. Group Manager, Bucks County Vineyards and Winery, Rt. 202, R.D. 1, New Hope, Pa. 18938. (215) 794-7449.

The art of wine making is something usually associated with those fine wineries in Europe and on the west coast of the United States. This may have been true in the past, but not today. Experienced wine makers have come to the east coast, and in such states as New York and Pennsylvania, successfully grown and harvested white and red grapes to produce a variety of wines. At Arthur Gerold's Bucks County Winery, (which stocks fifteen varieties of wine), a portion of the wine-making process may be observed. Well-informed guides give 15-

to 30-minute tours of the wine cellars, and bottling and aging rooms, all the while describing the processing procedure from grape to table. Following the tour, four varieties of wine may be sampled in the upstairs wine tasting room. A Wine Museum housed on the third floor of the building provides additional information and exhibits on this fine art.

While visiting the Winery, be sure to see the Fashion Museum housed on the third floor. It is fascinating. Mr. Gerold is President of the Brooks-Van Horn Costume Co. in New York, one of the oldest and largest theatrical costumers in the world. On display here is a portion of his personal collection of the original costumes of many Broadway stars, such as: Marlon Brando's suit from The Godfather, Mary Martin's Peter Pan outfit, and Richard Burton's magnificent King Arthur costume.

Directions: The winery is located three miles west of New Hope and 1½ miles east of Peddlar's Village on Route 202.

Nearby Attractions: See Peddlar's Village, New Hope, New Hope Mule Barge Rides, New Hope-Ivyland Railroad, Washington Crossing State Park, and Bucks County Covered Bridge Tour.

BUCKINGHAM VALLEY VINEYARD AND WINERY

Open all year: Weekdays, 12–7 p.m.; Sat., 10–6 p.m.; Sun., 12–4 p.m. Closed Mondays. No fees. Wine shop. Buckingham Valley Vineyard and Winery, Rt. 413, Buckingham, Pa. (215) 794-7188.

A small family-owned enterprise, this winery produces Bucks County wines made from their 14 acres of French-American vines. Using traditional old world methods tempered by present-day knowledge, these wines are produced on the premises, then aged (the reds for up to three years in oak casks) and bottled by hand upon reaching maturity.

Self-guided tours of this small winery may be taken. You are invited to browse through the vineyards and wine cellars, then sample a variety of wines in the upstairs shop.

Directions: The Winery is located on Rt. 413, a few miles south of the juncture of Rts. 413 and 202 at the town of Buckingham.

Nearby Attractions: See Peddlar's Village, New Hope, New Hope-Ivyland Railroad, and New Hope Mule Barge Rides.

BURPEE'S FORDHOOK FARMS AUGUST GARDEN TOUR

Tours provided during select days in August. Consult current Burpee Catalog or write for dates. No admission fees. Rest rooms. Gift shop. Museum. W. Atlee Burpee Co., 300 Park Ave., Warminster, Pa. 18974.

Did you ever wonder what an "All America" variety is, or how a hybrid plant, such as the Big Boy Tomato is produced? Well, here is your chance to find out! For a few select days in August, the Burpee Seed Company opens up its Fordhook Farms to the public. This farm is an outdoor laboratory where Burpee annually tests seeds and conducts experimental research in the breeding and growing of over 2,000 samples of fruits and vegetables.

A tour of this working farm lasts 45 minutes and is conducted by guides well versed in Burpee garden lore. The tour includes the Annual Flower Garden, a colorful display of flowers and ornamental vegetables, which, for the most part, are not yet on the market; The All America Garden, a competition among seed companies, independent plant breeders and horticultural research departments to search out and encourage new varieties of established plants; the Lathe House in which new varieties which grow in partial shade are planted; an experimental field of cultivated wildflowers; trial fields of marigolds and geraniums; and the Show Garden of Vegetables. In the popular Show Garden, the famous Burpee varieties are combined with good gardening techniques to produce a showcase of gardening expertise. The twelve sample gardens provide many exciting ideas for a successful and productive vegetable garden of your own.

Fordhook Farms has been in operation since 1888, and plays an important part in deciding which seeds and plants Burpee will make available to the public. It's fascinating to see the failures, as well as successes like the famous Burpee white marigold. In addition to the gardens, the farm also contains a small museum housing old pictures and equipment from Burpee's past, and a store which sells gardening supplies.

Directions: The farm is located near Doylestown, ¼ mile south of the juncture of Rts. 202 and 611 on New Britain Road.

Nearby Attractions: See The Mercer Mile, Green Hills, and The National Shrine of Our Lady of Czestochowa.

CHRISTIAN SANDERSON MUSEUM

Open year round Saturdays and Sundays plus Memorial Day, July 4th, Labor Day, and September 11th (Brandywine Battle Reenactment) from 1–5 p.m. No admission charge but donation requested. Rest room and gift counter. The Christian C. Sanderson Museum, Chadds Ford, Pa. 19317.

If you're in the Brandywine area on a weekend and have some time to spare, visit the Christian C. Sanderson Museum. Sanderson, who lived in the Chadds Ford environs from 1905–1966, was somewhat of a local legend. As a history teacher and buff, he was instrumental in convincing the State to declare the Brandywine Battlefield a memorial park. He was also a lecturer, fiddler, square dance instructor and caller, and most notably a pack rat who died poor but surely not forgotten. This is due to the efforts of his close friend and fellow fiddler Tom Thompson who followed through on Sanderson's request to have his biography written. Thompson was also instrumental in sorting through the wide-ranging collection of historical treasures, memorabilia, and just plain junk which Sanderson left in his seven-room house when he died. The house has now been converted into the Sanderson Museum and Thompson himself serves as one of the volunteers who escorts visitors through the attractively displayed collection.

The highlight of the collection is the paintings and other memorabilia of the Wyeth family, including Andrew Wyeth, who still lives about a mile north on Rt. 100. Sanderson was himself the subject of several Wyeth paintings, including portraits, "Sandy," "The Schoolmaster," and "Christmas Morn," based on the death of Sanderson's mother. These as well as pencil sketches, a local sign painted by W. C. Wyeth, an historical Chester County map on which Andrew Wyeth and Sanderson collaborated, and various photos showing the Wyeth's themselves are all on display at the museum. A second feature of the museum is the collection of battlefield artifacts that relate not only to Brandywine but also to the Civil War and more recent encounters. Next, there are the odds and ends revolving around Chris Sanderson's own life, ranging from his high chair and early Valentines to his fiddles, and autographs collected by establishing contacts with notable personalities throughout his 84-year-long life. Last but not least there's an eclectic assortment of Americana and truly unusual items such as magic lantern slides, a poster from the Lindbergh kidnapping, melted ice from the South Pole, and a jar of sawdust from revivalist Billy Sunday's "Sawdust Trail."

Directions: Take Pa. Turnpike 276W to Rt. 100 (Exit 23) and follow south towards U.S. Rt. 1. The Museum is 100 yards to the north of this intersection. If coming west on Rt. 1, go about 1 mile past the Brandywine Battlefield entrance and turn right on Rt. 100 for 100 yards to the Museum.

Nearby Attractions: See Brandywine Battlefield, The Brandywine River Museum, The Brinton 1704 House, Longwood Gardens, Newlin Mill Park, and Hillendale Museum.

THE ELMWOOD PARK ZOO

Open daily 10–4:30 p.m., closed Mondays. Outdoor areas and Children's Petting Zoo open in late spring. No admission fees, but donations accepted. Rest rooms. Picnics. Snacks. Zoo Curator, (215) 272-8089.

"Mommy, this flamingo has pink knees! And look at those ponies, they're rolling in the mud!" Children laugh, comment and marvel at the animals and their antics at this charming small zoo in the Valley Forge area. A visit to Elmwood Park provides a nice break for the children from historical monuments and battlefields. Here they can run down paths and see their favorite animals housed in cages and paddocks. One large building houses an assortment of birds, reptiles, monkeys and lions. The Macaques, Baboons, Gibbons and White–Faced Capuchins are guaranteed to delight young and old with their constant activity. The two lions, Caesar and Elsa, lie languorously in the sun while onlookers "ooh" and "ahh" over their massive size and sharp teeth. Corn Snakes, Boas, Pythons and other members of the snake family lie curled in their glassed-in habitats, ogled by the curious.

Beyond the buildings lie two outdoor areas, The Children's Zoo and Zoo America, 1776. A large paddock filled with baby sheep, goats, and other friendly animals provides children with the opportunity to get close to the animals and pet them. Nearby this paddock, wooden steps and a long bridge lead through what is considered the highlight of the park, Zoo America 1776. This unique look at animals in their environment at the time of the American Revolution is a project of the Norristown Zoological Society and was constructed by students of the Montgomery County Technical School. Zoo America is broken up into geographical areas of the United States, with each featuring animals common to it in 1776. Wooden plaques along the fence explain the history of the times and the important part these animals played. In the "Wild West" you'll see the bison grazing next to an adobe hut; in New England, there are elk wandering around the typical New England Salt Box; in the South, you'll see a stockade house surrounded by a small herd of Chincoteague Ponies; and in the Central States, the invaluable white-tailed deer. Also included in this display is a prairie dog town and a paddock full of donkeys.

Directions: The zoo is located in Norristown, Pa. about 10 miles east of Valley Forge. From the Pa. Turnpike (276W), take Rt. 422 towards Norristown. Turn left onto Rt. 202 South and follow this through Norristown. Just before you cross a large bridge, turn right onto M. Marshall Street (there are two gas stations, a Mobil and a Shell at this juncture). Follow M. Marshall for three lights, then turn right onto Stanbridge. At the next light, turn right onto W. Sterigere St. At the large yellow sign, bear left onto Harding Blvd. and follow this to the Zoo entrance.

Nearby Attractions: See Valley Forge, Peter Wentz Farmstead, and Audubon Wildlife Sanctuary.

GREEN HILLS: HOME OF PEARL BUCK

Tours conducted year round (except legal holidays), Mon.–Fri., at 10:30 a.m. and 2 p.m. Reservations required for large groups. Fees: Adults, $2.00; children, $1.00. Rest rooms. Gift shop. Picnics. Green Hills Farm, 520 Dublin Road, Perkasie, Pa. 18944. (215) 249-0100 or CH2-6779.

She lies buried under the lovely ash tree on the grounds, surrounded by acres of rolling farmland. In her lifetime, she won both the Nobel and Pulitzer prizes, the only woman to have ever done so. She wrote over a hundred novels, children's books, non-fiction works and countless magazine articles. She was an outstanding humanitarian, concerned with developing a greater understanding between the world's races. In 1964, she created a Foundation to aid in the care of half-American children left in Asia by American GI's. She was a remarkable woman who bequeathed her home of 35 years, Green Hills, to this Foundation, with the hope that proceeds from it and the sales of her books would further her humanitarian efforts. It is fitting that she rest here, for the spirit of Pearl Buck lives on in the work of the foundation (which is housed in the large red barn at Green Hills), and in the large fieldstone house which contains her furniture, books, memorabilia, and all those material things that accompanied her through her long and interesting life.

Within the sturdy walls of the 1835 stone farmhouse, the eclectic taste of a woman who was able to bridge the civilizations of East and West is displayed. An oriental influence highlights a charming blend of Early American and European furnishings. Having spent many years in China (her parents were missionaries there), Miss Buck acquired such handsome pieces as hand-carved Asian tables, Chen Chi watercolors, Chinese chairs with stone pictures in the backs, and the famous desk on which she wrote her well-known book, *The Good Earth.* Oriental rugs lie on polished wide-plank wooden floors, and a carved Korean chess set graces an unusual antique table flanked by two English court chairs. Pennsylvania antiques such as a library table and money chest go hand in hand with English pewter plates, Egyptian trays, and hand-carved Indian ivory lamps.

In the midst of all these treasures are more personal items that reflect the personality and life of this exceptional woman. In a bedroom are hung the countless humanitarian and literary awards she received. Pictures of her ten children (of whom seven were adopted, two were foster children, and one her child by birth), and her husband, Mr. Walsh, grace the walls and furniture of the master bedroom. In the two libraries, her literary tastes as well as her husband's are quite evident, with one entire room dedicated to rare books and first editions. And, in the secluded wing of the house, where she did the majority of her writing, hangs the 200-year-old Chinese saying which was a favorite of hers, "All under Heaven are one . . ."

A guided tour of Green Hills can last up to two hours. The house (which was declared a National Historic Landmark in 1980), is large, interesting, and full of stories. On some days, Florence, Miss Buck's housekeeper for almost twenty years, conducts these tours.

Directions: Green Hills is near the small town of Dublin (not far from Doylestown). Take Route 313 to the town of Dublin. Go west onto Dublin Road (there's a Dairy Queen on the corner). At the fork in the road bear right onto Maple Ave. Go for one mile, cross over the bridge, and the driveway will be on your right.

Nearby Attractions: See The Mercer Mile, Lake Nockamixon, and The National Shrine of Our Lady of Czestochowa.

THE HILLENDALE MUSEUM

Open year round Mon.–Sat., visits to start anytime between 9:30 a.m. and 1:30 p.m. Reservations recommended. Fees: Adults, $3.00; children 12–18, $1.50. Children must have completed 6th grade to be admitted and those under 16 must be accompanied by an adult. Rest rooms. Handicapped: Contact the Public Services Supervisor, ramp access through rear door for wheel chairs. Hillendale Museum, Hillendale Rd., Mendenhall, Pa. 19357. (215) 388-7393.

In 1492, when Christopher Columbus sailed in search of a northwest passage to Asia, the entire continent of North America was an unknown entity. Explorations were filled with excitement, mystery and danger. Who knew what lay beyond the horizon? Would it be endless stretches of ocean opening a more direct route to Asia's profitable markets, or inhospitable lands with hostile natives and impenetrable coastlines? Would they encounter fierce tropical storms with tidal waves, or a frigid sea of treacherous icebergs? You can share in the unraveling of this exciting mystery by taking a two-hour walk through 400 years of North American history at the Hillendale Museum.

Through dim and silent aisles of time you are guided by a cassette player past exhibits placed in chronological order like dates on a Time Line. By way of dioramas and paintings you relive the lives of famous explorers as they discover sections of the "mysterious unknown"— North America. You see Cortez in Mexico ordering his men to burn their boats so that they would be forced to explore inland for the elusive Northwest passage. You are with Joliet and Marquette as they discover there is no Northwest passage south of the Missouri, and you travel with Lewis and Clark as they become the first Americans to cross the Continental Divide.

Your trip with the explorers is broken up into four sections: Spanish Exploration, French Exploration, English Exploration, and American Exploration. At the end of each section is a lounge decorated in the style of the period in which you can rest and review what you have seen.

The major emphasis on this tour through time and terrain is the impact geographical features had upon the discovery and exploration of North America. Mountains, rivers, and accessible coastlines figured strongly in determining which areas were discovered first and by whom. The British, primarily land-oriented, didn't explore westward for years, their progress impeded by the Appalachian Mountains. The French, on the other hand, used the rivers as highways into the unknown and discovered large areas in Canada.

The tour places historical fact into a geographical perspective, creating a new dimension in historical education. Throughout the tour, there are sections of the globe displayed which depict the progressive westward expansion of the then-known world. To cap off the exhibit there is a magnificent twenty-eight- by thirty-nine-foot terrain model of North America.

For those who wish to explore this field in greater depth, there is a Major Waterways of the United States tour available at the museum which lasts for one hour and describes the influence major rivers, bays, lakes and harbors played in the development of the United States.

Directions: The museum is located southwest of Philadelphia near the Delaware Border. From Philadelphia, take Route 1 South to Route 52 South. Follow 52 for approximately one mile, then turn left onto Hillendale Rd. The museum will appear on your right.

Nearby Attractions: See Longwood Gardens, Brandywine Battlefield, Brandywine River Museum, Christian Sanderson Museum, and Brinton 1704 House. For a quick lunch, stop at Phillips Mushroom Place on Route One at Kennett Square, the Mushroom Capital of Pennsylvania. You can get mushroom delicacies here (mostly sandwich fare) and browse through the small mushroom museum and gift shop.

HISTORIC FALLSINGTON

Open March 15–Nov. 15, Weds.–Sun., 1–5 p.m. Closed Mondays unless holiday. Last tour starts at 4 p.m. Large groups need reservations. Fees: Adults, $2.00; students 12–18, $1.00; children 6–12, 50¢. Rest rooms. Gift shop. Historic Fallsington, 4 Yardly Ave., Fallsington, Pa. 19054. (215) 295-6567.

In the midst of the bustling traffic of U.S. Rt. 1 and the surrounding sprawl of suburbia, there is an historical oasis, a quaint little village in which two dozen 18th century houses still survive. As you enter Fallsington and see the three Quaker Meeting houses facing on Meetinghouse Square, you're immediately enveloped by a tranquility reminiscent of days gone by. The large gambrel–roof Meeting house dates from 1728 and faces the other two, which were built later to accommodate a growing congregation. Around the square are clustered fieldstone and frame houses—a picturesque scene from the past when

William Penn would come here to worship, a time when farmers, blacksmiths, artisans and others formed an integral part of a thriving community.

From their headquarters in Gillingham Store, hostesses from Historic Fallsington Inc. give one- to one-and-a-quarter-hour guided tours through three buildings near Meetinghouse Square, and describe others of historical interest. The Burges-Lippincott House, with its original portion being built in 1685, is a fine example of colonial architecture. The handsome doorway with glass fan above, the carved mantlepiece and catty-cornered fireplaces have all been carefully preserved. Each room is decorated with period furnishings, some of which are quite unusual. The Stagecoach Tavern, which operated as a stage stop between Philadelphia and New York from the 1790's until the 1920's has been restored and furnished. The Tavern Room with its card table, clay pipe holder, and pewterware displayed on a simple wood table served the needs of the men, while the Ladies Parlor, decorated in a more subdued style, with old books rather than card playing providing the entertainment, catered to the "gentler sex." Upstairs, where the travelers once slept, is an interesting collection of fashions and quilts dating from 1810 to 1940. The third structure, the Moon-Williamson House, is said to be the oldest log house standing in its original place in Pennsylvania. Built in 1685 of entire logs split down the middle, the house was put together without nails. At a later period, an English cottage was added to the back of the house. Primitive furnishings such as deerskin rugs, rope beds with straw mattresses, and a settle table which converts to a bench, reflect the simple life of the early pioneers, most probably Swedish, who first settled here.

A brief slide presentation augments information gleaned from the tour and provides an overall look at this curious village. After the guided tour, you may want to take a walk through the town. There are many old homes restored and occupied by local residents. If you can come on the second Saturday of October, which has been declared Fallsington Day, many of these private homes are open to the public. Craft demonstrations and sales are also held at this time.

Directions: Fallsington is located three miles South of Trenton, N.J. and five miles from Pennsbury Manor. From Pa. Turnpike Exit 29, go north on Route 13 for five miles, then follow the historical markers to the town which lies just south of the junction of Rts. U.S. 1 and 13.

Nearby Attractions: See Pennsbury and Sesame Place.

LONGWOOD GARDENS

Gardens open daily: Conservatories, 10–5; outdoor areas, 9–6 (9–5 from Nov. 1–March 31st). Fees: Adults, $3.00; children 6–14, $1.00. Rest rooms. Gift shop. Picnic areas nearby but not at gardens. Handicapped: Most areas accessible to wheel chairs. Seasonal programs including an Open Air Theatre during the summer. Longwood Gardens, Kennett Square, Pa. 19348. (215) 388-6741.

Walkways lined with trees and blossoms, cascading fountains, fields of wildflowers—you may think you're in paradise as tensions and worries fade away. It's a 300-acre country estate garden which was dedicated to the public in 1908 by the late Pierre Samuel du Pont and named Longwood Gardens. There are formal gardens with bulbs blooming from spring through fall, a topiary garden with elaborately-shaped bushes, and a lake area reminiscent of English estate gardens. You may just want to sit on a bench and watch water surge from the fountains or down the water staircase at the Italian Water Garden. If you need suggestions for your own garden at home, get inspired by the vegetables, herbs, fruits and flowers grown at the Idea Garden. Climb the Chimes Tower that broadcasts short concerts three times a day and look from a dizzying height at the showering waters of a nearby falls. If you can be there at 9:15 on a Tuesday or Saturday evening from mid-June through August, you can witness a breathtaking half-hour display of brilliantly illuminated fountains.

When the wind blows cold, Longwood has another surprise—one available at other times of year, but especially appreciated when winter holds you in its icy grip. It's the Conservatories—nearly four acres of gardens under glass. They are filled year-round with fragrant blossoms and non-indigenous plants such as chocolate trees, air plants, and vanilla orchids. You can see hyacinths and daffodils blooming in January, chrysanthemums at Thanksgiving, and thousands of poinsettias with 50,000 colored lights at Christmas. Longwood truly has something for everyone!

While there, don't miss the tour of the Pierce-du Pont house which effectively combines elements from two fascinating periods in American history. The West Wing of the house is the old 1730 Quaker farmhouse of the Pierce family and it's decorated with antiques from the pre-revolutionary era (the opening skirmish of the Battle of Brandywine was fought on the Longwood grounds). The East Wing was added by du Pont and reflects the prestige and opulent trappings of one of America's leading industrial titans during the early 1900's. One example of this contrast is the West Wing's gaily painted hardwood floors, used instead of carpeting during the 1700's, and the mechanical rug rollers in the East Wing. You'll begin the tour in the open-air Conservatory which divides the two wings and peer up at towering banana stalks. From there on, you'll be escorted by gracious and well-informed guides through tastefully decorated rooms filled with unusual artifacts. The house tour runs every twenty minutes during peak times and the admission is $1.00. It is not recommended for children.

Directions: About 30 miles southwest of Philadelphia, located northeast of Kennett Square on U.S. Route 1.

Nearby Attractions: See Brandywine Battlefield, Brandywine River Museum, The Christian-Sanderson House, Brinton 1704 House, and Hillendale Museum. An interesting and quick lunch may be had at Phillip's Mushroom Place which features mushroom delicacies and a small museum.

THE MERCER MILE: FONTHILL, MORAVIAN TILE WORKS AND MERCER MUSEUM

FONTHILL

Tours conducted Tues.–Sun., March 1–Dec. 31, from 10 a.m.–3:30 p.m. Reservations recommended. Fees: Adults, $2.00; students, $1.00; family (2 adults & children), $4.50. Fonthill, East Court St., Doylestown, Pa. 18901. (215) 348-9461.

There is a bit of whimsey in historic Bucks County. On the outskirts of Doylestown stands a medieval castle, complete with turrets, balconies, and pinnacles. It was the dream house of a brilliant but eccentric bachelor, Dr. Henry Chapman Mercer. Built of poured concrete in the early 1900's, Fonthill was designed by Mercer (who was not an architect and worked without floor plans) and constructed room by room. Multi-vaulted and strangely shaped ceilings, decorated in lovely tiles from all over the world, cover the twenty-seven oddly shaped rooms. Twisting concrete stairways, often decorated with paw prints from Mercer's favorite dog Rollo as well as pithy sayings such as "Through varied misfortune," lead to a crazy patchwork of chambers, each having at least two exits. Artifacts from all over hang in nets suspended from the ceilings, and concrete and wood bookshelves hold over 7,000 books, a monument to the curious intellect of this unusual man who was, at varying times, a lawyer, archeologist, writer, artist, builder and museum curator. A guided tour of Fonthill can last up to an hour and a half, so wear comfortable shoes as there is a lot of walking and climbing of stairs.

MORAVIAN POTTERY AND TILE WORKS

Open Weds.–Sat., 10 a.m.–5 p.m. (Last tour leaves at 4), from March 1–Dec. 31. Fees: Adults, $1.75; students, $1.00; family (2 adults & children), $3.50. Rest rooms. Gift shop. Moravian Pottery and Tile Works, Swamp Rd., Rt. 313, Doylestown, Pa. 18901. (215) 345-6722.

A short walk from Fonthill takes you to another architectural oddity, the Moravian Pottery and Tile Works. This "mud pie" building, which resembles a California mission with red tile roof, is Mercer's contribution to the preservation of the art of the Pennsylvania German potter. Once he had built the Tile Works (an arduous task utilizing labor from nearby farms and a hard-working horse named Lucy), Mercer commenced to make pottery and tiles in the same manner as did the potters of old. Unfortunately, the clay he used was unsuitable for pottery, so he had to concentrate his efforts on producing tiles and mosaics of unusual design and color. His efforts were a success, and his craftsmanship may be viewed in such buildings as the Casino at Monte Carlo, the State House at Harrisburg, and the library at Bryn Mawr College.

After Mercer's death in 1930, the Tile Works continued to operate under a succession of owners until 1967 when it was acquired by Bucks County for use as a museum. In 1974, the Tile Works were reactivated, and today guided tours may be taken through this living history exhibit. Long dark passages lined with tiles and molds lead past three small kilns (still in use), and down into the basement where the clay is stored and a gravestone rests (a monument to Mercer's grim humor). Potters may be observed creating the same tiles Mercer once designed, and a well-informed guide describes the art of making tiles and molds in the old tried and true ways. The tiles themselves may be purchased in the museum's gift shop.

THE MERCER MUSEUM

Open Tues., 10 a.m.–9 p.m.; Weds.–Sat., 10 a.m.–5 p.m.; Sun., 1–5, March 1–Dec. 31. Fees: Adults, $2.00; students, $1.00; family (2 adults plus children), $4.50. Rest rooms. Gift shop. The Mercer Museum, Pine Street, Doylestown, Pa. 18901. (215) 345-0210.

Spruance Library: Open Tues. 1–9; Weds.–Fri., 10–5. Fee for non-members: $2.00

A one-time archeologist who was appalled at the paucity of artifacts marking the passage of a civilization, Mercer determined that the culture of early America would be preserved. The result of this determination is the Mercer Museum. This imposing concrete building houses over 30,000 artifacts of pre-industrial America in a most unusual and fascinating manner. Suspended from this "castle's" high vaulted ceiling hang covered wagons, boats and plows. Passageways along either side of the main hall contain exhibits such as a country store, butcher shop, and candy store, all authentically furnished. Twisting stairways (there are also elevators) lead to balconies which overlook the main hall. Each of these contains numerous alcoves rich with historical treasure. The uppermost section of the museum is a labyrinth of dark passages and stairways which house old stove plates, stoves, and a grim collection of caskets, hearse and gallows. Hours may be spent in a self-guided tour of this museum.

Also located at the Mercer Museum is the Spruance Library of the Bucks County Historical Society. Primary and secondary sources which document early Buck's history as well as the Mercer Museum collection are housed here and may be used on the premises.

Directions: Both Fonthill and the Moravian Pottery and Tile Works may be reached by taking Route 313 to Doylestown. The Tile Works are on the northwest side of Doylestown, and you can see the unusual building right from Rt. 313. Follow the road that leads to the Tile Works to get to Fonthill. To get to the Mercer Museum (which is located in Doylestown about a mile away from the other two buildings) take Route 313 South to Court Street. Turn right onto Court and proceed for six blocks to Pine Street. Turn left onto Pine and go 4 blocks to Scout Way. Turn right on Scout Way for entrance to Museum.

Nearby Attractions: See Peddlar's Village (a ten-minute drive and fun to go to for lunch), Green Hills, and the National Shrine of Our Lady of Czestochowa.

THE MORGAN LOG HOUSE

Open April 1–Nov. 1, Sat. and Sun., 1–4 p.m. Other times by appointment. Fees: Adults, $1.50; students, 75¢. Group rates for ten or more available. Towamencin Historical Society, Box 261, Kulpsville, Pa. 19443. (215) 368-2480.

Eight thousand red oak shingles were hand-split on the premises of the Morgan Log House to provide an authentic roof for the restoration of this 1695 two-and-one-half-story structure. Built by Welsh Quakers, the house is an excellent example of medieval-style architecture. The log "mansion" features construction details such as horizontal logs mortared with stones set in an unusual diagonal pattern, a 32-foot-long summer (support) beam in the main house, medieval-style windows with slanted jambs, and the familiar Dutch doors. Over 90 percent of the building is intact, and the restoration performed on it is accurate down to the antique tools used to do the repair work.

The house was built by the Morgans, Welsh immigrants who settled here on 800 acres. One of their children, Sarah Morgan, later gained renown by being the mother of one of our nation's great heroes, Daniel Boone. The house was modelled after the Morgans' home in the Old Country. It contains a dining room with walk-in fireplace, a downstairs bedroom, living room, root cellar, and two upstairs bedrooms, one for the boys, the other for the girls. Each room is furnished with authentic 18th century antiques, many of them supplied by the Dietrich Foundation, the Philadelphia Museum of Art, and the Finkelstein Collection. You'll see clothes presses with rat-tail hinges, antique rope beds, a curly maple linen press, gate-leg tables, and other lovely furnishings. The setting for them is often plain with whitewashed walls, wide-plank wood floors, and wood-beamed ceilings.

Guided tours by hostesses in Quaker dress take you through the two stories of the house. Interesting tidbits about how the restoration was accomplished are interspersed with the history of the house and its occupants. Throughout the house are exposed sections of the walls so you can see what the construction of a log dwelling consists of, and at the tour's end you are welcome to browse through a scrapbook which contains pictures of the house in the various stages of restoration as well as photographs of the Morgans' elegant home in the Old Country.

Directions: Take the Northeast Extension of the Pa. Turnpike to Exit 31, Rt. 63. Immediately after exiting, turn east on Sumneytown Pike. Follow this one mile to Troxel Road and turn left. Go to the next road and turn right onto Snyder Rd. Follow this for a short distance, then turn left onto Weikel Rd. The house will appear on your left. The house is also easily accessible from Rt. 363, Valley Forge Road (turn left onto Sumneytown Pike from 363, then turn right onto Troxel).

Nearby Attractions: See Peter Wentz Farmstead.

THE NATIONAL SHRINE OF OUR LADY
OF CZESTOCHOWA

Shrine open to the public every day from approximately 11:30 a.m. (after the last Mass has been said) to 7:00 p.m. No admission fees. Picnics. Cafeteria open on Sundays and Special Days. Rest rooms. Films, lectures, and Cultural Tours arranged upon request. Gift shop. Pilgrimage Director, P.O. Box 151, National Shrine, Doylestown, Pa. 18901. (215) 345-0600.

Centuries ago, when Czestochowa, Poland was still a medieval town, a small wooden church in the center of it was dedicated to the Virgin Mary. In 1382, the Prince Wladyslaw Opolski brought a miraculous image of the Mother of God to this church. This image, purported to be painted by St. Luke, depicts the Virgin Mary in a sorrowful and pensive mood. The Prince dedicated the image to the Pauline Fathers who were eventually to found a monastery at this location. From this moment on, the fame of this image and the church spread far and wide, and Czestochowa became known throughout history as the spiritual center of Poland.

In 1951, a group of Pauline Fathers emigrated to the United States, and in 1953 purchased land near Doylestown, Pa. on which they desired to build an "American Czestochowa." Today, the shrine is virtually completed, and stands as an American tribute to the Polish struggle for religious freedom and as a center dedicated to Our Lady of Czestochowa in the United States. To complete the picture, a copy of the miraculous painting was enshrined in the basilica of the new building.

A visit to the National Shrine is awe-inspiring, and you don't have to be Catholic or Polish to appreciate it. The massive concrete structure built on the summit of Beacon Hill (483 feet above sea level) commands a sweeping view of the surrounding countryside. A large spiral concrete staircase leads to the entrance of the shrine. Inside the main church (which can seat up to 1,700 people) are magnificent stained glass windows which form, with the help of supporting beams, two complete sides of the large shrine. One wall of windows is dedicated to Poland and depicts a variety of Polish scenes such as the Martyrdom of St. Adalbert, the famous Sword of Kings, and the Polish Eagle. The opposite wall is dedicated to the United States and portrays important moments in American history including the signing of the Declaration of Independence. Both windows are executed in a brilliant kaleidoscope of colors fantastic to behold. Also situated at this site are a monastery, outdoor stations of the cross and small museum.

During Labor Day Weekend and on the 23rd Sunday of the year Polish Festivals are held at the Shrine. These feature folk dancing, crafts, food and other ethnic activities.

Directions: The Shrine is located a few miles north of Doylestown, just off of Rt. 313 (between its intersection with Rt. 611 to the north and Rt. 202 to the south). From 313, turn west onto Ferry Road in the town of Fountainville (there are directional signs). Follow Ferry Road and the entrance to the shrine will appear on your right across from a Retirement Village.

Nearby Attractions: See Green Hills, Lake Nockamixon and The Mercer Mile.

NEW HOPE

Shops open year round 10–5 p.m. Food: Restaurants; snacks. Rest rooms. Handicapped: Many shops too small for wheelchairs, some hills. New Hope Chamber of Commerce, New Hope, Pa. 18938. (215) 862-5880.

Eighty years ago a group of internationally-famous artists settled along the Delaware River and formed an art colony. Known as the New Hope Group, they settled here because of the impressive landscape with its picturesque canal, rolling hills, wooded countryside, and lovely old stone houses. By the 1920's, New Hope, as the village soon became known, had become home to a multitude of painters, craftsmen, and writers. Today New Hope still remains a center of the arts, and many artists of all types live in the village and on nearby farms.

New Hope is a curious spot, part eighteenth, nineteenth and twentieth century. Its quaint treelined streets and alleys lead to almost a hundred shops and restaurants. Here you can purchase "one-of-a-kind" items such as original works of art, fine antiques, and unusual crafts. A virtual labyrinth of paths, brick sidewalks, and alleys lead you past scenes harboring delightful surprises—hidden courtyards filled with impatiens, a work of modern art in a formal garden, a gargoyle door knocker. There's much to explore, appreciate, and buy (if you can afford the prices). One word of caution, children are welcome but many shops are crowded and filled with breakable antiques.

There are a number of annual festivals and events held at New Hope, and if you don't mind the crowds, it's a fun time to visit. In June there's the annual New Hope Street Fair which features rides, food, and games. During August, the Annual New Hope Automobile Show is held. Featuring over 40 divisions, this has become known as one of the best antique car shows east of the Mississippi. In the late fall and spring, the New Hope Historical Society holds its annual antique shows. Write for times and details.

BUCKS COUNTY PLAYHOUSE

Bucks County Playhouse, New Hope, Pa. 18938. (215) 862-2041.

While in New Hope, plan to see a play at the famous Bucks County Playhouse. This is housed in an old grist mill which was converted in 1939 into the playhouse. Now known as the State Theatre of Pennsylvania, it features a number of popular plays each summer. Its season has been extended to include some of the winter months, so write or call for details and reservations (group rates are available).

PARRY MANSION

Open 1–4 p.m. Fri.–Sun. and all holidays. Fee: $1.50. Call for group reservations. Parry Mansion, S. Main & Ferry Sts., New Hope, Pa. 18938. (215) 862-2194.

On Connor Square in the center of New Hope stands the lovely old Parry Mansion. If you have time, take a tour of this historic homestead, which was occupied by five generations of the Parry family. Ten rooms are on display and are furnished to depict the changing lifestyle from the colonial period to the 1900's.

Directions: New Hope is just one hour from Philadelphia, and 1½ hours from New York City. It is located near the border of Pennsylvania and New Jersey at the junction of Rts. 202 and 32.

Nearby Attractions: See Peddler's Village, Washington Crossing State Park, Bucks Co. Winery, and Bucks Co. Covered Bridge Tour.

THE NEW HOPE AND IVYLAND RAILROAD

Rides available Easter Weekend through Oct., Sat. and Sun. at 1, 2, 3, and 4:30 p.m. Fees: $3.00 for adults; $1.00 for children 3–12. Group rates available. New Hope and Ivyland Railroad, New Hope, Pa. 18938. (215) 862-5206.

The massive black steam engine with its accompanying coal car is being fired up. Steam and smoke come billowing out, creating an aura of awesome power. After much steaming and a loud whistle, the train's wheels start to turn, taking you slowly through the town of New Hope and into the lush surrounding countryside of Bucks County. The nine-mile excursion takes you across the curved trestle made famous in Pearl White's "Perils of Pauline" movie serials, and into a scenic rural region that's become a favorite of local artists—old stone houses, streams, meadows, rolling hills, cornfields, and dairy farms with neat red barns. The steam engine pulls the cars to Lahaska, then a diesel engine, hooked to the rear of the train pulls the cars back to New Hope. It's a good way to experience both the joy and excitement of the old Railroading days, and the clean efficiency of the new. The entire ride lasts about an hour and is a pleasant excursion for old and young alike.

Directions: If coming from Route 202, the train station will be on your left just after entering the town of New Hope. It is located off of Bridge Street just before the bridge crosses the canal.

NEW HOPE MULE-DRAWN BARGE RIDES

Season: April 1–Nov. 15. April 1–30: Wed., Sat., Sun. 1, 3, & 4:30 p.m. May 1–Sept. 15: daily 11 a.m., 1, 2, 3, 4:30 & 6 p.m. Sept. 15–Nov. 15: Wed., Sat., Sun. 1, 3, 4:30 & 6 p.m. Trips at other times by group reservations, private barge parties available. Fee: Adults, $3.50; children 3–12, $1.75. New Hope Barge Co., P.O. Box 164, New Hope, Pa. 18938. (215) 862-2842.

Sit back, relax, and let your cares subside as you slip back in time and take a 45-minute mule-drawn barge ride along the scenic Delaware Canal. Performers with banjos and guitars sing folk songs in the bow of the barge, accompanied by the clip-clop of the mule's hooves as he patiently pulls the barge up and down the canal. Your senses are regaled by the music, the heady smell of blooming flowers, the verdant green of the surrounding countryside, and the sight of the picturesque cottages lining the canal's banks. The trip will take you back in time to when life was slower and the barges made their way down the Delaware Canal, each carrying up to 100 tons of coal from Easton to New Hope. It is estimated that at one time there were up to 3,000 boats and barges travelling the canal. Today, the surrounding area is a national landmark—The Roosevelt State Park, but the old barges still ply the waters, not in as great a number, and carrying a decidedly lighter load. It's a peaceful interlude to a busy day of shopping in New Hope.

Directions: The Barge rides leave from New Hope, and the Barge landing with parking lot is located on New Street. From Rt. 179 (Ferry St.), (202 East leads into this) proceed into town. Turn right onto Stockton Ave., left onto Mechanic St., and a quick right onto New Street.

NEWLIN MILL PARK

Park Grounds open year round 7 a.m. to 8 p.m. No admission fee. Buildings and Facilities open March–Dec. Tours of historic buildings offered daily from 10 a.m. to 5 p.m. Fees: Adults, $1.50; children 12 and under, 50¢. Picnics: Reservations required on weekends and holidays. Fees for picnics: Adults, $1.00; children, 50¢. Trout fishing: Fees—adults and children $1.00 plus $2.00 per fish caught. No license required. Tennis Courts: Reservations required. Fees: $1.00 per hour per person. Nature Walks—no charge. Newlin Mill Park, Box 307, R.D. 4, Glen Mills, Pa. 19342. (215) GL9-2359.

A small stream meanders through woods and fields filled with wildflowers. Small bridges cross its quiet waters, leading to nature paths that pass through groves of dawn redwood and giant Sequoia. Interspersed throughout the three miles of trails are picnic groves where those lucky enough to catch a trout can cook and eat a delicious fish dinner. A playground provides entertainment for the younger set, and for would-be Babe Ruths, there is a baseball diamond. Even the tennis enthusiast will find courts to accommodate him. For an hour or a day, this 140-acre Park has recreational opportunities for practically everyone.

If there is a history buff in the family, Newlin Mill Park also features some interesting buildings that are open during the day. A 1704 Stone Grist Mill stands at the headquarters of the West Branch of the Chester Creek. Its wooden cogs, gears, wheels and pinions have been restored to working order and spectators can see corn ground right before their eyes. Adjacent to the mill is the restored 18th century miller's house built by an Irish Quaker, Nathaniel Newlin. It is completely furnished with authentic period furniture and consists of four rooms, two downstairs and two upstairs, with a fireplace in each. Nearby is a blacksmith shop built in 1976 around the remains of an old forge. The shop is completely equipped with old tools of the trade. There is also an old spring house on the grounds.

Directions: The park is located at the intersection of Rt. 1 (Baltimore Pike) and South Cheyney Road and is about three and one half miles northeast of the Brandywine Battlefield, and seven miles southwest of Philadelphia.

Nearby Attractions: See the Brandywine Battlefield, The Brandywine River Museum, The Brinton 1704 House, The Christian Sanderson Museum, and Longwood Gardens.

NOCKAMIXON STATE PARK

Park grounds open 8 a.m. to dusk. Most facilities available Memorial Day to Labor Day. Pool open daily 11 a.m. to 7 p.m. Memorial Day to Labor Day. No admission fee. Snacks. Rest rooms. Boat rentals. Bike rentals. Handicapped: Special picnic tables and parking spaces designated. All comfort stations accommodate wheelchairs. Nockamixon State Park, Dept. of Environmental Resources, R.D. 3, Box 125A, Quakertown, Pa. 18951. Park Office—(215) 847-2785. Boat Rental—(215) 536-5153. Bike Rental—(215) 536-8282.

A visit to Nockamixon State Park can be an enjoyable experience for the entire family. On hot summer days, a favorite spot for visitors is the large swimming pool complex situated up on the hill overlooking the 1,450 acre Nockamixon Lake. This guarded pool has a shallow wading area, a large swimming section, and a deep diving tank with three-meter boards. All for free! Adjacent to it is a fantastic playground for the children which features see-saws, rubber tire swings, a wooden maze of a jungle gym, a sandbox, swings, and slides. Also in this area are public dressing rooms, bathrooms, a food and refreshment concession and nearby picnic grounds.

After swimming, you may want to try fishing in the lake for wall-eye pike, bass, musky, and panfish. There is even a small fishing pond just for the children. Non-powered boats and registered boats up to ten horsepower are permitted on this large and scenic lake. Four public launching areas are provided and marina slips may be rented on a seasonal basis. If you don't have your own boat, you may want to rent one here. There are canoes, pedal boats, small and large sail boats, and motorboats—all of which may be rented for one to two hours. If you are a reluctant sea person, try taking the tour boat ride. These are only available on the week-ends, and take you on a half-hour tour of the lake.

In addition to the water activities, this 5,253-acre park offers bicycle and bridle trails, and hiking (self-guided hiking tour maps are available at the Environmental Study Area). Hunting, trapping and training of dogs is permitted from the fall archery season through March 31st.

If you are a fan of winter, you might want to try ice fishing, skating, boating and sledding at the park. These winter sports are quite popular here. It is requested, however, that you check with the Park Superintendant before attempting any of them.

Directions: The park is located on Rt. 563 near Quakertown, Pa. From Rt. 309, take Rt. 313 to Quakertown. Follow Rt. 313 through Quakertown, then turn north on 563. The park is also accessible via Rts. 611 and 412.

Nearby Attractions: See Green Hills.

PEDDLER'S VILLAGE

Shops open year round Mon.–Sat. 10–5, Fri. 10–9 p.m. Extended hours during Christmas season which starts the day after Thanksgiving: Mon. & Tues., 10–5, Weds.–Sat., 10–9 p.m. Open every night Christmas Week. No fees. Restaurants. Shops. Rest rooms. Handicapped: wide paved walkways with benches. Some shops too small for wheelchairs. Peddler's Village, Rts. 202 & 263, Lahaska, Pa. 18931.

Set amidst the gently rolling hills of Bucks County, Pa., Peddler's Village provides the visitor with a lovely setting in which to discover a large and varied world of shopping. Winding brick paths, bordered by a variety of flowers, lead to 42 distinctive shops specializing in cookware, nuts, clothes, bath accents, cheeses, brass fittings, folk art, handicrafts, and a number of other items. If a unique gift is needed for the person who has everything, there is a good chance that it will be found here. The appeal of these attractively-built shops is enhanced by the lovely landscaping that surrounds them. In addition to the abundant flowers, there is a waterwheel, pond, stream and miniature waterfall. For children (and husbands) who tire of the endless stream of shops, there are grassy areas in which to romp, and outdoor benches to sit on.

Located within the perimeters of the village are restaurants for both formal dining (The Cock 'n Bull), and for less formal meals (the open-air Pollywog's Porch and Punch & Judy). Annual events held at the village include a Strawberry Festival the first weekend in May; an Apple Festival the first weekend in November; and a Christmas Festival the first Saturday in December.

Directions: The village is located on Rts. 202 and 263 in Lahaska, four miles southwest of New Hope.

Nearby Attractions: See New Hope, Bucks Co. Winery, The Mercer Mile (10-minute drive), Washington Crossing State Park, and Bucks County Covered Bridge Tour.

PENNSBURY

Open all year. Daylight Savings Time: Weekdays, 9–5 p.m.; Sun., 1–5 p.m. Closed Monday. Winter hours; Weekdays, 9–4:30 p.m.; Sun., 1–4:30. Closed Mondays. Hours subject to change. Fees: Adults, $1.50; children under 12, free. Rest rooms. Picnics. Handicapped: Wheelchairs available; can see outbuildings and gardens, but stairs in main house. Pennsbury, R.R. 9, Morrisville, Pa. 19067. (215) 946-0400.

"A country estate I like best for my children . . ." so wrote William Penn about his favorite summer home, Pennsbury. He had started constructing the spacious mansion, modeled after an English manor house, shortly after his arrival in Pennsylvania in 1682. It was to be a part of a self-supporting plantation consisting of some 8,000 acres along the Delaware River. During its construction, Penn had to return to England for 15 years, but this did not deter him. He managed the construction details by mailing instructions to his overseer. When he finally returned to the colony in 1700, a finished estate awaited him.

The Penn family lived in the lovely manor house for almost two years. Its large and formal rooms were filled with many visitors and servants, and Penn was well content to remàin in his country estate. Unfortunately, in 1701 financial difficulties forced the Penns to return to England, and never again did they see their American home. After William Penn's departure, the manor was used for a brief time by his son John, but it gradually fell into a state of disrepair. By the American Revolution the place was in ruins.

The Pennsbury of today is a re-creation of William Penn's country home. It is the result of interest stimulated in 1932 by the celebration of the 250th anniversary of Penn's arrival in America. Ten years of historical and archeological research went into this reconstruction. Letters from Penn to his overseer and the discovery of some of the original foundations of the home and outbuildings aided in making the work more accurate.

Tours by costumed hostesses guide you through this commodious estate. Attractive pastures with split-rail fences contain horses, sheep and fowl. Flower gardens add bright splashes of color to the landscape. An Ice House, Smoke House, Plantations Office and Wood House are open for the visitor as guides explain the role these buildings played in the managing of a self-sufficient plantation. Near the main house is the Bake and Brew House, considered the center of activity for the large staff of servants. This unusually large building contains numerous rooms, which include the wash area with big copper kettles; The Malt Room, where grain was soaked in large wooden vats, then baked and ground; the Brew Room where the grain was again cooked and hops added in a massive vat to produce the well-loved beer; and finally, the spacious servants' kitchen where most of the cooking was done.

Dominating the landscape is William Penn's formal brick mansion. The ceilings are high, the rooms, spacious. Wide plank floors, rich wood panelling and bright colonial accent colors provide the background for the 17th century antiques considered to be the largest collection of its kind in Pennsylvania. From the brick-floored basement to the attic with its tiny rooms for the servants, the manor house displays an elegant simplicity reflecting the refined taste of its originator.

After the house tour, you are free to wander about the grounds and visit the boat house, which contains a replica of the personal sailing barge Penn used to travel to Philadelphia, the gardens, stone stable, and small graveyard.

Directions: Pennsbury is located near Levittown, Pa. From the Pennsylvania Turnpike (Rt. 276 East) take Exit 29 to Route 13 towards Levittown. Immediately after exiting, turn right at the traffic light onto Green Lane. Go for about a mile, then turn left onto Farragut Ave. Take this to Radcliffe St. Turn left onto Radcliffe (which follows the river). Continue on Radcliffe through Tullytown, bearing right at the police station. You will cross over a lake, and shortly thereafter see a large sign for Pennsbury on your right. Turn right at this road and follow it to the Manor. It should only take you about ten minutes from the Turnpike Exit, and there are small directional signs guiding you through this labyrinth of roads.

Nearby Attractions: See Historic Fallsington and Sesame Place.

PETER WENTZ FARMSTEAD

Open year round: Tues.–Sat. 10–4, Sun. 1–4 p.m. Closed Mon. No fees, but donations accepted. Rest rooms. Gift shop. Provisions to accommodate handicapped have been made, but call in advance. Peter Wentz Farmstead, P.O. Box 240, Worcester, Pa. 19490. (215) 584-5104.

True to the custom of selecting the grandest home in the neighborhood, when George Washington needed a place to stay while planning the Battle of Germantown, he chose the Peter Wentz Farmstead. The 1758 mansion of English Georgian architecture with German overtones fitted his needs exactly. His cook could use the winter kitchen to prepare the meals (no one else could be trusted for fear of poisoning), and there were two upstairs bedrooms available for use—one for sleeping, the other for planning battle strategy. That he found this farm conducive to his needs is evident, for he stayed here twice during the Revolutionary War.

Today the farmhouse looks much the way it did in 1777. Black and white shutters contrast sharply with the house's fieldstone exterior. The interior walls with their unusual decorations of spots, squiggles and cross-hatch lines must have fascinated Washington as they do us. The front portion of the mansion is finished off with plaster, while the rear half is a rougher version with exposed beamed ceilings. The furnishings are typical of the era and class of people, and one piece, a five-plate stove in the dining room, is quite unusual.

A slide-tape shown in the Reception Center (a 20th century converted poultry barn) introduces you to the farm and its history. This is followed by tours of the house given by volunteer guides in colonial costume. Once the tour is over, you are free to browse through the quaint German Kitchen Garden that is adjacent to the house, and see the 1744 barn which was completely restored by Amishmen. The grounds of the farmstead are quite scenic and many of the fields are planted with crops such as flax and fruit trees.

Throughout the year, 18th century craft demonstrations using authentic tools and methods are presented on Saturday afternoons or by special arrangement. These include weaving, block printing, wood carving, broom making, fraktur painting, embroidery, spinning, quilting, basket making and fireplace cooking and baking. In October and December, special candelight tours are given and the bake oven is in use.

Directions: The Farmstead is located right off Rt. 363 (Valley Forge Pike) and is accessible via Rts. 73, 422, and Exit 31 of the N.E. Extension of the Turnpike. From Exit 31, turn left (East) onto Sumneytown Pike and follow this until it intersects with 363. Turn right (South) onto Rt. 363 and go under the Turnpike. Shortly after this you will see the Central Schwenfelder Church on your right. At this juncture, turn left at the directional sign to the farmstead, then turn left at the split rail fences.

Nearby Attractions: See The Morgan Log House and The Elmwood Park Zoo.

POTTSGROVE AT POTTSTOWN

Open May–Sept.: Weekdays except Monday, 10–5; Sun. 1–5 p.m.; Oct.–April: Weekdays except Monday, 10–4:30; Sun. 1–4:30. Fees: Adults, $1.00; children under 12, free. Pottsgrove, Rt. 422, Pottstown, Pa. (215) 326-4014.

The stately brown sandstone mansion has withstood the passage of time for over two hundred years. Its 24-inch-thick walls and 11-foot ceilings surround elegant 18th century furnishings such as Chippendale furniture, oriental rugs, crystal chandeliers, built-in corner cupboards, and thick window seats covered in comfortable cushions. The mansion's decor reflects the simple refined taste of a gentleman of means, Mr. John Potts. A wealthy ironmaster, Mr. Potts built this dream house for his wife in the 1750's. People came from as far away as forty miles to view its splendor, and at one time, even George Washington and wife Martha came for a visit, sleeping in an upstairs bedroom.

Today the home stands much the way it did when John Potts and his descendents lived in it. In 1941, the estate was given to the Commonwealth of Pennsylvania and the Pennsylvania Historical and Museum Commission, who carried out some restoration to return the home to its original state.

Half-hour guided tours take you through ten rooms of the Georgian interior, which is considered, in simple elegance, to be one of the finest of its day. All have been furnished with authentic 18th century antiques. Fireplaces can be found in every room, and painted chair rails and woodwork add color and life to the interiors. Along with the typical furnishings encountered in a mansion owned by a wealthy family, there are some unusual items on display such as a rocking potty chair, a nightcap reputably belonging to Martha Washington, a large linen press, and a man's 600-pound walnut wardrobe. When your tour is completed, you are free to walk through the charming 18th century herb and flower garden adjacent to the mansion.

Directions: Pottsgrove is located just off Rt. 100 on Business Rt. 422 (not the new bypass) just west of Pottstown. If coming from Rt. 100, turn east onto King St. (there's a traffic light at the intersection, and a Gulf Station on the corner), Pottsgrove will appear directly on your right across from the Holiday Inn. There are directional signs from both directions on Rt. 100.

Nearby Attractions: See Mary Merritt's Doll Museum, and Daniel Boone Homestead (both listed under Berks Co. Area II).

SESAME PLACE

Open year round, 9:30 a.m. to 8 p.m. Memorial Day–Labor Day, 10 a.m.–6 p.m. Labor Day–Nov. 9. During winter, only *indoor* areas open 10 a.m. to 10 p.m. Fees: Adults and children, $4.95; 2 and under, free. Rest rooms. Restaurant. Snacks. Sesame Place, P.O. Box 579, Langhorne, Pa. 19047. (215)752-7070.

Entering through orange and blue metallic gates, you pay your admission fee (under 2 are free) and climb the bright yellow stairs leading into the opened beak of none other than Big Bird. Sounds of children laughing and screaming assail you as you gingerly walk across Big Bird's suspension bridge and gratefully make it to a platform set high up in the air. There's nowhere to go but down, so you bravely opt for the covered tunnel slide (there are stairs) which slips you like a newborn babe into the midst of a unique innovative play park called Sesame Place.

This elaborate playground is the result of the heady combination of the Children's Television Workshop (which produces Sesame Street) and Busch Gardens. There are forty outdoor play activities that will delight and thrill children ages three to thirteen (there are age and height restrictions for certain activities), and older folks can watch and admire them in the benches and seats provided throughout. Everything is powered by the energy of children. They can climb, swing, play, and test their abilities in countless ways. Watch them take a 120-foot pulley ride through the air (hanging safely from a rope a few feet above the ground), climb rope nets hanging high above the play area, crawl through a water maze, bounce on the Ernie Bed Bounce, and bury themselves in a sea of green balls. Even the toddlers can get into the act, playing in the dripping faucets in the sandbox and gleefully hurling light blocks in the building area. Each activity is closely monitored by helpful aides. Be sure to bring bathing suits (or at least a change of clothes) and flip-flops. Many of the activities involve getting wet, dirty, and going barefoot (a veritable children's paradise).

There are indoor activities which will also captivate both children and adults. A large gallery containing close to seventy computer games offers challenges to all ages. The games range in difficulty from the relatively simple Mup-o-matic in which the identity of a gradually emerging Muppet character is guessed, to rather sophisticated problem-solving situations. Tokens to play these games may be purchased in the gallery. Next to this gallery is Mr. Hooper's Emporium, where all types of Sesame Street products may be purchased. Nearby is the Food Factory, a restaurant which sells "healthful" but tasty foods (their pizza is delicious!) at reasonable prices. Finally, there is a building which houses the famous Sesame Street TV studio set where kids can watch themselves on closed-circuit television. Oscar's trash can and the well-known steps leading to a front door are the two main items featured in this setting. Also in the building is the Shadow Room (where children can dance about and have fun with their shadows), and a light gallery which contains more than twenty participatory science exhibits.

Directions: Sesame Place is located five miles north of the Rt. 1 Exit of the Pennsylvania Turnpike, and just off the intersection of U.S. Rt. 1 and I-95. Take Route 1 to just beyond the Oxford Valley Mall, and then turn left on New Oxford Valley Road. The Park will be on your left.

Nearby Attractions: See Historic Fallsington and Pennsbury.

SWISS PINES

Open March 15–Nov. 15: Mon.–Fri. 10–4; Sat. 9–11:30. Closed Sundays and holidays. Admission free. If guided tour desired, call or write in advance. Swiss Pines, P.O. Box 97, Upper Darby, Pa. 19082. (215) 933-6916.

"If you have a mind of peace, a heart that cannot harden, Go find a gate that opens wide into a lovely garden . . ." So reads the inscription at the gates of Swiss Pines, an oriental trail garden set in the lush Valley Forge countryside. Started as a hobby in 1956 by Mr. Bartschi, a Swiss-born American businessman, Swiss Pines now encompasses twenty acres of gardens. Mr. Bartschi has travelled extensively, and studied the art of the oriental garden both overseas and in the United States. His knowledge, interest in, and love of the simple beauty inherent in oriental gardens is evident throughout his own. Flowering trees, bubbling brooks with rock-lined beds resembling jigsaw puzzles, moss gardens, goldfish ponds, stone gods and goddesses—all present a carefully arranged and beautiful scene echoing the Far Eastern philosophy. It took Mr. Bartschi ten years to fully understand the art of Japanese gardening and each year he adds something more to his extensive trail garden (which is the only one in the United States to cover both flat and hilly terrain).

Lovely surprises will await you as you take a self-guided tour of the gardens. Gravel lined paths lead around ponds filled with goldfish and frogs. Hotei, Benten and Jurajin, the stone gods of health, elegance and longevity, watch over all from their small side garden while up on the hilltop a Buddha sitting in the lotus position gazes benignly from his pedestal. Flowering azaleas color the hillside and circular stone steps lead past a moon mound, a pile of stones so arranged as to reflect the moonlight, to a miniature temple. Water cascades down the hill into a series of pools accented by flowering trees and gardens. Everywhere you look there are scenes to refresh the mind, and stone benches are situated throughout the area providing the ideal opportunity to rest and drink in the quiet beauty.

There are other visual delights here in addition to the oriental trail garden. On your walk you will see gardens containing herbs, heather, roses, iris, ferns, rhododendron, flowering crabapple and migratory bird ponds. It's a pleasant oasis where you may want to spend an hour or an afternoon.

Directions: Take the Pa. Turnpike West Ext. to Exit 24 (Valley Forge-Rt. 363). Follow Rt. 363 north to Rt. 23. Go west on 23 towards Phoenixville, then in the middle of town turn left (south) onto Route 29. Follow 29 until just before it goes under the Pa. Turnpike, then turn right onto Charlestown Rd. Go 1.7 miles and Swiss Pines will be on your right with a small parking lot across the street from the entrance.

Nearby Attractions: See Valley Forge and Audubon Wildlife Sanctuary.

VALLEY FORGE PARK

Park open daily 9–5 p.m. (hours vary for historical buildings). No admission fees for self-guided tours. Bus tours: available Mid-April through October. Fees: Adults, $3.00; children 5–15, $2.00. Rented audio tours, $5.00. Handicapped: elevators in Visitor's Center, paved walkways and roads. Rest rooms. Gift shop. Picnics with grills. Snack Bar near Washington's Hdqrs. Bike and bridle paths. Superintendent, Valley Forge Historical Park, Valley Forge, Pa. 19481. (215) 783-0177.

The time is December 19, 1777, a cold and bitter day for the Continental Army under Washington's command. They have lost both the Battles of Brandywine and Germantown, and have been forced to abandon Philadelphia to the British. Their retreat has lead them to an elevated plain known as Valley Forge. Here they will establish their winter quarters and stay for six months without adequate food, shelter or clothing. Of the 11,000 men who have come here, 3,000 will die from exposure, starvation, and disease. It will be a harsh winter for these troops, more difficult perhaps than any battle they will have to fight. But for those who manage to survive, a new spirit and determination will be forged due to the discipline and training of an unusual and talented Prussian officer, Baron von Steuben.

When Benjamin Franklin heard of General Washington's travails with his amateur and undisciplined army, he sent Baron von Steuben over from Paris. For six months the Prussian drillmaster trained the often barefoot and suffering troops. His voice could be heard from dawn to dusk directing the men through series of maneuvers. Raw youths were turned into effective fighting men and soldiers were infused with the will to win. When the troops broke camp on June 19, 1778, they were prepared to do battle with and defeat the British Army. Although the war would continue for another five years, the winter at Valley Forge is regarded as the turning point in the American fighting spirit.

You can relive these moments in history by visiting Valley Forge and seeing the reproductions of the meager huts in which the men huddled through the long winter nights, the fields where they trained, and the house in which their commander planned his strategy. Over 2,400 acres of the encampment area have been preserved as an historical monument to this phase of the Revolution. Since the area is so large, it is best to start your visit at the Visitor's Center. The exhibits will introduce you to the important events in the winter of 1777–1778, and are augmented by a 15-minute audiovisual program that is shown every half–hour. After leaving the Center, you may decide to take a bus tour of the park (these are supplied with a tape narration and stop at seven spots in the park where you are free to disembark and pick up a later bus); drive in your own car and rent one of the audio-tapes available at the Center; or more simply rely on a map keyed to numbered stops available free of charge at the Center. These stops include the numerous remains and reconstructions of forts, Officer's Quarters, earthworks, Artillery Park, Washington's Headquarters, and the Grand Parade Ground where von Steuben rebuilt the tattered army. During the year, living history programs are held at certain stops.

Located within the park but on private property is the Washington Memorial Chapel and the Museum of the Valley Forge Historical Society. The Episcopal Chapel has thirteen beautiful stained glass windows which are executed in shades of red and blue. Ornate hand-carved woodwork decorates the pews and choir stalls, on the walls are military honor rolls etched in metal, and the ceiling is covered with the seals of all the States of the Union. The Church's Bell Tower features concerts every Sunday from 2 to 3 p.m., and special tours of the tower may be arranged from the last week in June until the end of August. The Museum, which is adjacent to the Chapel and charges a nominal admission fee, contains articles relating to the Revolution. These include a $120,000 check given to Lafayette by the U.S. Government in payment for his services, a unique powder horn collection, Revolutionary weapons and ammunition, locks of Washington's hair, well-known paintings including the original of Tregor's "Washington Reviewing His Troops" and a host of other relevant articles and documents.

A lovely time to visit the Valley Forge area is in the spring when the landscape is filled with the colors of flowering dogwood trees. It's the ideal place and time to bring picnics, kites for flying in the fields, and bikes for riding down the scenic and numerous trails.

Directions: Valley Forge is located 18 miles northwest of Philadelphia. From Rt. 276 (the west extension of the east-west Pa. Turnpike) take Exit 24 (the Valley Forge Exit), Rt. 363 North. Follow 363 to the junction of Rts. 23 and 363, and the Visitor's Center will be on your left.

Nearby Attractions: See the Elmwood Park Zoo, The Audubon Wildlife Sanctuary and Mill Grove, and Swiss Pines. If you come during the week (Mon.–Fri., 10–4) or on weekends (May–Sept., 10–4), you might want to stop and visit The Freedoms Foundation which is located along Route 23. The Foundation houses important documents relating to the struggle for liberty, from the Magna Carta in the 13th century to the present day; the Patriot's Hall of Fame, in which are the complete records of our Nation's greatest heroes; and an extensive library which combines information on our economic system, history and government. The Visitor's Center features twelve exhibits, dioramas, and slide-film programs revolving around patriotic themes. The actual medals and records of the 3,400 Americans who have received the Medal of Honor are on display in the General Henry Knox Building. Also on the premises are the Independence Gardens which feature a collection of stones and bricks from the homes of each of the 56 signers of the Declaration of Independence.

WASHINGTON CROSSING STATE PARK

Park open year round. Buildings open—Daylight Savings Time: Tues.–Sat., 9–5 p.m., Sun. 12–5 p.m. Closed Mondays. Grounds open 9–8 p.m. Standard Time: Tues.–Sat., 10–4:30 p.m., Sun. 12–4:30 p.m. Grounds open 9–4:30. Grist Mill open summer months only. Fees (which include admission to all the historic buildings): Adults, $1.00; children and adults over 65, free. Picnics. Rest rooms. Handicapped: certain historic buildings and facilities are accessible. Superintendent, Washington Crossing State Park, Washington Crossing, Pa. 18977. (215) 493-4076.

In the bitterly cold winter of 1776, George Washington and his Continental Army, having suffered defeat by the British at the Battle of Long Island, had retreated across New Jersey to the Pennsylvania side of the rapid-flowing Delaware River. Here his ragged troops, suffering from starvation and exhaustion, regrouped awaiting new orders.

On Christmas night, Washington assembled his troops near Bowman's Hill and McKonkey's Ferry. Snow and sleet fell on the shivering men. In a daring plan, Washington had decided to backtrack his path of retreat, cross the black ice-choked Delaware River, and surprise the celebrating Hessian garrison at Trenton. With 2,400 men, Washington crossed the formidable river in sturdy Durham boats, marched to Trenton and attacked the unsuspecting Hessians. His victory over the enemy was resounding. The success of this bold maneuver was a great morale booster for the faltering Continental Army. Under adverse conditions, with meager supplies and suffering men, Washington had achieved the impossible and breathed new life into the American fight for independence.

Today, a park consisting of 500 acres of forests, hills and scenic paths marks the spot of this memorable crossing. Comprised of two sections three-and-one-half miles apart, the park runs along both sides of Rt. 32 (River Road). The best place to commence a visit would be at the Memorial Building and Visitor's Center which is located in the southern or lower section of the park. A thirty-minute movie about Washington's crossing of the Delaware is shown here continuously during the day, and provides a good historical background with which to start your tour. A copy of the famous painting of Washington's crossing is displayed in the Auditorium as well as numerous other paintings depicting scenes in America's history.

Within walking distance of the Memorial Building are a number of historical houses. Two restored 19th century homes provide the setting for spinning and weaving demonstrations by the Hand Weavers of Bucks County. These are usually held during the spring and summer months on alternate weekends (Fri. and Sun.). Nearby is the Durham Boat House, which contains reproductions of the 18th century cargo boats used to carry the troops across the river. Each Christmas, starting around 2 p.m., these boats are used in a re-enactment of Washington's famous 1776 crossing. It is a colorful event open to the public. Down the path from the boat house is the well-known McKonkey Ferry Inn. The Inn and Ferry landing were the focus for historical gatherings of the time. It is believed that Washington ate here prior to his momentous crossing. Tours may be taken of this Inn. Guides dressed in colonial costumes describe the period furnishings (none original to the house but genuine antiques nonetheless), relate the history of the old Inn, and recreate important moments in America's fight for freedom.

A short drive north along the scenic River Road takes you to the "upper park." Dominating the landscape in this section is Bowman's Hill Tower, which unfortunately can no longer be climbed for safety reasons. This stone observation tower was erected in 1930 and marks the lookout where sentries watched the river for enemy activity. It is the highest elevation for miles. Along the road is the famous Thompson-Neeley House where Washington and his commanders held important staff conferences. This lovely stone home was originally built in 1702, with two sections added on in 1757 and 1788 respectively. There are guides stationed in the various rooms of the home who explain the relevance of what you are seeing to the historical events of the time. All furnishings are authentic pieces of the period. One room of the house is used as a museum to display pictures and colonial artifacts contributed by donors. If you ever wanted to see what Washington's teeth really looked like, here is the opportunity! On Washington's Birthday weekend gingerbread is baked in the large bake oven and the public is invited to partake and help celebrate.

Across the road from the Thompson-Neeley House is an old grist mill which has been fully restored. In the summer months the mill is operable and guided tours may be taken through it. These are a real treat, for you see the entire milling process in operation. The six-ton wooden water wheel, powered by flowing water, provides the energy required to turn the massive millstones which grind the grain into flour. There are three floors in the mill, each one containing systems of wheels, pulleys and chutes which contribute to the overall operation. It's a fascinating lesson in the early use of technology.

One hundred acres of the upper park have been developed as a Wild Flower Preserve. When you tire of visiting historical buildings, escape to this natural haven and hike down the nature trails which pass through hundreds of wildflower beds. From March to November there is always something blooming. Guided tours and lectures may be arranged for groups.

Before leaving the park, take the road that leads from the Thompson-Neeley House, cross the Delaware Canal, and visit the Soldiers' Graves. These small headstones and monument were placed in memory of the many unknown soldiers who died in these fields during the encampment prior to the Battle of Trenton. The base of the memorial flagstaff is comprised of thirteen sections each set with native stones from the original thirteen colonies.

Directions: The park is located about 3 miles south of New Hope on Route 32.

Nearby Attractions: See New Hope attractions, Peddler's Village, Bucks Co. Winery, and Bucks County Covered Bridge Tour.

THE FARMERS' MARKETS

A trip to the Pennsylvania Dutch countryside would not be complete without a visit to one of the local farmers' markets. It is here that seasonal produce and flowers may be purchased fresh off the farmer's fields. Stall upon stall is filled with the bright colors of golden sweet corn, red ripe tomatoes, deep green peppers, and the lovely purple of eggplant. Bright flowers add their assorted colors to this visual delight. The smell of freshly-baked goods fills the air (this is a good place to buy the famous shoo-fly pie and fresh-baked bread), as well as the pungent spices used to flavor such meats as Lebanon Bologna and sausage. There are butcher shops, cheese shops, fruit and nut stalls, and dry goods stores, all housed beneath one roof. The markets operate throughout the year and import fresh produce in the off-seasons. These are good places to observe and partake in the colorful goings-on of the Dutch marketplace.

The following is a list of the better-known farmers' markets throughout the area:

Lancaster

Central Market (the largest and best known of the Lancaster city markets, this is housed in an 1889 medieval-looking brick castle). Penn Square, Lancaster. Tuesdays and Fridays, 6–5.
Park City Farmers' Market: lower level Park City Center. Thurs. 10–9; Fri. 10–9; Sat. 9–5.
Southern Farmers' Market: Vine and Queen Sts., Lancaster. Sat. 6–3.
West End Market: 501 W. Lemon St., Lancaster. Tues, and Sat. 6–noon; Fri. 6–5.

Lancaster Environs

Bird-in-Hand Farmers' Market: Rt. 340 at Bird-in-Hand. Weds. 8:30–5:30; Fri. 8:30–6; Sat. 8:30–5:30.
Columbia Market (this is housed in an interesting building over 100 years old, which was built on top of seven jail cells known as ''The Dungeon.'' The Dungeon has been restored and is open to the public.) Third Street, Columbia. Fri. 11–4; Sat. 10–1.

Ephrata Market: Ephrata Square, Ephrata. Friday 9–9; Sat. 9–3.

Green Dragon Farmers Market (see also additional article on the Green Dragon). Off of Rt. 272, north of Ephrata. Fri. 10–10.

Meadowbrook Farmers Market: Rt. 23 between New Holland and Lancaster. Fri. 10–9; Sat. 8–4.

Roots Country Market: Rt. 72N near Manheim. Tues. 2–10 p.m.

Twin Slope Farmers Market and Flea Market: at intersection of Rts. 10 and 23, Morgantown (1 mile from Turnpike Exit 22). Fri. 11–9; Sat. 9–3.

Reading

Downtown Reading Local Market: Farmers'–Kissinger Market, 828 Penn St., Reading. Thurs., Fri. and Sat. hours (215) 372–4334.

Fairgrounds Farmers' Market: 5th St., Reading. Fri. 8–9; Sat. 8–6. Flea market Sundays, 8–5 p.m.

Leesport Market and Auction: Leesport (a few miles north of Reading on Rt. 61). Weds. 1–11; Sat. 1–11.

Shillington Farmers' Market: Shillington Market House, West Lancaster Ave. & Shillington Blvd., Shillington. Thurs. 12–7; Fri. 7–7.

Allentown

Allentown Farmers' Market: Between Chew and Liberty Sts. at the Allentown Fair Grounds, downtown Allentown. Fri. 9–5; Sat. 9–12.

Bucks County & Environs

Buckingham Farmers' Market: Rt. 202 and Burnt House Hill Road, Buckingham. Sat. 9 a.m. until produce is sold.

Quakertown Farmers' Market: 201 Station Road, Quakertown. Fri. & Sat. 10–10; Sun. 11–5.

FAIRS AND FESTIVALS

This is a list of Festivals mentioned in the book. For a full list of Pennsylvania Festivals and dates for the current year, write: Bureau of Travel Development, Pa. Dept. of Commerce, South Office Bldg., Harrisburg, Pa. 17120.

February: Washington's Birthday Celebration at Washington Crossing State Park, 204

Washington's Birthday Celebration at Valley Forge, 202

April: Last Saturday, Spring Steam-up at Rough 'N Tumble Engineer's Museum, Kinzer, 53

May: Spinning & Weaving Frolic and Spring Folklore Festival, Schaefferstown, 69

Bach Festival—Bethlehem, 117

Shad Fest—Bethlehem, 117

Memorial Day Weekend, Lehigh County Covered Bridge Festival, Allentown, 130

June: 23rd Sunday of the year, Polish Festival at National Shrine of Our Lady of Czestochowa, Doylestown, 189

Cherry Fair, Schaefferstown, 69

Historic Bethlehem Folk Festival, Bethlehem, 117

July: Last Week in June and First Week in July, Kutztown Folk Festival, Kutztown, 90–1

Bavarian Summer Festival, Octoberfest in July, Lakewood Park (Barnesville), 71–2

July 4th Festival of Lights Celebration at Lititz Springs Park, Lititz, 41

August: First Weekend in August, Das Awkscht Fescht, Macungie, 132–3

Burpee's Fordhook Farms' August Garden Tour, Warminster, 175

Third week in August, four day Thresher's Reunion at Rough 'N Tumble Engineer's Museum, Kinzer, 53

Last week in August, The Allentown Fair, Allentown, 110–1

September: Labor Day Weekend, Polish Festival at National Shrine of Our Lady of Czestochow, 189

Saturday before Labor Day, Duryea Day at Boyertown, 74

Weekend after Labor Day, Pennsylvania Dutch Farm Festival at Kempton, 97–8

Sept. 11, Re-enactment of Battle of Brandywine, Brandywine, 166

Mid-Sept.—Harvest Fair, Schaefferstown, 69

2nd Weekend in Sept.—Duryea Hill Climb, Reading, 100

October: A Day In Historic Bethlehem, 117

Columbus Day Weekend, Harvest Festival at Quiet Valley Living Historical Farm, Stroudsburg, 152

Second Saturday, Historic Fallsington Day, 182

Enschine-O-Rama at Rough 'N Tumble Engineer's Museum, Kinzers, 53

December: Christmas Night Light Tours, Bethlehem, 123

Moravian Community Putz, Bethlehem, 123–4

Dec. 25th at 2:00: Re-enactment of Washington's Crossing of the Delaware at Washington Crossing State Park, 205

Topical Cross References

FOR THE HANDICAPPED

Brandywine Battlefield, Brandywine, 166-7

Eckley Miner's Village, Poconos, 138-9

Hillendale Museum, Mendenhall, 180-1

Lehigh County Velodrome, Trexlertown, 147-8

Lil-Le-Hi Trout Nursery, Allentown, 148-9

Lockridge Furnace, Alburtis, 141-2

Longwood Gardens, Kennett Square, 183-4

Merritt's Museum of Childhood & The Pennsylvania Dutch, Douglassville, 93-5

National Watch & Clock Museum-Columbia, 43-4

National Wax Museum of Lancaster Co. Heritage-Lancaster, 44-5

Peddler's Village, Lahaska, 194-5

Pennsbury, Morrisville, 195-7

Peter Wentz Farmstead, Worcester, 197-8

Plain & Fancy Farm and Dining Room, Bird-In-Hand, 47-8

Railroad Museum of Pa., Strasburg, 50-1

Rough 'N Tumble Engineer's Museum, Kinzers, 53-4

Saylor Park Cement Industry Museum, Allentown, 142-3

Toy Train Museum (see Strasburg's Railroads in Miniature), Strasburg, 56-7

Trexler-Lehigh Game Preserve, Schnecksville, 158-9

Valley Forge Park, Valley Forge, 202-4

Washington Crossing State Park, Washington Crossing, 204-6

FOR THE CHILDREN

(* starred items not recommended for children under 6)

FOLKWAYS, ARTS AND CRAFTS

HISTORICAL HOUSES AND MUSEUMS

National Wax Museum of Lancaster County Heritage, Lancaster, 44-5
Parry Mansion, New Hope, 190-1
Pennsbury, Morrisville, 195-7
Pottsgrove, Pottstown, 198-9
Rock Ford Plantation, Lancaster, 51-2
Thompson-Neeley House, Washington Crossing, 205-6

Tulpehocken Manor Plantation, Myerstown, 103-5
Wheatland, Lancaster, 59-60
Wright's Ferry Mansion, Columbia, 61-2
Zeller's Fort, Newmanstown, 106

HOBBIES AND SPECIAL INTERESTS

Antique Doll Museum, Plain 'N Fancy Farm and Dining Room, Bird-In-Hand, 48
Boyertown Museum of Historic Vehicles, 73-4
Bucks County Vineyard's Fashion Museum, New Hope, 174
Choo-Choo Barn, Strasburg, 55-6
Eagle Americana Museum, Strasburg, 26-7
Freedom's Foundation, Valley Forge, 204
Hillendale Museum, Mendenhall, 180-1
Lost River Caverns Lapidary Shop and Display—Hellertown, 149-50

Mary Merritt Doll Museum, Douglassville, 93-4
National Watch and Clock Museum, Columbia, 43-4
Railroad Museum of Pennsylvania, Strasburg, 50-1
Roadside America, Shartlesville, 101-2
Rough 'N Tumble Engineer Museum, Kinzers, 53-4
Strasburg Steam Railroad, 54
Toy Train Museum, Strasburg, 56-7
WK&S Steam Railroad, Kempton, 105-6

INDUSTRIAL TOURS (CURRENT AND HISTORICAL)

A. Bube's Brewery and Catacombs, Mount Joy, 17-8
Anderson Pretzel Bakeries, Inc., Lancaster, 21-2
Ashland's Pioneer Coal Mine & Steam Lokie, Ashland, 70-1
Bethlehem, Pa.: Eighteenth Century Industrial Area, 121-3
Bucks County Wineries, New Hope, 173-4
C. F. Martin Guitar Co., Nazareth, 126-7
Candy Americana Museum, Lititz, 42
Cornwall Furnace, Cornwall, 75-6
Crayola Factory Tours, Easton, 131-2

Ebersole's Chair Shop, 36, 47
Eckley Miner's Village, Poconos, 138-9
Haines Flour Mill, Allentown, 139-40
Hershey's Chocolate World, Hershey, 81-2
Hugh Moore Park Canal Museum and Mule Boat Ride, Easton, 140-1
Lancaster County Winery Tours, 36-7
Lebanon Bologna Free Plant Tours, 91-2
Lockridge Furnace, Alburtis, 141-2
Michter's Distillery, Schaefferstown, 95-6
Mount Hope, Schaefferstown, 76-7

NATURE TRAILS, PARKS AND GARDENS

OUTDOOR THRILLS AND AMUSEMENT PARKS

RELIGIONS

RESTORED VILLAGES, PARKS, HISTORICAL TRAILS AND WALKING TOURS

SHOPPING MARKETS

(Food, Bargains, Arts, Crafts and Antiques)

WILDLIFE AND ANIMALS

General Index